MODERN SPORTS ETHICS

Selected Titles in ABC-CLIO's
CONTEMPORARY
WORLD ISSUES
Series

For a complete list of titles in this series, please visit
www.abc-clio.com

Books in the Contemporary World Issues series address vital issues in today's society, such as genetic engineering, pollution, and biodiversity. Written by professional writers, scholars, and nonacademic experts, these books are authoritative, clearly written, up-to-date, and objective. They provide a good starting point for research by high school and college students, scholars, and general readers as well as by legislators, businesspeople, activists, and others.

Each book, carefully organized and easy to use, contains an overview of the subject, a detailed chronology, biographical sketches, facts and data and/or documents and other primary-source material, a directory of organizations and agencies, annotated lists of print and nonprint resources, and an index.

Readers of books in the Contemporary World Issues series will find the information they need to have a better understanding of the social, political, environmental, and economic issues facing the world today.

MODERN SPORTS ETHICS

A Reference Handbook

Angela Lumpkin

**CONTEMPORARY
WORLD ISSUES**

A B C 💮 C L I O

Santa Barbara, California
Denver, Colorado
Oxford, England

Library of Congress Cataloging-in-Publication Data
Lumpkin, Angela.
  Modern sports ethics : a reference handbook / Angela Lumpkin.
    p. cm. — (Contemporary world issues)
  Includes bibliographical references and index.
  ISBN 978-1-59884-197-8 (hardcopy : alk. paper) —
ISBN 978-1-59884-198-5 (ebook)
  1. Sports—Moral and ethical aspects. I. Title.
  GV706.3.L84   2009
  175—dc22   2009006161

12   11   10   2   3   4   5

This book is also available on the World Wide Web as an eBook.
Visit www.abc-clio.com for details.

ABC-CLIO, LLC
130 Cremona Drive, P.O. Box 1911
Santa Barbara, California 93116-1911

This book is printed on acid-free paper ∞

Manufactured in the United States of America

Contents

List of Tables

List of Figures

Preface

Examples of unethical conduct in amateur sport are reported nonstop by the electronic and print media. These ethical issues are associated with an overemphasis on winning and commercialism that have taken amateur sport away from the ideals of playing sports for the inherent joy and personal satisfaction of challenging oneself against a respected opponent or a performance standard. Cheating to gain unfair advantages, gamesmanship ploys, the use of performance-enhancing drugs, recruiting scandals, academic misconduct associated with athletes, discriminatory practices against females and African Americans, and other breaches of principled behavior have become everyday realities in sports. Many fans, who want to be entertained as they cheer their favorite teams, have come to accept questionably ethical actions as normative behavior and the way the game should be played to help secure the all-important victory.

For well over a century, millions in the United States have claimed that youth, interscholastic, intercollegiate, and Olympic sports teach positive values. Yet, many people argue that sport ethics is a contradictory combination of words, or an oxymoron. If ethical conduct is to characterize sports, coaches, players, administrators, parents, and fans need to teach, model, and reinforce character development and positive values. To address ethical challenges like taunting, disrespect for opponents and officials, and cheating, this handbook on sport ethics emphasizes sportsmanship, respect for the game, fair play, and making morally reasoned decisions as essential to ensuring that positive values and character will be taught, learned, and demonstrated.

Chapter 1 includes a historical context for examining sport ethics, specifically how character development and sports are linked. A description of ethics, ethical theories, and moral reasoning helps the reader gain a deeper understanding of the interface between amateur sport, ethical conduct, and morality in sports. Achieving positive values through sport programs sponsored by educational institutions is challenged by unethical behaviors. Numerous examples of violence, gamesmanship, violations of academic eligibility rules, sport dropout due to physical and psychological burnout, cheating, gambling, and the use of performance-enhancing drugs demonstrate the adverse effects of unethical behaviors in sports. Specific suggestions are described to show how character education can reduce unethical actions in sports.

Chapter 2 examines contemporary issues, controversies, and problems that confront all levels of amateur sports in the United States. This chapter stresses that an overemphasis on winning is a leading culprit contributing to unethical actions in sports. Cheating, gamesmanship, violence, discrimination, and the use of performance-enhancing drugs are examined topically. Then, specific ethical problems that threaten the achievement of positive outcomes in youth, interscholastic, and intercollegiate sports are presented. Recommendations for teaching positive values to youth, adolescent, and young adult athletes are offered.

Chapter 3 transcends national boundaries by placing sport ethics in an international context. The Olympic Games are described historically with an emphasis on these controversies: amateurism; nationalism and politics; racism and human rights; sexism and discrimination against females; bidding scandals; unethical behavior of officials; and use of performance-enhancing drugs and doping scandals. Examples of gamesmanship, cheating, gambling, and fixing outcomes of competitions show how unprincipled behaviors have become commonplace in international sports. Given the global interconnectedness of sport, codes of ethics have been enacted to guide athletes, coaches, officials, and fans in acting in morally appropriate ways, essential if sport is to achieve the lofty goals of friendship, respect, and fair competition.

Chapter 4 provides the reader with a chronology of significant events starting with the beginning of the modern Olympic Games to the present that have impacted ethical conduct in sports. More than 50 examples chronicle the erosion of positive values; a dozen examples applaud the highest levels of principled behaviors.

All of these examples are provided chronologically to contextualize unethical actions in sport. This chapter describes several awards and recognitions given by national sport associations to honor outstanding sportsmanship.

Chapter 5 personalizes this examination of sport ethics by providing 35 biographical sketches of athletes, coaches, and leaders whose ethical conduct in sport has been outstanding. Each profile shows how teaching and modeling positive values has made a difference in the lives of those who have been influenced to demonstrate positive values in sports.

Chapter 6 includes 4 documents, 12 figures, and 15 tables that provide evidence of existing ethical problems as well as positive approaches for addressing them. These data and documents provide key facts or statistics to help understand important ethical issues in sports. These data-based entries are placed into historical context. The reader is challenged to draw morally reasoned conclusions about ethical issues in sports based on the facts and evidence presented.

Chapter 7 describes 125 sport and sport-related organizations, which are placed into brief historical context. Web sites and contact information are provided for each organization, along with the connection of national sport governing bodies in the United States to international sport federations. As appropriate, each description connects the organization's scope of work with ethical behavior in sport.

Chapter 8 provides 175 citations of reference works, books, magazine and journal articles, other print works, DVDs, videotapes, databases, and Internet sites, each with an annotation describing its relationship to sport ethics. These print and nonprint resources are the best available for learning more about and staying current with the latest challenges to ethical morality in sports and possible ways to recapture the moral fabric of amateur sports.

The glossary provides brief definitions of over 70 key terms associated with ethical conduct in sports.

Acknowledgments

Parents are the first teachers who begin the process of developing and modeling moral values for their children. I would like to express my deepest appreciation to my parents, Carol and Janice Lumpkin, who taught me what was morally right and helped me learn an ethical code of behavior that has shaped who I am as a person. I dedicate this book to honor them in appreciation for their guidance and love.

1

Background and History

Sport ethics has been called an oxymoron because many believe that sport and ethics are incongruent or contradictory. Sport describes competitive physical activities governed by rules. These competitions usually involve one or more opponents playing for fun and/or reward. Involvement in sport often begins early as balls are some of the first toys given to children, with parents often teaching their children how to throw, catch, and kick. Playing sports and attending sport competitions are frequently shared between children and parents as enjoyable bonding experiences. Many children realize the significance placed on sports; plus, sports are often integrated with friends, food, and fun. Also, everyone is surrounded by mediated sports on television, radio, and the Internet.

Brief Origin of Sport

Even though the exact origin of rule-governed sport is unknown, it is generally assumed that individuals in prehistoric, Chinese, Native American, and other early civilizations engaged in competitive sporting activities. Sports in early eras were usually linked with religion, war, and rites of passage into adulthood. While competitions may have been recreational, the early Mayan civilization took their ball matches more seriously than most, since the losers were often killed.

Most historians credit the Greeks with formalizing competitive sports based on historical documents recounting warrior/athlete competitions. These competitions began as informal, spontaneous displays of athletic prowess but later evolved into pan-Hellenic festivals, including the ancient Olympic Games. Athletic competitions in early Greece were held in honor of various gods and linked directly with religious observances. These festivals included competitions in which athletes ran, jumped, wrestled, boxed, threw the discus and javelin, drove chariots, and rode horses as they demonstrated their skills as warriors.

Sport for men in subsequent civilizations was associated with military preparedness, such as during the Middle Ages in jousting, and in Germany, Sweden, and Denmark in gymnastics and fencing. The British were instrumental in promoting sport competitions through colonization, leading to the worldwide spread of soccer, rugby, field hockey, rowing, tennis, badminton, golf, boxing, and horse racing. The British and other predominately European immigrants brought their love of sports to what became the United States of America.

Sports in the early years in the United States were primarily recreational in nature as individuals of all ages played various ball games. While a few females became sport enthusiasts, mostly males competed in baseball, cricket, bowling, pool, horseshoes, rowing, fox hunting, horse racing, running, boxing, and other physical activities. Baseball, which had become the favorite ball-and-stick game in rural pastures as well as on city streets, and benefited from a set of written rules, was spread during the Civil War as soldiers wearing blue and those wearing gray played in military encampments as well as in prison camps. As the popularity of baseball as a participant sport grew nationwide, it became professionalized when Harry Wright paid all of the Cincinnati Red Stockings players in the late 1860s. With professional baseball players helping to popularize the game, baseball truly became the national pastime as many males (and a few females) played pickup, and later organized, games.

The baseball nine, as a team was called on mostly men's college campuses, was soon supplanted in popularity by the football eleven. As football, a uniquely American game that evolved from rugby and soccer, gained supremacy in colleges, it fostered the construction of stadiums that seated thousands. Newspapers promoted games between teams like Yale and Princeton as their annual contest became a highlight on the social calendar. Male collegians also played baseball and tennis, rowed, ran track, boxed, and engaged in gymnastics, although these sports were never as popular as football. Designed as a winter sport to be played between football and baseball seasons, basketball remained on the periphery on most campuses until after World War II. While played on most campuses, more importantly, it was spread worldwide by the Young Men's Christian Association (YMCA). Basketball did, however, become the most popular participatory sport for females at women's colleges. These women also informally played baseball, field hockey, tennis, and golf, shot archery, fenced, ran track, rowed, and engaged in gymnastics.

Boys' high school sports followed the lead of college sports, with an emphasis on the team sports of football, baseball, and basketball, and track and field. Economic factors limited the breadth of sport programs, but did not deter the enthusiasm displayed by communities in cheering for their local teams. In some small towns, girls' basketball at times rivaled the popularity of boys' basketball. The girls, however, usually played by rules that restricted their movement to a portion of the court due to societal perceptions that the full-court game was too vigorous for females.

Organized youth sports for boys can be traced back to the 1920s, when local communities began to establish teams, especially summer baseball teams, to prevent juvenile delinquency and promote local businesses (as sponsors). Illustrations of the beginnings of national competitive sport programs included American Legion baseball in the 1920s, Pop Warner Football in 1930, Little League Baseball in 1939, and Biddy Basketball in 1950.

Youth, scholastic, collegiate, and Olympic sports mushroomed in fan popularity, participation, and competition in the years after World War II due to economic prosperity, expanding educational opportunities, and the media. Radio, network television, cable television, and the Internet joined the print media in publicizing sports and dramatically increasing the revenues associated with sports. With greater financial benefits to coaches and institutions, most often associated with winning, however, have come ethical concerns.

What Is Ethics?

Ethics is the study of morals, moral values, and character. A person's morals are those motives, intentions, and actions that are right and good, rather than wrong or bad. Moral values describe the relative worth an individual places on virtuous behaviors like honesty, respect, and responsibility (Lumpkin, Stoll, and Beller 2003). People's moral values characterize who they are and what they will do. Family, religion, peers, and societal influences help shape moral values.

In sport and in all aspects of life, people usually make decisions and act based on their moral values. Even though it is assumed that people's lives reflect what they believe is right and wrong, there is the possibility that they may act differently in their personal lives than they do in their professional roles or differently depending on the situation. For example, sometimes when confronted with problems, individuals may fail to rationally analyze the issues, think through the ramifications of different resolutions, or act based on their moral values. Time constraints may lead to hasty actions that under other circumstances would not go against the expectations of others, rules, or laws. Sometimes self-interest or personal advantage may cloud a person's judgment leading to actions with unintended consequences. Peer pressures or unique circumstances may lead to people acting in ways that harm others.

Given these issues and possibly as a way to address these challenges, ethical pluralism suggests taking multiple approaches to the same problem—that is, values may be situational, contextually based, or absolute. Considering the five ethical theories briefly described in the following section could help each person understand how differently people may view the same situation.

Ethical Theories

Utilitarian theory, or utilitarianism, states that the ultimate standard of what is morally right is dependent on the greatest amount of good for the greatest number of people—that is, there is no specific standard of right because it depends on the circumstances and the resultant consequences. Individuals adopting utilitarianism make ethical decisions based on what they think the anticipated short- or long-term consequences will be for most people. The goal is to maximize utility, or amount of satisfaction, benefit, or enjoyment for most individuals. The challenge, however, is determining exactly what this collective human welfare could be. For example, if a collegiate athlete maintains his or her eligibility by receiving an unearned grade from a professor and subsequently helps the team win a championship, this would benefit the team, institution, and maybe thousands of fans. It could be argued that this produces the most benefit, thereby offsetting the fact that the other students in the course did not receive preferential treatment in the grades they received.

The theory of ethical relativism argues that each individual determines what is true, so all points of view are equally valid. Since people believe different things are true, there are no moral absolutes and no definitive right or wrong. The relativist claims that social norms and cultures differ, so morals evolve and change. A relativist might believe Caucasian males deserve preferential treatment in athletics because they are more skilled, even though females did not receive similar treatment. For example, the ethical relativist would not have supported the banning of South Africa, due to its apartheid practices, from the Olympic Games from 1964 to 1992, because discrimination against ethnic groups was acceptable in South Africa at that time. Most reject the theory of ethical relativism because underlying moral values relative to the treatment of others are violated.

Situational ethics is an ethical theory based on love as the only absolute law. Proponents of this theory willingly permit the casting aside of all other moral values. In the absence of a universal standard or law, what matters is the outcome or consequences; so, the end can justify the means. Possibly the following contrasting realities can help illustrate the application of situational ethics. In a pickup game of basketball played among friends, everyone is expected to call his or her own fouls or acknowledge knocking the ball out-of-bounds. Caring about one's friends and maybe getting to keep playing with the group leads to these actions. But, once an organized game is played with officials, most athletes will not admit to the same fouls or violations as the end goal of winning is more important than expressing concern for opponents. Situational ethics has been extended by many athletes and coaches to mean trying to get away with (i.e., not penalized by the officials) as many actions on the field or court as possible to gain advantages.

Non-consequential (Kantian) theory states that there is an absolute moral code of behavior. Whatever is morally right is always right, and wrong behavior is always wrong. In its strictest application, an inherent rightness, or a categorical imperative, exists and can be applied consistently and without partiality in every situation. It is the moral duty of an individual to do what is morally right without regard to the circumstances. In application of this theory, if a volleyball player touches the ball as it goes out-of-bounds, she or he is morally obligated to admit touching the ball, even though it results in the loss of a point. This emphasis on doing one's duty builds moral courage because of the universal standard that applies without exception. This belief in inherent rightness, while making it easier to resist compromises to ethical standards, is sometimes challenged when there are conflicting duties, such as loyalty to teammates and conformity to the rules.

Justice as fairness, another ethical theory, advocates guaranteeing equal rights and equality of opportunity while providing the greatest benefit to those least advantaged. The justice part of this theory states that not everything has to be equal as long as each person has an equal opportunity to succeed or reach a desired outcome. This is balanced by fairness to ensure that those least advantaged will be provided additional benefits in addressing existing disparities. For example, Title IX of the 1972 Education Amendments requires that all students in educational institutions have equal opportunities to participate in sports and are provided with equivalent treatment, benefits, and opportunities. Justice mandates an end to discriminatory treatment. Fairness, however, means equal opportunity, not necessarily spending equal dollars or offering the same number of teams.

Although not an ethical theory, it is important to include a brief overview of moral development. The study of moral development examines how and through what processes people learn and develop morally, even when confronted with psychological and social detractors. Social learning theorists advocate that moral values are learned and developed through a cognitive-developmental approach—that is, experiences with parents, other adults, peers, environmental influences, and the process of socialization progressively shape moral values. These individuals learn principles of right and wrong and develop their reasoning abilities. Some philosophers have suggested that moral judgments advance from a lower level focusing on obedient actions performed to avoid punishment through following rules for self-interest and in conformity to the expectations of parents, peers, and society in general. Ideally, individuals will advance to an adherence to universal ethical principles (Kohlberg 1981).

Moral Reasoning

Those who adhere to principle-based morality advocate using moral reasoning, which is the process of evaluating personal values and developing a consistent, impartial set of moral principles by which to live (Lumpkin, Stoll, and Beller 2003). In order to reason morally, the first step is moral knowing. This means that an individual cognitively learns about moral issues and how to resolve them. The second step is moral feeling, which describes what each person believes along with the beliefs, values, and principles that guide interactions with others. The third step is moral acting, which describes how each individual behaves based on what is known and believed (Kohlberg 1981). Thus, to reason morally, a person identifies what is known about moral values, believes in these values, and, most importantly, has the moral courage to act based on these values.

As will be examined in this book, there are problems with the moral reasoning of athletes. For example, Beller and Stoll (1995) found that the moral reasoning of youth, interscholastic, and intercollegiate athletes is less consistent, impartial, and reflective than is that of nonathletes. The study on "Impact of High School Sports on the Values and Ethics of High School Athletes" reported that interscholastic athletes cheat more in school than do nonathletes. This study also found that boys who play baseball, football, and basketball cheat more (injure, intimidate, and break rules) than do boys playing other sports. Other studies have shown that lower levels of moral reasoning characterize collegiate athletes in revenue-producing sports, athletes in team sports show less moral reasoning than do athletes in individual sports, and male athletes behave less morally than do female athletes (Beller and Stoll 1995; Bredemeier and Shields 1995; Rudd and Stoll 2004; Silva 1983). Of particular concern is the fact that the longer athletes participate in sport, the lower their moral reasoning (Bredemeier 1995; Rudd and Stoll 2004)—that is, as athletes progress through youth, school, college, and professional athletics, they demonstrate less moral courage to reason morally and act based on moral values.

One possible explanation for lower scores on moral reasoning inventories may be the application of groupthink to sport. The concept of groupthink occurs when agreement among group members is the expectation and when individuals wanting to make right decisions are discouraged because group members disagree with these decisions. The cultures of some sports that emphasize winning, or a specific sport's culture, such as the widespread acceptance of throwing at a batter after he hits a home run in baseball, illustrate the existence of groupthink. To apply this concept further, groupthink may lead to the expectation of "taking out" an opponent in football or ice hockey in order to play against a lesser-skilled opponent, and thus increase the possibility of winning. Groupthink may lead to the use of performance-enhancing drugs as athletes seek to enhance their physical abilities to help win championships.

Some athletes try to make it seem that unethical actions are really ethical—that is, they may claim there is no rule against their actions, no one will ever know, or everyone else does it. Some athletes state that their actions are not unethical since no one was harmed or no fouls were called or penalties assessed. Or, they may argue that while rules of the sport were violated, the amount of good accomplished overshadowed the small amount of harm—the ends justify the means (Stoll and Beller 2006). Some athletes use what has been called bracketed morality (Bredemeier and Shields 1995) to justify acting unethically in sport to win or gain advantages. Yet, outside of sport, these individuals behave in congruence with their moral values. Given the behaviors of some athletes, is it possible that they are attempting to justify their unsportsmanlike actions? Do others perceive their actions as unfair, dishonest, disrespectful, and against the rules?

Obstacles and fallacies in moral reasoning can lead to unethical behaviors in sport. Table 1.1 provides several examples to illustrate how athletes, coaches, or others in sport may justify their actions.

Brief Historical Context for Amateur Sport and Character Development

Before exploring further the issue of whether or not there has been an erosion of values in sport as suggested by the examples in Table 1.1, it is important to establish whether or not sport can and should teach character and moral values. Socrates,

TABLE 1.1
Fallacies in Moral Reasoning in Sport

Fallacy	Description of this Fallacy	Sport Examples of Fallacy
Ad hominem	• Attacking the person rather than the argument, such as by name-calling	• A coach who has been violating recruiting rules lashes out against the person who reported these violations by calling him or her a whistle-blower whose word cannot be trusted.
Appeal to ignorance	• Claiming something is right just because it has not been shown to be wrong	• An athlete who has been accused of using performance-enhancing drugs claims that there is no evidence to prove that she or he has used these drugs.
Appeal to force	• Supposing that "might makes right" or that the biggest, strongest, or greatest number must be right	• Since every lineman in football holds, then holding is just an accepted part of how the game is played.
Appeal to tradition	• Resisting change because it is not the way things have typically been done	• College coaches have always been given preferential admissions for their star recruits, so there is no reason to change this successful practice.
Bandwagon effect	• Appealing to what everyone is doing or popular opinion	• Taunting members of opposing teams by fans is a part of the home court advantage.
Circular reasoning or begging the question	• Using one thing to justify or support the same thing	• Football teams bring in most of the revenue so, of course, they should be able to spend whatever they want on their teams.
Dogmatism	• Affirming that a person's subjective certainty (i.e., closed mindedness) is the only solution	• In baseball, everyone accepts that the pitcher is expected to throw at a batter who is crowding the plate.
Equivocation	• Using words incorrectly or those with the wrong meaning to prove a point	• Since the coach is in control, she or he can do whatever it takes to motivate athletes.
Exception to the rule	• Establishing something as true, rather than challenging its truth	• It is impossible for our team to be competitive and athletes adhere to the NCAA's 20-hour per week policy regarding the time they are permitted to be involved with their sports.
Fallacy of authority	• Claiming that something is true just because it was stated or done by someone with authority	• This product must be as good, because my favorite player endorses it.
False cause	• Assuming that one event always causes a second event	• Ms. Smith is too demanding in her English course, which is why three key players on the team are failing this course.
Single cause	• Claiming a simple cause to a complicated problem	• Requiring an athlete who misses classes to run laps in the early morning will motivate him or her to attend classes.
Slippery slope	• Assuming that a specific action, if not continued, will inevitably lead to a bad outcome	• Without a structured off-season conditioning program, athletes will not work diligently and enhance their fitness and skills to help win more games next season.
Straw argument	• Attacking one aspect or a minor point of an argument	• Since so many men's teams have been eliminated, this proves that Title IX is flawed and should not be enforced.

Plato, Aristotle, and other Greek philosophers revered those who attained their highest potential as shown through their superiority in knowledge. This process of demonstrating excellence and virtue, or areté, also was applied to prowess in athletic contests. The victorious athlete was respected and honored by the Greeks because he demonstrated his superiority over all challengers. This was particularly the case when upperclass men, the nobility, trained for war and occasionally competed in athletics, not necessarily for lucrative prizes, but to prove their superior abilities and prowess.

Greek athletes also professionalized sport. After centuries of competing with the goal of displaying their athletic superiority, warrior/athletes were replaced by specialists who, rather than develop as all-around athletes who could run, jump, throw, and engage in hand-to-hand combat, trained in the specific event that they believed they could dominate. Most of these athletes were motivated by the praise and financial rewards that they would receive if they won. The benefits of winning, however, led some athletes to sell their skills to the highest bidder instead of competing as representatives of their home cities. Eventually, because the rewards were valued so highly, some athletes cheated and bribed opponents to let them win. These and other corruptions led to the elimination of the Olympic Games around 400 AD.

By the nineteenth century, British upper-class males, who were leaders of the dominant international power at the time, were competing in sports in elite schools, universities, and private clubs. They claimed that sport taught socialization skills, initiative, loyalty, cooperation, sportsmanship, self-discipline, and leadership, which were viewed as important characteristics for the ruling class. This concept was called the British Amateur Sports Ideal because it was believed that social and moral values were learned, practiced, and reinforced through sport.

Many upper-class males in Great Britain praised those who played at their games (i.e., the amateur), while disrespecting those who worked at sport for financial gain (i.e., the professional). Through this differentiation, upper-class males separated themselves from those who depended on victory for a living or as a supplement to their incomes. Upper-class males advanced this ideal of "playing the game for the game's sake" by attending exclusive educational institutions and building private clubs, such as the All England Lawn Tennis and Croquet

Club (Wimbledon), which excluded those without the financial means and status to join. Working-class males who were eager to play sports for pay were viewed as social inferiors in the economically stratified society of Great Britain.

The British ideal of teaching character and moral values through sport influenced sport worldwide. Among the strongest advocates was Frenchman Pierre de Coubertin, the founder of the modern Olympic Games, who sought to use sport to promote world peace and friendship. When the modern Olympic Games were begun in 1896, de Coubertin and the International Olympic Committee (IOC) perpetuated the British (and Greek-influenced) ideal that sport should be played for the sheer joy of participation and competition, rather than for remuneration. This policy led to the early exclusion of working-class athletes from the Olympic Games, because they could not afford to stop working in order to train for competitions. For more than 80 years, IOC regulations stipulated that athletes had to verify their amateur status to be eligible to compete.

Since the 1980s, though, most Olympic athletes have been professionals because they have trained and competed year-round and supported themselves through appearance fees, prize money, and income from other sport-related activities. In accepting this reality, the IOC permitted each international sport federation to determine eligibility rules for its athletes. Another contributing factor to this elimination of the amateur requirement was the attempt to level the playing field, so the United States and other nations would have a better chance to win the all-important medal count.

Athletics in Educational Institutions

The concept of amateurism in sport has shaped educational sport in the United States as males and females in schools and colleges have played sports as a part of their extracurricular activities (i.e., as a supplement to their academic curriculum). For example, the National Federation of State High School Associations (NFHS) emphasizes that sport participation enhances the academic performance of athletes. This governing organization states that high school athletes have higher grade point averages, lower drop-out rates, better daily attendance, and fewer discipline problems than do nonparticipating students.

School administrators, coaches, and parents believe that the over 7 million high school athletes, in addition to enhancing their sport skills and physical fitness, also learn sportsmanship, self-discipline, and teamwork. This view of interscholastic sports harkens back to the British Amateur Sport Ideal, especially given the fact that the NFHS disallows any high school athlete from receiving financial benefits other than those provided by schools, leagues, or state associations.

The National Collegiate Athletic Association (NCAA) has always viewed college athletes as amateurs and athletics programs as integral to each member institution's educational mission (Falla 1981). The NCAA has attempted to maintain a clear distinction between college athletics and professional sports. The line between the amateur and the professional, however, has changed dramatically as a look at the evolution of athletic scholarships reveals (Sack 2005). When founded in 1906, the NCAA viewed the awarding of athletic scholarships as a violation of amateurism based on the premise that athletics were extracurricular activities for students to engage in during their free time. Despite this, in 1929 the Carnegie Foundation reported in *American College Athletics* that most colleges subsidized athletes in violation of NCAA rules (Savage, Bentley, McGovern, and Smiley 1929). Even though in 1948 the NCAA adopted the Principles for the Conduct of Intercollegiate Athletics (called the Sanity Code) that specifically banned athletic scholarships, several colleges continued to give them. After unsuccessful attempts to enforce this ban, and because of the widespread practice of paying the educational and living expenses of athletes in violation of the NCAA's amateur code, in 1957 the NCAA permitted the awarding of athletic scholarships in its rules. This change was tantamount to sanctioning a practice previously defined as professionalism (Sack 2005).

The NCAA now defines a professional athlete as someone who receives any type of payment for athletic participation other than what its regulations allow. Even though by the late 1900s the British and the IOC realized that amateurism had become historically obsolete and a hypocritical myth, there remains a persistent belief that youth, interscholastic, and intercollegiate sports in the United States should be played by amateurs. This is not the model internationally, however, because seldom do educational institutions sponsor and provide sport teams for students. Rather, individuals participate in a variety of sports through independent clubs that have no connection with schools and colleges.

Another challenge facing amateur sport in colleges is a commercialized arms race (Knight Commission on Intercollegiate Athletics 2001). In an attempt to keep up with conference members or highly ranked teams, institutions are continuously building new athletic facilities for practices, physical conditioning, and competition, or at least making renovations to improve athletic facilities. These expansive and increasingly plush facilities are used to impress potential recruits with the latest and greatest accommodations and possibly to appease the athletes who spend many hours using these facilities. With no constraints on spending, other than how much private funding can be raised, the millions spent on athletic facilities continue to escalate annually. Many schools are modeling their interscholastic sport programs, especially football, after this commercialized concept of building bigger and more elaborate facilities.

Sport for over a century has been used to promote schools and colleges. Since sport is the beneficiary of free publicity in the media, institutions of higher education have used athletics to influence political favor in state capitals and as a key factor in student recruitment. Being able to brag about having outstanding facilities for athletes and luxury boxes for wealthy fans of football and basketball teams gives departments of athletics significant power and influence on their campuses. It could be claimed that intercollegiate athletics has become a model for the transmission of economic, rather than educational, values.

The Knight Commission on Intercollegiate Athletics was formed to examine abuses that were threatening the integrity of intercollegiate athletics and the institutions in which they operate. Based on its examination of numerous areas, such as recruiting and revenues, this Commission recommended a "one-plus-three" model for reform (Knight Commission on Intercollegiate Athletics 1991). Its report suggested that presidential control should lead the way for academic integrity, financial integrity, and certification. A decade later, this Commission reported that despite some reform efforts, the problems in big-time intercollegiate athletics had grown, rather than diminished (Knight Commission on Intercollegiate Athletics 2001). Among these were continued academic abuses, an expensive arms race, heightened commercialization based on television and corporate interests, and a widening chasm between educational values and intercollegiate athletics. The Commission characterized some aspects of intercollegiate athletics as corrupt due to extensive unethical conduct. To address these serious issues, the Commission recommended academic reforms, a reduction in the arms race, and a de-emphasis on commercialization.

Despite the issues identified by the Knight Commission, many still claim that sport builds character and teaches moral values. Sport competitions and seeking to win are not the culprits. Rather, could it be that an overemphasis on winning, monetary outcomes, and moral relativism have overtaken more positive outcomes in importance?

Morals vs. Winning

Since sport heroes may harm their reputations, risk their livelihoods, and maybe even lose their freedom because of their unethical actions, why do they take such huge risks? Some athletes may decide that the financial and personal benefits from winning significantly overshadow the lesser likelihood of being caught. Erosion in character may occur if nonmoral values or other preferences become more important than, and conflict with, moral values, or when a person lacks the moral courage to do what is right. Some athletes, coaches, and fans believe that "winning isn't everything; it's the only thing." Without moral values as guides, the emphasis on winning at all levels of sport can lead to increased unethical and unsportsmanlike behaviors. Within the next paragraphs, frequent occurrences in sport will be briefly described in questioning whether or not these actions are ethical or unethical. These include taunting and intimidation, violence, eligibility, elimination, cheating, gambling, and using performance-enhancing drugs.

Taunting and Intimidation

A large number of athletes and fans believe that taunting is just a part of the game. Some fans assume that the price of admission gives them the right to mock or jeer opponents, since this is part of the home court (or field) advantage. For example, sometimes yelling "air ball" often occurs when an athlete on the visiting team misses the basket entirely on a shot attempt. Taunting attempts to distract and "throw off" the opponent's game. In youth sport through collegiate sport, some adults, including parents of athletes, indicate by their words and actions that taunting is acceptable.

Some athletes seem to take pleasure in showing up opponents when they score touchdowns, hit home runs, or dunk basketballs. Because of the hurtful nature of taunting in some youth, scholastic, and collegiate sports, no taunting policies have been adopted and enforced. Boston University, for example, in 2006 initiated a policy that banned obscene chants and racist and sexist comments at sporting events on its campus. Despite claims from students that this no-taunting policy was an infringement of their freedom of speech, university administrators emphasized that yelling obscenities is not supporting the home team.

One objective of taunting is intimidation, or behaviors intended to keep opponents from performing as skillfully as they potentially could. Physical and psychological intimidation have become normal actions for some athletes. A hard foul on a shooter, a crushing tackle on a wide receiver, a pitcher throwing a high and tight fastball to a batter, and a laser forehand hit toward the head of a player at the tennis net are examples of how athletes seek to instill doubt or timidity in opponents. Is this good strategy, playing fair, trying to injure an opponent, and/or intimidation?

Psychological intimidation is more subtle than physical intimidation. Is trying to get inside someone's head to throw him or her off just how the game is played? While Larry Bird and Michael Jordan were two of the all-time greatest players in the National Basketball Association, they also were two of the most prodigious trash talkers in trying to intimidate their opponents. Are their examples of trash talking what youth, interscholastic, and intercollegiate athletes should follow?

Some coaches use intimidation to motivate athletes. For example, a coach may use negative feedback, obscene language, and physical punishments in hopes of changing an athlete's performance or effort. While former coach Bobby Knight has been praised as an outstanding coach, many have questioned his use of vulgarity and in-your-face confrontations with athletes on his teams.

Violence

Athletes, especially in sports in which physical contact is integral to the game, sometimes have a difficult time drawing the line between adhering to the rules and breaking not only the letter of the rules but also the spirit of the rules. The spirit of the rules refers to playing the game without resorting to gamesmanship or strategies designed to exploit the rules to gain unfair advantages. Constitutive rules govern how a specific sport should be played and differentiate it from other sports. Proscriptive rules forbid or prohibit certain actions, such as undercutting in basketball or clipping in football. Often these rules have been developed and are enforced to reduce and prevent violent actions that cause serious injuries and harm athletes. Some proscriptive rules have been added to address behaviors such as hockey players using their sticks as weapons and athletes losing control and fighting. Sportsmanship rules have been added in an attempt to thwart out-of-control actions, such as when a soccer player receives a red card (resulting in disqualification) for repeatedly tripping opponents or 15-yard penalties in football for unsportsmanlike conduct such as spearing.

Is violence on the rise in sports because athletes view opponents as objects to be removed in the headlong pursuit of victory? It is easier to intentionally harm another person when she or he is viewed as an object, rather than a human being. For example, in 1994 the cronies of Tonya Harding hit her rival, Nancy Kerrigan, in the knee to incapacitate her so she would be unable to compete in the U.S. Figure Skating Championships, which was the qualifying event for selecting figure skaters for the Olympic Games. In 2006, Mitch Cozad, backup punter at the University of Northern Colorado, stabbed the starting punter in his kicking leg in order to better Cozad's chances of getting to play. Such actions seem to indicate that individuals will resort to violence if it will benefit them personally.

Has the seriousness of injuries increased because some coaches urge athletes to be more aggressive? For example, John Chaney, former basketball coach at Temple University, in 2005 directed an athlete on his team to rough up an opponent. ESPN's SportsCenter often shows vicious hits in football and ice hockey. This seemingly reinforces that violence is central to how these games should be played. During the telecast of a collegiate bowl game in 2008, the broadcasters in discussing a video of a youth football game praised one athlete who violently blindsided and knocked out his opponent. Is it any wonder that impressionable young athletes mimic their sport heroes?

In thinking about violence in sport, it is important to ask why violence is permitted in sports, why it is taught, why it is condoned, and why it is rewarded. Violence is used to intimidate and thereby gain competitive advantages. Violence increases whenever proscriptive and sportsmanship rules are not enforced—that is, athletes learn quickly what they can and cannot get by with and then act accordingly. For example, basketball players are coached to see how the game is being officiated and then to adjust their actions accordingly. So, if holding or hand-checking is not being penalized, athletes are coached to engage in these actions as aggressively as allowed. The bottom line is that overly aggressive and violent actions have become more acceptable; deciding where to draw the line between ethical and unethical behavior has become blurred for many.

Violence is taught by some coaches, teammates, and parents because it is perceived that it can help in gaining competitive advantages. What else would lead a father to sharpen the exposed edges of his son's football helmet in order to injure opponents and get the opposing team's best players off the field because they are bleeding? It is argued that some fans want to see hockey players drop their sticks and fight, deadly crashes on the racetrack, or incapacitating hits in football. Some sport administrators admit that they permit and encourage violence because it sells. Athletes realize that sometimes violent behaviors in sport are rewarded. A hard slide into the shortstop to break up an attempted double play or hacking the low post player on his or her way up for an easy two points are considered by many to be good aggressive play. Is there a point at which actions like these violate the letter and spirit of the rules?

Eligibility

Some people may question how eligibility issues relate to sport ethics. In youth sports, there are age and weight categories specifying who can or cannot play on teams so competition is more fair and equitable. However, it seems for every rule, such as age limits or number of years played in interscholastic sports, there are attempts to get around these rules. For example, some parents choose to gain developmental advantages for their sons by holding them back a grade in elementary or middle school so they will be physically more developed when competing in interscholastic sports.

A huge issue in interscholastic sports today deals with recruiting. Private schools and special interest or magnet schools, which do not have defined attendance areas as do public schools, are free to recruit skilled athletes to attend their schools and offer scholarships. Some argue that this is unethical because of the unfair advantages gained by teams with recruited athletes. Another controversial issue in schools is whether "no pass, no play," a policy that requires a specified level of academic achievement in order to be eligible to play, discriminates against adolescents based on socioeconomic status and associated learning opportunities.

The most controversial issue surrounding eligibility in colleges also relates to academics. As coaches identify prospective athletes who they want to play on their teams, they may learn that recruits have low grade point averages or earned low scores on admission tests. Some coaches seek and obtain preferential admissions for marginally prepared students based on the argument that these adolescents deserve educational opportunities. It may be more likely that these coaches simply believe these blue-chip athletes can help their teams win. Once these students are admitted, despite tutoring and other academic support services, many of these students struggle academically and fail, primarily because they did not have the requisite preparation for college-level work.

Intercollegiate athletics associations require that these athletes make normal progress toward their chosen program of study in order to maintain eligibility to compete. This sometimes results in athletes being given unearned grades and athletes taking a smorgasbord of courses that do not lead to degrees. The low graduation rates associated with sport teams at some institutions illustrates this ethical issue. The NCAA's Academic Progress Rate is one approach to reemphasize the importance of students earning a degree because it holds institutions accountable for the progress that athletes are making academically.

Elimination

In some cases, there may be ethical issues associated with the elimination of athletes from sports. Young athletes, when asked why they participate in sports, consistently respond that having fun is most important. Several studies and researchers have stated that 50 to 70 percent of youth have self-selected, for physical and psychological reasons, out of sports by age 13. These youth say they drop out because they are not having fun anymore, are not getting to play or to play a preferred position, have limited input because programs are controlled by parents and coaches, are tired of the intensity of their training, and are bothered by receiving so much negative feedback.

Many middle and secondary school students are cut from teams or choose not to even try to make teams because they perceive that they lack the skills. Some adolescents have grown tired of coaches or parents who push them too hard in sports, such as through the expectation to concentrate on only one sport year-round, even at times when they have been injured due to overtraining. Other young athletes do not want to deal with the expectations of their communities to lead their teams to championships or of parents who pressure them to succeed because of huge financial investments in their training programs.

Most students in high school do not play on sport teams. They have already opted out or been cut in the narrowing of the sport funnel as fewer participation opportunities are provided. This elimination process is even more significant at the collegiate level with fewer than 5 percent of scholastic athletes being recruited to play sports in college (National Collegiate Athletic Association 2007). Some college athletes leave sports because of year-round training, coaches' demands for improved performance, and pressures to win. To address the issue of dropout, maybe athletes, parents, and coaches should agree on the purpose of sports at each level. Is it for fun, fitness, character development, or competitions primarily among the highly skilled, or for winning?

Cheating

Winning is the primary culprit, many suggest, that leads to cheating in sports. While seeking to win is why sports are played, is it how the victory is sought after and attained that is the issue? It seems that the goal for some athletes and coaches is to try to outwit the officials. For others, it is how to circumvent rules for personal advantage. Cheating takes many forms, such as copying a classmate's paper or exam to help maintain eligibility, or giving a college athlete or family member financial benefits not permitted by the rules to influence the athlete's decision about which college to attend. Is it cheating to claim to catch a pass that you know hit the ground first or faking an injury to stop the clock so the kicker can get set up to attempt a potential game-winning field goal?

Some athletes and coaches claim that if they are not cheating, then they are not trying hard enough to win. Have unethical actions been accepted as just the way the game is played? Sometimes cheaters gain advantages and are praised for their creativity and rewarded for winning as long as what they do is not harmful or dirty; so, is any cheating right? Since many coaches cheat during recruiting, such as by giving inducements or making too many contacts with recruits, are the best recruiters those who cheat in signing the best recruits without getting caught?

Has cheating increased because winning has become so important? For example, did Major League Baseball ignore the known use of steroids and other performance-enhancing drugs because teams' revenues were increasing? Have the cultures of some sports accepted cheating, such as stealing signs, videotaping other teams' signals, and hand-checking on defense in basketball, as good strategies? That is, does today's apparent condoning of cheating in sport mean that athletes, coaches, and fans have developed a tolerance to cheating like a drug abuser builds up a tolerance for a physically dependent drug like cocaine or heroin? If this is the case, is this ethical?

Gambling

One specific example of cheating is gambling, such as when athletes are enticed by gamblers to fix games. By controlling the point spread, readily available in numerous media, athletes and gamblers can make money. Most, but not all, people view fixing games as unethical. When officials, such as Tim Donaghy, a former referee in the National Basketball Association, may have changed the outcome of games, most believe that such actions are wrong. But is gambling wrong when it is a small wager among friends on the golf course, or if a person joins an online pool for the NCAA men's basketball championship bracket?

Performance-Enhancing Drugs

The steroid era in Major League Baseball and the doping scandals in international cycling illustrate that the use of performance-enhancing drugs is more widespread among athletes than many imagined. To some, the use of performance-enhancing drugs is strictly a legal issue, since athletes were not tested for drugs and proven to have used them—that is, is the only question whether obtaining these drugs violated federal law? To others, the use of performance-enhancing drugs is a moral issue because the athletes who use them are intentionally gaining physical advantages in ways that make a mockery of the best athlete versus the best athlete (not the best pharmacist).

Why have many elite athletes risked harming their bodies, possibly permanently, to get stronger, faster, or more skillful? Is it because of the associated financial rewards and ego benefits of winning? Some athletes seem to want to win so intensely or are driven by multimillion dollar contracts, astronomical endorsement deals, and celebrity status that they will do whatever it takes to attain them.

Moral Callousness

Whenever athletes, coaches, and fans justify taunting, intimidation, violence, cheating, use of performance-enhancing drugs, and related behaviors, they may be illustrating *moral callousness* (Kretchmar 2005). This term describes how people harden their feelings, like forming calluses on the hands from manual labor, so they no longer feel that their actions are morally wrong. For example, athletes may justify their use of performance-enhancing drugs by stating that all other athletes are using these drugs, so they have no choice but to use them to compete on a level playing field or have a chance to win. Or, coaches may rationalize violating recruiting regulations by claiming that other coaches are cheating in recruiting, therefore, their cheating must be acceptable, too. When asked, athletes and coaches who violate the rules in these or similar ways may rationalize that they have done nothing morally wrong.

To further illustrate this concept of moral callousness, many athletes, when asked, acknowledge that their coaches teach them how to cheat. For example, some coaches teach basketball and football players how to gain advantages, such as through holding, in ways that are difficult to detect. Some soccer goalies are taught how to advance past the goal line on penalty kicks, even though the rules prohibit it. Basketball players who shoot free throws at higher success rates may be taught how to take the places of their fouled teammates who are less accurate shooters. Some coaches alter playing fields in ways that benefit their teams and teach their players to take advantage of how the field has been changed. Many coaches tell their athletes never to tell an official about knocking the ball out-of-bounds or not catching a pass, if the officials' incorrect calls are in their teams' favor. These same athletes are conditioned to believe that it is acceptable for their coaches to yell at officials when incorrect calls are not in their teams' favor. Many coaches ignore, condone, and even encourage trash talking as a psychological ploy against opponents.

Is sport ethics an oxymoron? Has there been a moral drift toward the acceptance of more unethical behaviors in sport? Or, can moral values and character be developed in and through sport? The next section will explore the interface between amateur sport, ethical conduct, and importance of character and moral values in sports.

Synergy between Character Development and Sport

Athletic ability and sport achievement are highly esteemed in this country, as verified by multimillion dollar salaries and nonstop mediated sport. Another reason for this status is the belief that sport teaches moral values and life lessons. Many people realize that behaviors learned in sport, whether good or bad, will last a lifetime. These individuals state that sport has the potential to teach social values like cooperation and teamwork and moral values like integrity, respect, and justice. Parents want their children to participate in sport programs that will help them learn these values.

Character education includes teaching athletes and coaches moral reasoning or knowing what is right, valuing what is right, and doing what is right. Initiating this process could begin with encouraging athletes and coaches to question what the media, other athletes, and other coaches may suggest is right. Since humans frequently model what they see, athletes and coaches may never have been challenged to ask why certain behaviors in many sports seem integral to and characteristic of them. For example, is it morally defensible for a wrestling or gymnastics coach to expect a normally maturing athlete to drop weight, such as through eating too little, wearing a rubber suit while working out, or failing to hydrate properly? Does sport give coaches the right to use obscene language and verbal abuse to motivate athletes?

Cognitive dissonance describes the questioning approach through which athletes and coaches could examine what is the right thing to do in sports. The key to developing cognitive dissonance necessitates that athletes and coaches question situations and issues to learn to differentiate between what is morally right and wrong. This can occur through formal and informal processes. For example, intervention programs, such as described below, could have a positive and long-term effect on moral reasoning.

Athletes can be educated about what character is, what it looks like, and how to live principled lives. Steps that coaches and parents can take to help achieve the goal of building character include: (a) modeling what character is, shaping and continuing to mold moral values, and consistently reinforcing and praising the ethical behaviors of young athletes; (b) teaching what it means to treat opponents, officials, and teammates honorably and respectfully while following the letter and spirit of the rules; (c) modeling how to behave when faced with morally challenging situations; (d) shaping players' thinking so effort, hard work, and doing one's best are more important than winning; and (e) reinforcing how character is displayed in sport, such as through sportsmanship and fair play, and how moral values can be applied in other aspects of life.

Four moral values of justice, honesty, responsibility, and beneficence will be described to illustrate how their underlying principles can contribute to the development of character. Justice means treating others with fairness, such as through the distribution of benefits, equitable application of policies and procedures, equity in punishments, and appropriate compensation whenever harm or unfairness has been suffered. A universal rule of conduct associated with justice is: do not violate the rules of the game. So, the athlete who tries to gain advantages without being penalized by an official is violating this principle. Honesty is about keeping promises, telling the truth, and being trustworthy. Honest athletes and coaches adhere to the principle of do not cheat or lie, even if they believe that a rule may be flawed or that it would be to their advantage to cheat or lie. Responsibility encompasses fulfilling one's duty and being a person who can be counted on to carry out what is expected. In order not to act irresponsibly, an athlete as a dependable teammate puts the team ahead of selfish interests. Beneficence refers to playing fairly or doing good. The beneficent athlete does not intentionally harm an opponent, helps prevent a teammate from getting into a fight, avoids a potentially volatile situation, and does good by being a role model for ethical behavior (Lumpkin, Stoll, and Beller 2003).

In addition to moral values like these four, a socially valued, moral virtue is a deeply held trait or disposition that causes a person to act morally. Moral virtues especially relevant to sports include civility, cool-headedness, courage, loyalty, modesty, persistence, and teamwork. When displaying these virtues, athletes can learn to be confident, dependable, determined, disciplined, eager to learn, enthusiastic, and poised. Athletes with these virtues are more likely to work hard, put the team first, learn from mistakes and failures, become mentally tough, develop and show moral courage by being willing to stand up for what is right, and win and lose with class.

Coaches of young athletes, with the support of parents, keep winning in perspective while establishing team cultures that nurture and develop moral values and moral virtues. They establish rituals and procedures, such as starting practices with comments emphasizing character, use trigger words and actions as reminders for ethical behaviors that should be repeated, such as thanking the passer for an assist, and utilize teachable moments to reinforce moral values. Through the process of transforming the culture in sport, winning is redefined (not focused on the scoreboard), players' efforts (not the outcome) are rewarded, specific, measurable, attainable, rewarding, and timely goals are set to stretch each player to work harder, and symbolic rewards are given to reward effort and achieving personal growth in character.

Athletes can be highly competitive, yet still demonstrate sportsmanship. Respecting opponents, officials, teammates, and the letter and spirit of the rule describes sportsmanship. It also includes gracefulness in losing, inevitably a part of the game, while working diligently to win. Learning sportsmanship can be an important precursor to learning about living. It includes the integrity to win with humility and lose without making excuses, throwing things, or starting fights. With these moral values and moral virtues as desirable outcomes, next comes a discussion about how to develop character.

Steps in Character Development

There are five key steps in character development. The first step requires each person to identify his or her core values, such as respect and responsibility. Respect is holding others in high regard and treating them the way you wish to be treated. It includes being considerate of others and expressing appreciation when others do things for you, accepting others along with their personal differences and speaking positively about them, resolving interpersonal problems amiably, and never intentionally hurting other people physically, mentally, or emotionally. Responsibility describes behaviors that result from being morally accountable for actions, accepting the consequences of these actions (admit mistakes and make corrections), making thoughtful choices that determine perceptions, thoughts, and actions, and taking an honest inventory of strengths and abilities and developing these. While not the only core moral values, these illustrate the importance of each person determining what guideposts will shape decisions and actions.

In the second step, each person develops the ability to reason morally. As discussed previously, the moral reasoning process encompasses knowing what is important, believing in these values, and having the moral courage to act based on these values. In the third step, each person learns from and follows role models of moral courage to do the right thing. The following three examples illustrate this vividly.

First, in 1948, John Wooden interviewed for a coaching position at the University of Minnesota and the University of California at Los Angeles (UCLA). It was arranged that Minnesota's athletic director (AD) would call at a specified date and time if an offer was to be made. When Wooden did not receive the job offer by this time, he accepted UCLA's coaching position. When the AD from Minnesota called late with the offer, he explained that a raging snowstorm had caused his delay in getting to a telephone and calling. Wooden responded that he would not renege on his commitment to UCLA, even though he had planned to accept Minnesota's job. It is no wonder that during his career Wooden developed his famous pyramid of success, which is a graphic representation of his values and those he taught and emphasized as he coached.

A second example occurred in 1940 in football. Dartmouth outplayed nationally ranked Cornell until Cornell scored a touchdown on a fifth down, which was mistakenly awarded to that team on the next-to-last play of the game. The game ended with the score Cornell 7, Dartmouth 3. The next day, the referee admitted his mistake in allowing a fifth down to be played after he reviewed data and pictures from the game. The president of Cornell immediately sent a telegram to the president of Dartmouth, awarding the victory to Dartmouth.

Example three comes from tournament golf, in which the code of honor expects each player to be a stringent and unwaveringly honest referee—that is, since each player adheres to the moral standard of honesty, she or he will immediately acknowledge moving a ball or violating any other rule of golf, even though this results in a penalty stroke.

The fourth step in character development occurs when a person learns from past lapses when she or he failed to act morally. Only time will tell if Marion Jones learned from her unethical and illegal behaviors of using performance-enhancing drugs and lying repeatedly about their use. Many athletes who have shaved points, gambled, taunted, and were violent have expressed remorse for their actions and changed how they made future decisions.

The fifth step expects a person to consistently live in conformity with moral values. For example, National Baseball Hall of Fame inductees in 2007, Cal Ripken Jr. and Tony Gwynn, have often been praised for not only their outstanding achievements as players, but also for the quality and influence of their lives as positive role models.

Successful Programs That Help Develop Moral Values and Character

There are numerous organizations and efforts focused on developing character through sport, possibly in response to how the moral reasoning of athletes lessens as the competitive level increases. Four examples will be briefly described. First, the Institute for International Sport promotes thoughtful discussions and activities by athletes, parents, coaches, and administrators about how sport can serve as a positive force in society and collaborates with *USA Today* in sponsoring a national essay contest to enhance the growth of National Sportsmanship Day. Second, Character Counts, the approach to character education established by the Josephson Institute of Ethics, promotes six pillars of character in schools and communities: trustworthiness, respect, responsibility, fairness, caring, and citizenship rules. It uses these six pillars as the foundation for its sportsmanship campaign, Pursuing Victory with Honor. Third, the Champions of Character program offered by the National Association of Intercollegiate Athletics seeks to instill an understanding of the core character values in sport of respect, responsibility, integrity, servant leadership, and sportsmanship. It provides practical tools for athletes, coaches, and parents to use in modeling exemplary character traits. Fourth, Winning with Character is a nonprofit organization providing character, ethics, and leadership training to high school and college athletic programs. Its educational programs and materials are designed to improve moral reasoning and social values among male and female athletes by challenging them to reach their full potential in the classroom, on the field, and in society, providing understanding, reasoning, and application of moral and ethical principles, and seeking to change students' values, thinking, and behavior.

Resolving Ethical Dilemmas

Programs like these seek to help athletes make reasoned decisions in sport. When faced with ethical dilemmas, it is important to understand the process that leads to behaving morally. The starting point is to define and interpret the situation by identifying the issue or issues and gathering the facts (who did what). In this data-gathering process, it is helpful to explore what actions are possible, who and how people might be affected by a specific course of action, and how these individuals possibly would react depending on what might occur.

In the analysis phase, each person tests what is right and wrong in comparison with his or her moral values. Three informal tests can help in deciding what a person believes is the morally right action to take. The "stench test" describes a negative, gut-level reaction to the situation—that is, if a person feels that an action is wrong, then do not do it. The "media test" suggests that if a person would be uncomfortable if the planned action or decision were to be reported in the national or local media, then do not do it. The "mom test" offers that if a person is considering violating the moral values of someone cared about, then do not do it (Blanchard and Peale 1988). In addition, during the analysis phase, it is important to identify any colliding values, because at times two right values may conflict. For example, what should be done when telling the truth would hurt a teammate's feelings and possibly be perceived as disrespectful? Whenever this may occur, the challenge is to determine how to prioritize or stack these values in order to resolve the dilemma. A caution, however, is to make sure that moral values trump personal preferences. Finally, each person decides whether to act morally. It takes moral courage to take the morally right action.

Several principles can help in resolving ethical dilemmas. First, it is essential to keep winning in perspective. It is important to educate coaches, athletes, sport administrators, and fans about values, such as sportsmanship, and stress playing the game by the letter and spirit of the rules. Helpful in this educational process could be to develop, publicize, and enforce codes of conduct. In order to make these codes effective, however, penalties may have to be assessed whenever unethical behaviors occur. When sport administrators keep winning in perspective, they will choose to hire and retain coaches based on integrity and their modeling of moral values (not based on their win-loss records). Coaches, athletes, and others who are committed to sport helping to build character will choose to follow the rules of sport governing organizations.

Conclusion

Sport ethics may have become an oxymoron. But, this current erosion in moral values and character development through sport does not have to be accepted as inevitable result. In some instances, sport has become morally bankrupt as numerous examples of unethical behaviors threaten fair play, sportsmanship, and character development. Some young athletes can become selfish, undisciplined, and act unethically when they realize that principles of fairness and integrity are not enforced. However, when parents and coaches teach, model, shape, and reinforce moral reasoning and influence learning morally sound lessons for life, athletes can learn about and strengthen their character. Moral values like integrity, respect, and responsibility are integral to sport when striving to perform to the best of one's abilities replaces an overemphasis on winning. Parents and coaches can emphasize pursuing victory with honor and playing the game by the letter and spirit of the rules.

As the outcome of the game hangs in the balance, so does integrity. Morally based actions can reflect the moral values integral to whom each athlete is. As stated in the Olympic Creed, "The most important thing in life is not the triumph, but the fight; the essential thing is not to have won, but to have fought well" (International Olympic Committee n.d.). After all, athletes would rather play, even on a losing team, than sit on the bench for a winning team, because it is playing a sport that is fun. Athletes playing to the best of their abilities while valuing others and the integrity of the letter and spirit of the rules are engaged in life-enriching activities.

References

Beller, J. M., and S. K. Stoll. 1995. "Moral Reasoning of High School Student Athletes and General Students: An Empirical Study versus Personal Testimony." *Pediatric Exercise Science* 7 (4): 352–363.

Blanchard, K., and N. V. Peale. 1988. *The Power of Ethical Management.* New York: William Morrow.

Bredemeier, B. J. L. 1995. "Divergence in Children's Moral Reasoning about Issues in Daily Life and Sport Specific Contexts." *International Journal of Sport Psychology* 26 (4): 453–463.

Bredemeier, B. J., and D. L. Shields. 1995. *Character Development and Physical Activity*. Champaign, IL: Human Kinetics.

Falla, J. 1981. *NCAA: The Voice of College Sports*. Mission, KS: National Collegiate Athletic Association.

Institute for International Sport. "National Sportsmanship Day." Available at: http://www.internationalsport.com/nsd/index.cfm.

International Olympic Committee. "The Important Thing...." Available at: http://www.olympic.org/uk/games/past/innovations_uk.asp?OLGT=1&OLGY=1908.

Josephson Institute of Ethics. "Character Counts!" Available at: http://josephsoninstitute.org/sports/index.html.

Josephson Institute on Ethics. "Impact of High School Sports on the Values and Ethics of High School Athletes." Available at: http://josephsoninstitute.org/pdf/sports_survey_report_022107.pdf.

Knight Commission on Intercollegiate Athletics. 1991. "Keeping Faith with the Student-Athlete: A New Model for Intercollegiate Athletics." Available at: http://www.knightcommission.org/images/uploads/1991-93_KCIA_report.pdf.

Knight Commission on Intercollegiate Athletics. 2001. "A Call to Action: Reconnecting College Sports and Higher Education." Available at: http://www.knightcommission.org/images/uploads/KCfinal-06-2001.pdf.

Kohlberg, L. 1981. *The Philosophy of Moral Development: Moral Stages and the Idea of Justice*. New York: Harper and Row.

Kretchmar, R. S. 2005. *Practical Philosophy of Sport and Physical Activity*, 2nd ed. Champaign, IL: Human Kinetics.

Lumpkin, A., S. K. Stoll, and J. M. Beller. 2003. *Sport Ethics: Applications for Fair Play*, 3rd ed. Boston: McGraw-Hill.

National Association of Intercollegiate Athletics. "Champions of Character." Available at: http://naia.cstv.com/champions-character.

National Collegiate Athletic Association. 2007. "Estimated Probability of Competing in Athletics beyond the High School Interscholastic Level." Available at: http://www.ncaa.org/research/prob_of_competing/probability_of_competing2.html.

National Federation of State High School Associations. "High School Sports Participation Increases Again; Girls Exceeds Three Million for First Time." Available at: http://www.nfhs.org/web/2007/09/high_school_sports_participation.aspx.

Rudd, A., and S. Stoll. 2004. "What Type of Character Do Athletes Possess? An Empirical Examination of College Athletes versus College

Non-Athletes with the RSBH Value Judgment Inventory." *Sport Journal* 7 (2): 1–10.

Sack, A. L. 2005. "Amateur vs. Professional Debate." *Berkshire Encyclopedia of World Sport*, Vol. 1: 44–49.

Savage, H., H. W. Bentley, J. T. McGovern, and D. F. Smiley. 1929. *American College Athletics.* New York: Carnegie Foundation for the Advancement of Teaching.

Silva, J. M. 1983. "The Perceived Legitimacy of Rule Violating Behavior in Sport." *Journal of Sport Psychology* 5 (4): 438–448.

Stoll, S. K., and J. M. Beller. 2006. "Ethical Dilemmas in College Sport." In *New Game Plan for College Sport*, edited by R. E. Lapchick, 75–90. Westport, CT: Praeger.

Winning with Character, Inc. "Providing Character and Ethics Education to Student Athletes." Available at: http://winningwithcharacter. org.

2

Problems, Controversies, and Solutions

Sport is a multibillion dollar industry with popularity across all ages, ethnicities, and socioeconomic strata. Relationships with various media have helped sport attain an unprecedented status in the United States and internationally—that is, the media promote sports, and sports increase the reach and popularity of various media. The reach of sport encompasses participation, products, and entertainment.

Millions of people participate in sports through Little League Baseball, Pop Warner Football, the Senior Games, the Olympic Games, and public and private sport organizations, clubs, schools, and colleges. Sport participation includes occasional golf outings with business associates, softball games at family reunions, pickup games of basketball with friends at recreation centers, and sport camps for youths and adolescents. Relative to sport products, most households have sport equipment and clothing as well as collectibles associated with favorite teams. Millions of dollars are invested in outfitting athletes with equipment and uniforms, purchasing sport-related video games, and equipping homes and businesses with various electronics that enhance the viewing of favorite teams and players. Sporting events are always available, with in-person and electronic spectating as people are entertained day and night with an endless array of sports and demonstrate a seemingly insatiable appetite for sports.

Overlaying the pervasiveness of sport, however, are numerous challenges. Many perceive that there has been a decrease in the integrity associated with sport because winning has become too important—that is, breaking rules to gain competitive advantages and a "winning is everything" mentality in many instances have replaced honesty, respect, sportsmanship, and fair play. Others, who claim playing a sport can and does teach character, argue that this is a desired outcome because sport helps prepare people for life. To examine whether sport, character, and winning can coexist in positive ways, this chapter will examine controversies and problems across all levels of sport, followed by sections specifically analyzing youth, interscholastic, and intercollegiate sports. Recommendations for addressing the controversies and problems confronting sport will be offered.

Controversies and Problems across All Levels of Sport

Whenever winning becomes the sole purpose of sport, then everything else, including moral values and the development of character, seems threatened. The identity of the United States as a global power, it seems, is predicated on winning—politically, economically, and being No. 1 in sport. Not only is the team representing the United States expected to win the most medals in the Olympic Games, but athletes from this country are expected to win the Davis Cup (men) and Federation Cup (women) in tennis, Ryder Cup (men) and Solheim Cup (women) in golf, the America's Cup (this cup is named for the first yacht to win the trophy), and other international sport competitions. Pressures to win on some athletes, coaches, and sport administrators may lead to actions that violate sport rules or rules of sport governing organizations, as they justify behaviors by stating that they just did these things to try to win.

But, why is winning such a powerful motivator that it can lead to unprincipled actions? The answer points directly to the benefits that accrue to the victorious. Winners become sport heroes and heroines and enjoy the rewards of victory. For example, winners get carried off the field or court, have their pictures in newspapers, appear on ESPN's SportsCenter, and get invited to meet the president at the White House. The big man (and sometimes woman) on campus phenomenon thrives in schools and colleges as athletes who win are recognized by others, and their achievements are celebrated. By way of contrast, seldom is heard a word about athletes who compete to the best of their abilities and serve as role models of sportsmanship. The fact that people in this country love a winner is a lesson not lost on the young, who are constantly bombarded with evidence of the celebrity status and financial benefits enjoyed by those who win.

Has Winning in Sports Become Too Important?

Given the overwhelming evidence that winners are rewarded handsomely, it is easy to understand why pressures to win increase. Parents and coaches may begin with encouragement for children to play sports, but too often they forget the ages of youthful athletes and begin to push, prod, berate, yell, punish, and demean them when they do not perform like professional athletes. Pressures to win may be physical, such as when a coach ignores an injury and plays an athlete to help win a game, despite the potential for a permanent injury. Or, athletes may hide their injuries from coaches and parents because they are fearful of harsh comments questioning their commitment to the team or constant reminders about the financial and time investments in their sport development made by these adults (Coakley 2009).

Pressures to win also may be psychological, such as when a coach questions an athlete's effort or heart in trying to motivate him or her to play better. When the stakes are higher, such as in a championship game, the pressures from coaches, parents, and fans usually are more intense. One sad example of the destructive consequences of such pressures to win in high school occurred several years ago in Pennsylvania. In the suicide note left by a sophomore quarterback, he stated that after leading his team to the state championship, he could not deal with the pressures of having to do this two more years. Of course, there are also the self-imposed pressures that athletes feel. The intensity of these pressures to win are related to numerous factors, such as the athlete's perceptions of and reactions to pressures from parents, coaches, and fans, confidence or lack of confidence in the athlete's abilities to succeed, and the attraction of the anticipated status and financial benefits that will accompany winning.

The pressures to win on youth, interscholastic, and intercollegiate athletes are disproportionate to the likelihood of achieving the desired outcome. For example, in every team sport there are as many nonwinners as there are winners on the scoreboard. In an individual sport such as golf or track and field, there is one winner and numerous nonwinners. The word *loser* was intentionally not used because it has become a negative—that is, calling an athlete a loser is so derogatory that it may lead to a verbal or physical response. As long as adults involved with sport praise and reward winners and ignore or disapprove of those who do not win on the scoreboard, many athletes and coaches may choose to do almost anything to win. Some athletes and coaches engage in unethical behaviors so they can avoid the negativity associated with not winning.

But, it might be asked, if it is not about winning, then why keep score? An essential differentiation needs to be made between winning (at any cost?) and seeking to win while playing ethically. To illustrate this point, Harold Abrahams in the movie *Chariots of Fire* is questioned about whether he is placing too much emphasis on winning. He responds that he is not trying to win at any cost, but he is seeking to win within the rules.

At most, athletes win only half the time. In contrast, seeking to win remains a viable objective whenever athletes compete. The athlete who is seeking to win tries to play as skillfully as possible. However, despite diligent preparation and effort, this may not result in a victory. So, if competing in sports is not primarily about winning, what are the goals? Shared goals for youth, interscholastic, and intercollegiate sports include having fun, developing sport skills, building character, and learning life lessons.

Maybe one way to help keep winning in perspective is to shape it differently. Winning could be defined as competing against one's self to become the best athlete possible—that is, learning sport skills and using these skills during competitions allow an athlete to measure his or her performance against a personal standard or potential. Another benchmark could be improvement as athletes continue to develop and expand their sport skills. Sometimes athletes compete against a standard like the clock, a course, or a specific distance. In this context, the process of seeking to win is characterized by exerting maximal effort, learning from mistakes, and appreciating incremental progress.

Despite these alternative perspectives, the emphasis placed on winning remains. When sport stresses and rewards only winning, problems emerge at all levels of sport. These include cheating, gamesmanship and violence, discriminatory actions, and the use of performance-enhancing drugs, which will be discussed in the next sections.

Cheating

Possibly the most widespread controversy related to winning is what is or is not fair, honest, ethical, or right within sport. Some athletes and coaches believe that it is only cheating if you get caught. They feel no ethical obligation to play by the rules, unless they are forced to comply. For example, Bill Belichick and the New England Patriots were suspected of stealing signs from opposing teams for years. In 2007, Belichick and the Patriots were caught videotaping hand signals from defensive coaches from the New York Jets. They were fined by the commissioner of the National Football League for intentionally defying a policy statement that such cheating would not be tolerated.

The driving force for cheating within sport is to gain competitive advantages—that is, some athletes and coaches behave as if they will do whatever it takes to win. This may mean intentionally teaching, learning, and executing actions in violation of the rules. For example, a football coach may teach offensive linemen how to hold defensive linemen in ways less likely to be flagged by officials. Athletes may learn and practice these techniques until they become proficient enough that their performances help win more games. Three questions could be asked to determine if this is cheating or not (Blanchard and Peale 1988). First, is using techniques to hold an opponent permitted within the rules? Second, is the use of these techniques fair to all concerned? Third, how does using these holding techniques make each athlete feel about himself? If the answer to any of these questions is "no," is this cheating?

What about this situation? Near the end of a closely contested basketball game, athletes on the team with fewer points intentionally foul opposing athletes hoping that free throws will be missed and possession of the ball can be regained and more points scored to try to win. Is this cheating since there is an intentional rule violation in opposition to the spirit of the rules? Is this an acceptable form of gamesmanship since fouling is permitted along with awarding of free throws to the person fouled? Is this good strategy in seeking to win? While most would argue that this is simply the way the game of basketball is played, important questions to ask are: "Should the game be played to use the rules in attempting to gain advantages?" and "Is playing the game this way right or ethical?"

The concept of moral callousness, as discussed in Chapter 1, suggests that over time individuals can grow hardened, such as when athletes make less morally reasoned decisions the longer they are involved with sports (Bredemeier 1995; Rudd and Stoll 2004). To emphasize how intentionally fouling at the end of the game to stop the clock may illustrate moral callousness, consider how the game was played decades ago. This type of rule violation did not occur, and the intentional grabbing or hacking of an opponent to prolong the game would have been viewed as unsportsmanlike. Has the perception changed because this strategy might help win the game? What about when a football player fakes an injury near the end of a game to get the clock stopped? Some affirm that this is cheating, while others argue that this is just good strategy. Has moral callousness in some sports changed intentional rule violations into good strategies?

Many coaches and athletes claim that certain behaviors are acceptable, and even expected, due to a sport's unique culture; others not engaged in a particular sport simply may not understand how the game is played. For example, fighting in ice hockey is often perceived as just a part of the game, but it is not in football. A runner attempting to score and knocking over the catcher who has the ball is the expectation in baseball, while knocking down a defender on the way to the basket is not. The goalie in soccer advancing ahead of the line to narrow the angle for a penalty shot is perceived by many to be gaining a strategic advantage, while trying to serve from inside the baseline in tennis would not be. Accidentally moving a golf ball is a penalty stroke for an intercollegiate golfer, but typically it is not for the weekend duffer. Is fighting in ice hockey, knocking over the catcher, reducing the angle in soccer, or failing to assess a penalty stroke cheating?

For some athletes, coaches, and fans, whether something is cheating depends on whether this action can be done without getting caught. Others state that there is no such thing as cheating inside of sport because as long as athletes and coaches are willing to live with the consequences of rule violations, then it is justifiable to try almost anything. Cheating becomes even more valued if athletes or coaches are not penalized for rule violations that help their teams win. Some would argue that cheating is permissible because they are playing by the letter of the rules as enforced by the officials (i.e., no penalty, no harm).

If the objective of the game is to see how effectively coaches and athletes can break sport rules to their advantage, is this cheating? The spirit of the rules dictates fair play, sportsmanship, and honesty. The good sport plays within the rules, as stated and implied, and does so with firm resolve. Athletes who are good sports play by the spirit of the rules and will not violate the rules strategically to gain advantages.

Cheating also includes actions that violate regulations of sport governing organizations, such as those dealing with recruiting and eligibility. The purpose of these rules is to equalize competition so outcomes are based on skilled performances, not on who can find ways to entice more of the best athletes to play for one team. But, many coaches and athletes circumvent these regulations because they believe that it will increase the possibility of winning. For example, Kelvin Sampson, former basketball coach at the University of Oklahoma and Indiana University, made hundreds of impermissible phone calls to prospective recruits. Was this cheating?

Violations of recruiting regulations also occur at the youth and interscholastic levels. Some youth sport coaches recruit the most highly skilled athletes for travel teams or when forming teams to represent communities in elimination tournaments, often through gifts like athletic shoes, apparel, and equipment. Some interscholastic coaches use financial benefits to influence families to move or change the legal guardians of athletes so they will live in a required attendance area associated with these coaches' teams. When select teams, private schools, public magnet schools, or foreign-exchange programs are involved, the family may not have to move so an athlete is eligible to play on a certain team, but recruiting is still happening. Some would argue that such actions cause no harm because an athlete should be able to maximize his or her competitive opportunities. Others claim that the recruitment of youth and adolescents is cheating because it violates the letter and spirit of the rules.

Sport is replete with violations of eligibility rules at all levels of sport. In youth sport, cheating often involves age requirements, which are set to equalize competition between youth at different developmental levels. For example, one father falsified his son's birth certificate, which enabled Danny Almonte to pitch his team to third place in the Little League World Series in 2001, although he was 14 years old (two years too old). In order to qualify for teams with weight limitations or to compete in a lower weight category in wrestling, some athletes are encouraged by coaches to change their developmentally appropriate weight through unsafe measures, such as running in rubber suits and not hydrating properly. The rationale given for such dangerous practices is so these athletes or their teams will increase their chances of winning or being successful.

In interscholastic sports and intercollegiate athletics, cheating is often associated with giving unearned grades or changing the grades of some athletes to keep them eligible. Despite pages of regulations governing intercollegiate athletes, some coaches knowingly play athletes who have not met the required standards of academic eligibility, such as transfer admissibility, minimum number of hours passed, progress toward degrees, and declaration of majors. Some argue, however, that athletes who struggle academically should be granted exemptions to these academic standards because they were not adequately prepared for college-level work. Some believe so strongly that these rules are unjust that they feel justified in breaking them to keep their athletes eligible to help win games.

Since many coaches' jobs depend on winning, rule-breaking behaviors are sometimes overlooked by sport administrators, encouraged by fans, and condoned by schools and colleges. What many coaches and sport administrators fail to acknowledge is that athletes often know when their coaches are intentionally violating the rules. Athletes realize that if coaches will seemingly do anything to win, they are more likely to cheat. These athletes are learning that cheating is the way the game is played.

Gamesmanship and Violence

Gamesmanship refers to devious or creative strategies and methods used to help win. While technically these actions are not against written sport rules, are they ethical? Gamesmanship is often about getting inside the head of an opponent to gain advantages. Many believe that the emphasis on winning, especially as popularized through the electronic and print media, is a major contributing factor in the increase in gamesmanship in sport. For example, many athletes accept that taunting and trash talking are just a part of the game. So, is the objective of sport to outperform other athletes, or is it to psyche out opponents so they perform at lower levels than they are capable?

Coaches and athletes acknowledge that sport instruction books provide information about fundamental skills and playing strategies but are silent about how to be effective in gamesmanship—rather, when the mental side of sport is discussed, it focuses on motivation, confidence, relaxation, and self-control. So, gamesmanship must be learned from coaches, teammates, and others within the context of sports. But, are these role models teaching positive or negative lessons?

One common approach to gamesmanship is to attempt to break the flow or concentration of an opponent. Some baseball players have been accused of using slow play as an intentional distraction to their opponents. A batter may slowly walk to the plate, take considerable time to get set in the batter's box, step out after each pitch, and only step back in after several adjustments to his batting gloves or parts of his uniform, and often ask for a time-out just prior to the pitcher's delivery. In college and professional football in 2007, several coaches waited until the last possible moment to call a time-out, often causing the field goal kicker to have to kick again since he had already begun his kicking motion before the whistle stopping play was heard. A glaring look at an opponent after making a successful move in wrestling may help in breaking his concentration.

Another gamesmanship strategy is to try to get opponents to over-think or under-think their play. Athletes may allege that a specific sport is just not their best or that they are not very skilled in this sport in trying to get opponents to let up or not play as well as possible. Another ploy often used in tennis occurs when players ask their opponents if there are weaker strokes that they would like more setups for during the warm-up prior to matches. In baseball, catchers try to get umpires to call pitches strikes by moving their gloves, and base runners on second try to steal catchers' signs to pitchers. Flopping, or faking being fouled, occurs in basketball, soccer, and football. Some defend actions such as these by stating that there are no criteria or lines drawn about whether these actions are or are not acceptable. Simply stated, athletes and coaches engage in gamesmanship to help win because they think they can get away with it without penalty or there is no specific rule against their actions.

Taunting, which derides or mocks another person, is another frequently used type of gamesmanship. Taunting often comes from fans that criticize the play of the opponents, call them names, or yell to try to get them off their games. A few years ago at a men's intercollegiate basketball game, the fans held up pictures of J. J. Redick's mother and sister and yelled disparaging comments about them at him. Some argued that this was unsportsmanlike; others claimed it was their right as fans to do whatever they could to distract the Atlantic Coast Conference's leading scorer at the time and maybe help the home team win. Taunting such as this continues to escalate as fans at lower levels of sport mimic intercollegiate and professional sports fans. For example, a casual observer at a youth soccer or basketball game might be shocked to hear the words some parents, siblings, and friends shout at children on the other teams, coaches, and officials.

Taunting occurs among players when they seek to show up their opponents after they score a touchdown, make a dunk, or hit a home run. At what point do individual and team celebrations intentionally humiliate or demean opponents? Some would argue that running up the score on an over-matched opponent is a form of taunting; others would defend running up the score as sending a clear message of superiority that tells the opponents that they must improve.

Moral suasion to change this form of gamesmanship has failed to eliminate taunting, with sport behaviors continuing to deteriorate and get more abusive. As a result, sport governing organizations and educational institutions have established policies limiting what can be said and done. Codes of ethics and personal conduct contracts are illustrations of initiatives to eliminate taunting and emphasize sportsmanship.

Trash talkers often challenge their opponents using boasts about their skills or insults about opponents' abilities. For example, an athlete might mockingly ask, "Is that the best you got?" as if to suggest that the trash talker is such a better player, and that there is no way the opponent can stop him or her from scoring. Trash talkers, who may believe that this is one of sport's most beloved practices, use this gamesmanship ploy to psyche out or get into the heads of their opponents and maybe throw them off their games. There are even Web sites for learning new insults to hurl at opponents, as well as commercials, such as sponsored by Nike, which encourage trash talking. Many athletes are able to ignore or disregard trash talking and focus on playing well; others are bothered, distracted, and insulted. Whenever these latter reactions occur, then the trash talker has succeeded in gaining an advantage to help win, which was the goal.

Intimidation includes intentional behaviors that cause a person to fear imminent injury or harm. Some athletes seek to intimidate through violent tackles and other physical contacts that send the message of "don't mess with me or you'll get hurt." The label of a dirty player or enforcer is associated with intimidation because this player has earned a reputation for intentionally hurting opponents. A disdainful stare is often used to intimidate a less-confident opponent. Verbal abuse, including taunting and trash talking, can also be used to intimidate.

Coaches often use intimidation when they pressure, threaten, or coerce athletes. Because of the significant power differential, some coaches attempt to control the behaviors of their athletes in ways that could be considered physically or verbally abusive. Under the threat of punishments, less playing time, loss of grants-in-aid, or expulsion from the team, most athletes feel forced to follow coaches' directives. With quitting their sports as the only perceived alternative, many athletes are sufficiently intimidated that they will violate sport rules or sport governing association rules, engage in unethical behaviors, or harm their bodies by playing while injured or training excessively.

Coercion, especially if linked with a threatened loss of favor with the coach, has resulted in some athletes being sexually abused by their coaches. A coach's intimidating control may begin when a highly skilled athlete comes under the influence of a coach who promises the likelihood of a college grant-in-aid, gold medal, or professional sport contract if this athlete will do what the coach says. Coaches spend considerable time with and have easy access to children and adolescents because they are trusted by the parents and athletes. So, extra practice times to further develop an athlete's skills can provide opportunities for a predatory coach to begin inappropriate touching, often leading to sexual assault. In addition, coaches must be held accountable for sexually harassing their athletes. In the case of Anson Dorrance, the women's soccer coach at the University of North Carolina at Chapel Hill, he and the institution settled a lawsuit out of court because of his inappropriate behaviors relative to the sexual activities of members of his teams.

Until recent years, behaviors by coaches were seldom questioned because the cultures of sports gave coaches almost total control over the lives of their athletes. As a result of intimidating and harassing behaviors by coaches, sport organizations and educational institutions have taken steps to reduce the abuse of power by coaches. Development and enforcement of codes of conduct and signed contracts of expected behaviors are examples of setting boundaries for the appropriate use of power by coaches. In addition, many programs now require background checks for coaches of nonadult athletes.

One more issue related to intimidation is the increasing level of violence in sports. Violence is directly related to what coaches teach and/or permit their athletes to do, what officials allow, and what is modeled by athletes at higher levels of competition. Since coaches stress aggressive play, especially in contact and collision sports, they may permit, encourage, and even teach their athletes to be so aggressive that they engage in violent actions—that is, coaches, through their verbal and nonverbal cues, shape and largely control how athletes play. Depending on whether violent hits are the standard expectation or disapproved by the coach, athletes will learn to respond accordingly by engaging or not engaging in violent play.

While rule books are quite clear about allowable and nonallowable actions by athletes, the officials determine how each game is called. So, the oft-heard comment that the officials are "letting them play" is actually stating that few penalties are being assessed for hard contact. The escalation of such actions to the point of violence often results because many athletes believe right is defined as whatever is not penalized. Athletes are highly influenced by what they see professional and collegiate athletes do on television (and on YouTube), as violent actions by professional and collegiate athletes are mimicked by younger athletes. Violent actions of athletes are more likely to occur when they see that their violent actions help the team win, and violence is cheered by fans. These benefits in the minds of impressionable athletes far outweigh the possibility of getting penalized.

The emphasis on winning has led to an increase in violence among parents, fans, and athletes outside of the actual game. For example, sadly, Thomas Junta beat Michael Costin to death in a fight after a youth hockey practice in which the sons of both men participated. Out-of-control actions such as this have become all-too-frequent occurrences, such as parents attacking young athletes, their coaches, the officials, and other fans. Coaches have attacked officials, opposing athletes, and fans. A T-Ball coach offered a player $25 if he would hit an autistic teammate in the face with a ball in an attempt to sideline him from a playoff game. These violent acts happen because those involved have forgotten that sport is only a game, not a life-or-death situation.

It is argued by many that gamesmanship, including taunting and trash talking, intimidation, and violence signal a decline in sportsmanship and illustrate a general loss of civility in sport. Is an emphasis on playing by the letter and spirit of the rules needed? Can ethical behaviors in sport replace gaining advantages in any ways possible to help win?

Discriminatory Actions and Societal Factors

Sport potentially offers a welcoming environment for the blending together of people and their experiences. Sport has been praised for being a melting pot as immigrant groups used sport to become assimilated into the culture of the United States. The question about whether sport leads society or sport reflects society has been discussed for years. For example, when Jackie Robinson began playing for the Brooklyn Dodgers in 1947, baseball was applauded for integrating the national pastime before many aspects of society were as welcoming. However, it also could be argued that the integration of professional baseball, football, and basketball occurred because it was financially beneficial (i.e., in order to field the best teams to make the highest profits, the teams needed the best talent available, which included African Americans). While sport overall can be a socializing influence, its success historically in accepting all athletes on an equitable basis has been less praiseworthy. Some argue that unethical behaviors in sport reflect a general erosion of moral values in society.

Social class, while not as stratified as in other countries, remains a significant reality of life in the United States. A person's socioeconomic heritage influences what sports may be played due to access to equipment, facilities, coaching, and competitions. For example, basketball is called the city game because all that is needed is a ball and goal; competitors are readily available, and then the game is on. This is quite different from golf, which requires a set of clubs, continuing supply of balls, greens fees for playing courses, and money to travel to competitions. Most of the best golfers come from families with the financial resources to support playing this sport; basketball players come from all socioeconomic strata, although, the numbers playing basketball are disproportionate from those less well off financially. From an ethical perspective, it could be asked if this situation is right, just, or fair. While interscholastic sports have removed some of the financial barriers for playing tennis, swimming, or wrestling, athletes who play certain sports largely reflect the limitations of their socioeconomic status.

Race, ethnicity, and racism remain controversial issues in sports, even though many of the discriminatory practices of the past have been eliminated. While the exclusion of African Americans and members of other races and ethnicities from some sports is today viewed as discriminatory, at one time their exclusion reflected the attitudes held by many individuals in the United States. Some segregated sport opportunities were enjoyed by African Americans and other ethnic minorities, while sometimes formerly all-Caucasian teams welcomed all athletes on equitable terms. For example, it took an entire season, but the Caucasian and African American athletes and coaches finally came to respect each other in a newly integrated high school in Virginia as chronicled in the movie *Remember the Titans*. While most discrimination against ethnic minority athletes has been eliminated relative to making teams, earning playing time, getting grants-in-aid, and securing living accommodations, some residual racism persists. For example, racial slurs and epithets are sometimes heard in taunting and trash talking.

Some ethnic minority athletes enter college through preferred admissions or are less prepared than their peers, often as a result of socioeconomic barriers at home or their educational programs ill prepared them for college-level work. While many benefit from the academic support services provided athletes, some athletes still are unable (or unwilling) to earn degrees.

Some doors remain barred to ethnic minorities because of prejudice, as progress to fully integrate the coaching and administrative ranks of sport has been much slower than acceptance onto teams. In contrast with the number of athletes, especially in basketball, football, and track and field, relatively few ethnic minorities have been hired as head coaches, athletic directors, and in other sport administration roles. Many argue that Caucasians who make hiring decisions are reluctant to hire, and even interview, ethnic minority coaches and sport administrators. Justice and fairness and federal laws demand that vacancies are open to the best qualified candidates and that hiring practices eliminate discriminatory treatment.

Just like for ethnic minorities, females continue to struggle to gain full acceptance as athletes, coaches, and sport administrators (Acosta and Carpenter 2008). While some females have broken through the glass ceiling, sport remains predominately a man's world. At times, sexism continues to affect societal attitudes toward the role of and the sports opportunities provided to females.

Females in the United States were usually excluded from sports until the twentieth century, although there were exceptions, such as in women's colleges. Societal attitudes restricted most females to their homes and the fulfillment of domestic responsibilities. Even during the early decades of the twentieth century, females were seldom competitive athletes. Exceptions to this exclusion included a limited number of Caucasian women at private clubs where they engaged in golf, tennis, and swimming, some African American females at segregated schools and colleges, and girls' basketball teams in some rural schools. While the women's rights movement helped lead the way for the elimination of many discriminatory practices in society, historically sport lagged behind, rather than led the way, in its acceptance of females as equals.

The role of females in sport continues to be shaped by males who direct, coach, and report on all levels of competition. Many males believe that females are not as interested in sport or lack the expertise to coach, manage, and lead sport programs. For example, men who are most often the scholastic and collegiate athletic directors hire coaches. For example, 78.7 percent of directors of athletics in NCAA institutions are males (Acosta and Carpenter 2008). More often than not, they have chosen to hire males. For example, in NCAA institutions, 57.2 percent of the coaches of women's teams are males (Acosta and Carpenter 2008). Maybe this is because more men apply, men are more qualified, or it is perceived that female candidates are less interested, qualified, or likely to continue in sport given family responsibilities. Or, maybe females are discriminated against because many in the "ol' boys' network" simply do not want to hire and work with them.

A breakthrough for females began in the 1970s as changing perceptions and federal laws resulted in a dramatic increase in playing opportunities for females in youth, interscholastic, and intercollegiate sport. Sometimes it required lawsuits or the threats of legal action before sport governing organizations, such as Little League Baseball, permitted females to play alongside males. Other sport organizations began to initiate teams and programs in response to increased interest expressed by females.

Title IX of the Education Amendments of 1972 states that no person can be discriminated against or precluded from participation in any interscholastic or intercollegiate sport program. As a direct outcome of this federal legislation, schools greatly expanded their sport offerings for girls and began to treat them more fairly, such as by providing teams, uniforms, equipment, coaches, access to facilities, and travel expenses, where once these were available only to boys. Since this law requires schools to cease historical practices of relegating girls to the stands to watch or the sidelines to cheer, these females could now dream of receiving grants-in-aid to fund their education and having professional careers in sports. Still, though, a few states provided interscholastic sport teams for females in nontraditional seasons, while males continued to play during traditional seasons. The rationale for this practice was to maximally use facilities. The courts found that this practice discriminated against females because they were disadvantaged in being recruited or having the opportunity to receive grants-in-aid.

While Title IX significantly impacted intercollegiate athletic programs, it was much more controversial. When this legislation was passed, intercollegiate athletics was almost exclusively the domain of males. Most males perceived Title IX as a threat to the status quo of having control over all the money, facilities, and benefits associated with sport. The first reaction of some directors of athletics, coaches, and the NCAA was so negative that some males attempted to get Congress to prevent the application of this law to athletics. These attempts met no success. Several regulations, interpretations, clarifications, and lawsuits have reinforced this law that requires equal opportunities in athletics for both genders.

Specifically, this legislation requires equal opportunity in interscholastic sport and intercollegiate sport in three areas: (a) financial assistance, which must be substantially equal to the ratio of male to female athletes; (b) equivalent treatment, benefits, and opportunities in program areas, such as the provision of equipment and supplies, travel and per diem allowance, and provision of locker rooms, practice and competitive facilities, and recruitment; and (c) the interests and abilities of male and female students must be equally effectively accommodated (Carpenter and Acosta 2005).

Since 1979 when these three areas were described, significant progress has been achieved by female athletes in schools and colleges. In some institutions, however, there has been resistance to providing equal opportunities for females with blatant and subtle discriminatory practices remaining. In almost all colleges, males continue to receive more funding for recruiting, grants-in-aid, and operations than females.

The most controversial requirement in Title IX deals with meeting the interests and abilities of male and female students. Institutions are given the option to choose between one of three ways to comply with this requirement: (a) they can demonstrate that the participation opportunities are substantially proportionate to the undergraduate enrollment; (b) they can demonstrate a continuing practice of program expansion in response to developing interests and abilities of the underrepresented sex; or (c) they can show that the interest and abilities of the members of the underrepresented sex have been fully and effectively accommodated (Carpenter and Acosta 2005).

The first of these, which has been called a safe harbor, has been adopted by many institutions because it was believed to be easier to demonstrate. The problem with this option is that proportionality has been accused of being the same as a quota—that is, since the percentage of athletes by gender is expected to mirror the percentage of undergraduate students by gender, some institutions have eliminated men's teams claiming that Title IX was the causal factor. Athletes and coaches from these teams have argued in their lawsuits that this was reverse discrimination. The courts have consistently disagreed by stating that Title IX does not require, and in fact does not support, the elimination of men's teams as a way to provide substantially proportionate participation opportunities for both genders. The use of roster management by limiting the number of male athletes, and especially walk-ons who are not recruited, is also not congruent with the spirit of Title IX, which supports increased opportunities for the underrepresented gender, not a reduction in the opportunities for the other gender. The other two options are equally effective ways to comply with ensuring equal participation opportunities. Both have been used by institutions as they continue to expand athletic opportunities for females, unless they have already met their interests and abilities.

In summary, although social class is initially influenced by economics, an adult's social class has less to do with circumstances of birth than with abilities, opportunities, and what is done with these. Still, societal factors, including race and gender, continue to present ethical challenges to sport as some discriminatory treatment persists. Athletes know when coaches, sport administrators, and fans treat others disparately due to their socioeconomic status, race, ethnicity, and gender. To ensure equitable treatment, adults can model that each person is respected on the basis of personal merit, not on some characteristic of birth or other circumstance. Behaving in morally acceptable ways demands this.

Performance-Enhancing Drugs

The use of performance-enhancing drugs has touched the lives of youth, adolescent, and young adult athletes. The term *performance-enhancing* reveals why athletes choose to use these drugs—that is, they are seeking competitive advantages to help them win (some would argue to level the playing field because other athletes use them). While the use of performance-enhancing drugs is not a recent phenomenon, the extent of the current use by athletes may not yet fully be known. For example, Major League Baseball has been accused of ignoring the widespread use by its players of steroids, amphetamines, and other performance-enhancing drugs. Only when published evidence and Congressional hearings exposed what was happening did owners and players take action with expanded drug testing and stiffer penalties for using banned drugs. It is unknown how many youth, interscholastic, and intercollegiate athletes have been influenced to use performance-enhancing drugs by record-setting performances, celebrity status, and multimillion-dollar contracts of drugged sport heroes.

Athletes can easily obtain performance-enhancing drugs from some teammates, coaches, athletic trainers, personal trainers, doctors, and parents. Many athletes believe these drugs can help them quickly become bigger, stronger, and faster, which they believe will lead to greater success in sports. Naively, many athletes ignore the risks of side effects associated with these drugs even though they may be jeopardizing not only their playing careers but also their lives. Has an overemphasis on winning clouded their judgment? For example, in a 1995 survey, aspiring Olympic athletes revealed that well over half of them would take a performance-enhancing drug if it would guarantee winning every competition for five years, even though taking this drug would kill them (Longman 2001). Is this an example of winning at all costs?

Opposition to the use of performance-enhancing drugs is not universal. Some believe that athletes have the right to do whatever they choose to do to win, and hence they would not condemn Olympic athletes who decide that the money, notoriety, and other benefits outweigh any personal harm. Some claim that taking performance-enhancing drugs is no different than taking vitamins, training intensely, or using various methods or drugs to rehabilitate from injuries. Others argue that taking performance-enhancing drugs is acceptable as long as athletes are smart enough not to get caught, especially if their competitors are taking drugs. Still others emphasize that it is acceptable to take performance-enhancing drugs as long as there is no rule against it. (This is the position of some baseball players who claim that no rules of the game were violated when they used performance-enhancing drugs.)

Those who stress that taking performance-enhancing drugs is wrong, dishonest, and unfair believe that this practice destroys the integrity of sport. These individuals emphasize that sports should be competitions between athletes who have trained and worked hard in their skill development and physical and mental conditioning, not contests between pharmacists focused on the most effective drugs or the drugs that will not get detected in drug tests.

Drug testing is controversial because some athletes believe that this practice singles them out as likely drug users and violates their constitutional rights. Specifically, they claim that the Fourth and Fourteenth Amendments to the Constitution guarantee their rights against an unreasonable search, which they argue urinalysis is. Because so many athletes have found ways to avoid being caught for using drugs, such as through the substitution of the urine of others, urine samples in many cases are no longer obtained in private. This has raised the issue of drug testing as an invasion of privacy. Another issue with drug testing is that many claim that it has failed to achieve the desired goal of eliminating drug use in sport—that is, new performance-enhancing drugs are being developed and used because they cannot be detected with existing tests or they require taking a blood sample, a more invasive and expensive procedure. Another problem is that there is currently no test for human growth hormone, even though it is used by athletes in several sports.

Despite these claims, for years the NCAA has required drug testing of college athletes at its championships and football bowl games. In addition, most intercollegiate athletic programs require their athletes to take drug tests during the season and off-season as a deterrent to the use of performance-enhancing drugs. Some states require drug testing of high school athletes. Even in youth sport at some championships, athletes must take drug tests, because some athletes at the youth level are using performance-enhancing drugs.

Lacking in most sport programs, however, are educational programs that potentially could help athletes decide not to use performance-enhancing drugs, rather than just reduce their use for fear of getting caught. Rather than requiring athletes to sign statements that they have not used performance-enhancing drugs in order to be eligible to play, and thereby possibly perjuring themselves, ethical behavior in sport emphasizes that athletes learn the morally right decision of choosing not to violate the letter and spirit of the rules. Many believe that the use or nonuse of performance-enhancing drugs in sport rests upon athletes demonstrating honesty, responsibility, and integrity.

Having discussed several problems and controversies characteristic of several levels of sport, the next discussion examines issues specifically confronting youth, interscholastic, and intercollegiate sport. Each section will begin with a description of the goals, or the rationale for why individuals believe that sport should exist at these levels. Next, specific problems will be discussed in order to gain a better understanding of how they threaten the integrity of sport at each level. Finally, recommendations will be offered for addressing the issues as sports at these three levels seek to achieve potential benefits in morally responsible ways.

Youth Sport

Youth sport enjoys a somewhat idyllic status in the United States. Many parents, coaches, and other volunteers in youth sport claim that laudatory and beneficial outcomes accrue to children who play sports. They state that young athletes develop sports skills and physical fitness, learn how to play sports, learn and develop self-confidence, discipline, sportsmanship, and teamwork, and develop and maintain friendships. A perusal of purpose statements of community recreational programs and many youth sport organizations verifies these goals as established by adults.

The goals from athletes' perspectives, however, are not always the same as those listed by adults. Consistently, children emphasize that the first and foremost goal is always to have fun. This should not be surprising since children love to play, which to them is fun. In addition, children say that they want to learn sport skills through their participation in sport, spend time with their friends, have something to do, and feel successful. Probably the more noteworthy difference is that adults advocate that sports teach character and moral values, while this is absent from the children's list. This is not to say, however, that children would resist this. In fact, they are likely to learn whatever is taught, good or not so good.

Problems and Controversies in Youth Sports

The problems and controversies affecting youth sports will be discussed in three specific areas. First, there is a concern about children not having fun playing sports. Second, most children want to learn sport skills, and this is not always happening. Third, winning dominates most aspects of youth sports (Citizenship through Sports Alliance 2006).

Fun

When children choose not to participate in sports, the primary reason given is often that the sport is not fun. Young athletes are quite clear in wanting to have fun in sports, which they usually define as getting to play and not sitting on the bench. Children want to be actively engaged and avoid unpleasant experiences. Since too often coaches forget this obvious reality, it is no wonder that children quit or do not join teams the next year as they choose to participate in activities that are more fun.

Children are often relegated to the bench because they are not as skilled, physically fit, or developmentally advanced as other children. None of these mean that children do not want to play. Children are not nearly as concerned about dropping a fly ball or missing a tackle as their coaches and parents are. Many youth sport coaches believe winning a game is more important than giving every child an equitable opportunity to play. So, most youth sport programs have established written rules requiring at least a minimum amount of playing time for each child in each game, because otherwise many children would not get to play—that is, instead of adults keeping winning in perspective by focusing on treating each child fairly, it had to be required.

While ensuring playing time for each young athlete may be an important guarantee, just being in the game does not automatically make sport fun. Children also want to play their favorite positions. Not every child who wants to play quarterback or pitcher can do so all the time because others will have similar preferences; but, this should not mean that children never get these opportunities. Similarly, children do not think it is fair to be forced to play certain positions, such as right field or on the offensive line, that they do not enjoy. Sometimes, instead of allowing themselves to be relegated to these positions, they drop out of the sport. Also, anyone who has ever watched a youth sport game knows the attraction is the ball. So, if a child never gets to touch the ball, the fun may quickly disappear. Again, has playing the most skillful child in key positions emphasized winning over fun and skill development?

Children did not establish youth sport national championships—adults did. Yet, for every 10-year-old national champion, there are thousands of children who would much prefer to have fun just playing games with their friends. Rather than winning trophies that quickly collect dust on shelves, should the goals of youth sports return to children being physically active and interacting socially with friends?

Children did not establish youth sport travel, elite, or select teams—adults did. These teams attract highly skilled players who are provided opportunities to compete against other talented athletes. Those who support these teams believe that these competitions accelerate the skill development of those chosen, who it is assumed have the potential for sport stardom. There is, however, an ever-present threat of exploitation. Often, these young athletes are pressured to practice for and compete in the same sport year-round lest they fall behind, often leading to overtraining or overuse injuries. These young athletes may become consumed by the practices, competitions, travel, and pressures to win. The latter is particularly a problem with team sponsors expecting victories in return for their financial support, thus increasing the pressures to win, maybe at any cost.

Many athletes on travel, elite, or select teams lose opportunities to spend time with peers and interact with them in other sports and social activities. The costs associated with these teams may create problems for parents and other children who do not receive the same type of parental investments. Or, athletes without the financial means to join these teams may be excluded or receive benefits that jeopardize their eligibility to play sports in high school or college. Coaches and others involved with these travel or select teams may influence the choices of educational institutions these athletes attend—as these adults advance their own careers. Has developing the skills of a few youth on travel or select teams replaced an emphasis on fun for all?

Learning Sport Skills

Some children learn skills that enable them to participate in and enjoy sports throughout their lives. But, this does not always happen. Most youth sport coaches have limited expertise in how to teach sport skills and especially how to teach them in developmentally appropriate ways to children. Youth sport coaches are largely volunteers and often parents who agree to help provide sport experiences for their children and others. Often these volunteers have played sports in high school, and maybe college, or they may only have an interest in the sport they are coaching. As a result, these coaches often coach as they have been coached or model their behaviors after those they have learned through the media.

Whenever youth sport coaches are poorly prepared for their roles, the children do not learn sport skills or they learn them incorrectly. The lack of coaching preparation may result in practices during which children are expected to engage in disorganized activities that are boring or potentially harmful and do not lead to skill development. Whenever practices are filled more with athletes getting yelled at by the coach than with getting to catch, hit, or kick balls, little skill is developed.

Often, youth sport coaches possess limited knowledge about effective instructional strategies, motivational techniques, or risk management. Even though these coaches frequently make mistakes due to their limited preparation, they still expect skillful play by young athletes. Coaches seldom are required to demonstrate their knowledge of the basics of their sport or how to prevent and care for injuries, and largely they coach their athletes without supervision. These volunteers determine what types of experiences these young athletes will have and if they learn sport skills.

Winning as the Only Measure of Success

While not having fun or not learning sport skills cause many children to drop out of sport activities, an even more serious problem in youth sport may be the overemphasis on winning. Did children decide they needed manicured fields, uniforms modeled after those worn by professional athletes, and year-round practices and competitions in one sport to have fun and learn sport skills? No, but youth sport athletes enjoy these fields, uniforms, and organized programs now as pickup games have largely become a relic of the past—that is, youth sports have become super-organized and imitators of professional athletics.

Ask any youth sport program director about who causes their problems and for whom more and more rules must be written, and the answer is inevitably coaches and parents who have gotten over-invested in youth sport. Many controlling, and sometimes even abusive, adults have imposed their emphasis on winning and overly competitive inclinations on child's play. Many adults invest significant amounts of time and money, and they usually expect winning teams.

This adult measure of winning as the only measure of success in sport now permeates youth programs with adverse consequences, such as when adults engage in physical confrontations with officials, coaches, and opposing players whenever their team does not win or they believe it has been treated unfairly. Most children would not dedicate their childhood years to mastering their backhands, jump shots, or balance beam routines without considerable urging from parents and coaches. Many coaches and parents push children into sports based on a professional model as fun gets short shrift. The emphasis on winning keeps some children on the bench or away from positions that are more likely to impact the outcome of a game or competition. The bodies of the most highly skilled and developmentally advanced may be taxed to the point of overuse injuries and permanent incapacitation. Overtraining, in the guise of getting bigger, stronger, and faster, may lead to physiological and psychological issues, such as interruption of normal growth and maturation, eating disorders, and use of performance-enhancing drugs. If these stressors become unbearable, athletes burn out and leave sport entirely. Have youth sports become miniature versions of professional sports?

Some out-of-control coaches and parents yell, scream, and verbally abuse young athletes. A few coaches seek to build their reputations based on the winning percentages of their teams to help secure coaching positions at higher levels of sport. Some coaches and parents victimize young athletes when they pressure them relentlessly to win, often leading to physiological and psychological problems. When parents disproportionately focus their lives and resources on a highly skilled child hoping that she or he will become a collegiate and professional athlete, this almost always causes financial and interpersonal problems in the family.

In seeking to keep parents under control, some youth sport programs have begun to require them to attend sessions about sportsmanship so they can learn to keep winning in perspective. Codes of conduct for parents have been established and enforced. Some youth sport programs have initiated 24-hour rules (i.e., cooling off time before parents can talk with coaches) to hopefully reduce confrontations. Some programs have enforced silent days when parents are forbidden to speak during youth competitions. Occasionally, behaviors have become so abusive or unsportsmanlike that parents have been removed from the stands and banned from attending future youth sport competitions. Such actions lead to questions about what values these parents are modeling.

Children seldom mention winning as a reason why they participate in sports. Young athletes learn from adults about the importance placed on winning. So, many respond that they like to win because parents and coaches reward winning, such as when adults buy treats for athletes after the game or lavish praise on the player whose play directly led to a win on the scoreboard. While young athletes soon forget scores, they do remember whether they had fun and played well.

Teaching Values in Youth Sports

To emphasize having fun and learning sport skills, a few suggested changes might be considered. First, youth sport organizations could educate parents to help them model proper behaviors at competitions, de-emphasize winning, and keep children as the focus of all decisions. Second, coaches of young athletes could be taught the importance of, and held accountable for, playing every child in each game and in different positions during the season, teaching skills, strategies, and rules in developmentally appropriate ways, giving each child an equal opportunity to strive for success, and de-emphasizing winning. Third, the emphasis could be shifted from outcome to process— that is, winning as the singular goal could be replaced by seeking to win while doing one's best. This approach potentially can reinforce developing character, young athletes learning moral values, and young athletes making the right decisions in sport.

Keeping winning in perspective means playing hard and playing fairly, as coaches and parents can redefine winning so athletes do not focus solely on the scoreboard—that is, reward young adults for effort and sportsmanship regardless of the outcome. In child-centered programs, coaches and parents will reinforce determination, persistence, and incremental progress through symbolic rewards more so than tangible awards and the scoreboard.

Fair play, sportsmanship, teamwork, honesty, respect, responsibility, and integrity do not automatically result from participating in youth sport. Rather, it is important to focus on educating everyone involved with youth sport about these values. Coaches and parents can help shape the character of young athletes by ensuring that sport experiences are fun, being supportive and encouraging, emphasizing treating opponents fairly and respectfully, reinforcing the importance of respecting the authority of coaches and officials, and modeling ethical behavior. Most importantly, if parents and coaches diligently teach, model, and reinforce these values, children will view them as integral to sport and how games are to be played.

Interscholastic Sport

Most people in the United States believe that interscholastic sport is an important part of educational and extracurricular activities of adolescents. Public school sport programs are funded from state appropriations in ways similar to academic programs because it is claimed that through sports adolescents learn valuable lessons and enjoy positive outcomes. The goals of interscholastic sport programs are for adolescent athletes to develop sport skills and physical fitness, learn values like teamwork, cooperation, self-discipline, and sportsmanship, compete in organized, supervised, and safe environments, learn how to work as a member of a team, and enhance their academic work. An extended goal is to provide a shared activity for students, schools, and communities.

Interscholastic athletes want to enjoy their experiences, but not in the same way that younger athletes emphasize having fun. These adolescents take more seriously the development of their sport skills because sport at this level excludes them if they do not meet coaches' standards. Being a member of a team and enjoying associations with peers are important to many athletes. Most also begin to realize they may be playing in their last level of competitive sport as the ever-narrowing funnel of sport will most likely preclude their opportunity to play intercollegiate athletics. A small minority of high school athletes, however, will work diligently to hone their skills in hopes of receiving grants-in-aid and advancing to the next competitive level.

Problems and Controversies in Interscholastic Sport

Some of the problems and controversies that confront youth sport also plague interscholastic sport, such as when athletes drop out when sports are no longer enjoyable and burn out due to physiological and psychological factors. Some parents and coaches require adolescent athletes to specialize in one sport. These adults emphasize that only through dedicated, year-round physical conditioning, skill development, and competition can an athlete realize his or her potential and maybe even qualify to play this sport in college. Sport specialization also may mean that an athlete is forced to choose between playing on the school's team or on a team sponsored by a sport organization. This oftentimes places pressure on an adolescent athlete to choose between wanting to play and socialize with friends while representing his or her school and wanting to take advantage of competitive opportunities nationally and even internationally.

In addition to sport specialization and those issues discussed broadly for all sports, interscholastic sport is challenged by specific ethical problems and controversies associated with academics, eligibility, conduct, and the emphasis on winning. Each of these issues will be discussed along with possible ways to address them to keep character development as a desired outcome.

Academics

The National Federation of State High School Associations and schools throughout the United States have found that interscholastic athletes achieve at a higher level academically than do nonathletes. They report that athletes attend classes more regularly and stay in school at higher levels as well. Like their peers who are actively involved with band, debate, or other extracurricular activities, athletes psychologically and socially benefit from being part of groups with shared interests (National Federation of State High School Associations 2004).

One reason why interscholastic athletes may do better academically is that many states, schools, or coaches have implemented "no pass, no play" policies. These typically require a minimal grade in each course or passing all courses to play sports. These policies, some of which were mandated at the state legislative level, were enacted because some athletes were not taking advantage of their educational opportunities. Where these policies exist, interscholastic athletes can no longer ignore their academic work and are encouraged to take a more conscientious approach to being a student first so they can earn the privilege of playing sports. Yet, some have argued that these policies or laws discriminate against students with learning difficulties or those who may have had fewer or inferior educational opportunities. Some also claim that without sports as an incentive, some students will drop out of school.

A common issue related to academics is that some athletes choose to cheat, rather than study, learn, and pass their courses. These athletes may be helped with cheating by classmates or have classmates do their homework assignments. Some coaches who also teach give unearned grades or influence other teachers to give passing grades to athletes, even though these athletes do not attend class, turn in assignments, or pass their tests. Some people emphasize that when this occurs, these athletes are being exploited academically because they are not learning essential knowledge for their adult lives. They are cheating themselves of opportunities to qualify for college and the potential financial benefits associated with earning a college degree.

Athletes who get to keep playing without completing the prerequisite academic work are learning that athletic abilities can exempt them from rules and the responsibility to play by these rules. It is an easy transfer of this feeling of entitlement onto the court or field so that sport rules are ignored or violated to gain advantages. Is this a lack of morally based decision making that could lead to a feeling of being above the law relative to drinking alcohol, violating traffic regulations, and getting into physical altercations?

Eligibility

In addition to interscholastic athletes maintaining their eligibility academically, they also must meet the requirements of their schools, leagues, and conferences. The legitimacy of athletes attending particular schools is the rule most often violated. For example, some exceptionally skilled basketball players may enroll at a different school each year in high school as they seek to play under an acclaimed coach, to compete against better competition, or to increase the likelihood of being recruited by coaches of the best college teams. Sometimes transfers between schools include private schools, because requirements about living in a specified attendance area do not apply. In other cases, creative, but not always allowable, approaches are used to change an athlete's legal guardian so this athlete can meet the technical details of this eligibility requirement. The new schools attended seldom have anything to do with academics and everything to do with playing sports. Should such school transfers be allowed?

Another eligibility issue deals with the age of athletes. Most state high school associations have rules that specify the maximum age, usually 19 or 20, for the eligibility of athletes. These rules were enacted because older and more mature athletes would have physiological advantages in interscholastic sports. Similarly, these governing associations limit the number of years of competition in interscholastic sports so adolescents cannot continue to play year after year instead of making progress in attaining their diplomas.

Some parents decide to have their child, most often boys, repeat an elementary or middle school grade so he can gain a developmental advantage over other athletes. Thus, the concept of redshirting that often occurs in intercollegiate athletics has moved down to precollegiate athletics. The goal in the minds of parents is that their sons throughout high school will compete against boys who are one year younger and less mature physically. This advantage, they posit, could be just enough to lead to greater success for their sons. While maybe beneficial athletically, what are the implications academically, socially, or ethically?

Because state high school associations exist primarily to provide competitive opportunities and to establish rules that govern athletic competitions, most are not staffed with enforcement personnel to monitor compliance with eligibility rules. Often violations go undetected, with games and championships won by teams and individuals who according to the rules were ineligible. When adolescent athletes observe that violations of the rules can lead to winning championships, what lessons are they learning?

Conduct

Interscholastic sport is not exempt from unethical conduct on the part of athletes, coaches, and fans. Sometimes these individuals have chosen to follow the examples of those involved with intercollegiate and professional sports, such as through taunting, cheating, and violence. Another example of unethical behavior is hazing, which is defined as meaningless, harassing, and humiliating. Older team members sometimes use hazing to initiate new players into the team by requiring them to do tasks that often harass and humiliate them. While some argue that hazing is harmless and just adolescents having fun, what might have been intended as a way to socialize with new teammates has become hurtful and degrading. For example, some freshmen and sophomores have been forced to eat inedible items and drink alcoholic beverages. Sometimes hazing has included sexually harassing these young adolescents. Many guilty of hazing, but not all, have been disciplined and sometimes lost the opportunity to play on teams; some coaches who have condoned hazing have lost their jobs. Teaching respect and responsibility to athletes, modeling appropriate treatment of all teammates, and reinforcing how to respectfully welcome new teammates is likely to prevent hazing.

Interscholastic sport participants represent their schools. For most athletes, this is a new level of responsibility they can learn about, accept, and fulfill. In the absence of concerted efforts on the part of coaches, and reinforced by parents, to help these young people understand how to follow team rules, treat opponents as honored guests, respect officials, play by the letter and spirit of the rules, and win and lose with grace, many of these athletes will model their behaviors after collegiate and professional athletes. This may lead to irresponsible actions, disrespectful behaviors, and violations of rules. Educational programs through which athletes understand their responsibilities as representatives of their schools and as role models for younger athletes in their communities are important in helping to ensure that interscholastic athletes behave in responsible ways. Whenever athletes help establish codes of conduct, they are more likely to internalize a commitment to behaving appropriately. Should coaches be held accountable for teaching athletes to play fair, show sportsmanship, and take pride in their conduct?

Emphasis on Winning

Many state that as an extracurricular learning experience for adolescents, the primary purpose of interscholastic sport should not be winning. Many others disagree with this statement because they believe that winning elevates the status or prestige of their schools, communities, coaches, athletes, and fans. The intense desire to claim "we're No. 1" is associated with some interscholastic sports, especially football and basketball. Driving into towns, it is not unusual to read a sign listing state championship teams. Should it be the responsibility of adolescents to enhance the identity or bragging rights for fans in a town? Many young people have learned, however, that they carry a heavy responsibility to win, as the book, movie, and television series *Friday Night Lights* about high school football in Texas illustrate so dramatically. Winning football games for many has become more important than school work, athletes' physical and psychological well-being, and families. The pressures on adolescent athletes to maintain winning traditions or to win championships are intense and can be relentless as coaches, parents, and fans demand victories or else. The else can be abusive treatment, withholding of love, or loss of status.

Oftentimes, coaches pressure athletes to win because they believe their jobs depend on winning. These coaches demand year-round conditioning, specialization in one sport and position, and unquestioning compliance with coaches' directives. Coaches praise athletes who have adopted similar levels of drive, intensity, and commitment, with everything else in life as secondary to sport. Some athletes are subjected by coaches to demeaning treatment, abusive punishments for failure to perform at expected levels, and vulgar language—that is, many coaches believe that their positions entitle them to do anything and everything it takes to win, even if this means sacrificing the physical, psychological, or emotional well-being of athletes in the process. For these coaches, winning has become the only outcome that will be accepted.

Teaching Values in Interscholastic Sports

Rather than this overemphasis on winning, striving to win in sport does not have to be characterized by abusing athletes or ignoring moral values. If it is assumed that interscholastic sport can help prepare adolescents for their adult lives, then life lessons, character, and moral values should be taught and reinforced through sport. Since for every sporting event there is at least one team or individual who does not win on the scoreboard, has the importance of winning gotten out of balance? Given there will be more nonwinners than winners, should the emphasis be on rewarding or reinforcing effort and how well the game is played? How can school administrators and members of boards of education temper their expectations of winning? Should they expect all coaches to develop athletes physically, psychologically, and in character?

Intercollegiate Athletics

Mission statements of intercollegiate athletic programs usually state a commitment to the development of athletes academically, athletically, socially, and ethically. Intercollegiate athletics is typically dedicated to helping athletes achieve their potential in sports, enrich their educational experiences, and prepare for life. It is claimed that intercollegiate athletic programs, including coaches, players, and administrators, comply with institutions' and intercollegiate athletic organizations' regulations, respect each individual, and promote integrity within the context of fiscal responsibility. Many who applaud the lofty aspirations of intercollegiate athletic programs do so to justify their status within institutions of higher education.

Intercollegiate athletes realize that they compete at a much higher level than in high school with the expectations for winning increasing significantly. In many cases, they have received grants-in-aid as recruited athletes. In essence, their sports have become their jobs, with all the requisite demands on their time and effort. Pressures to win are most often associated with recruiting, academics, and commercialism, as well as the problems and controversies associated with each. An emphasis on winning is intertwined with recruiting, academics, and commercialism as recruiting the most highly skilled athletes, keeping athletes eligible, and maximizing revenues become a self-perpetuating and ever-growing cycle. In seeking to operate winning programs, sometimes developing character is not emphasized by coaches and sport administrators.

Recruiting

The NCAA, National Association of Intercollegiate Athletics (NAIA), and National Junior College Athletic Association (NJCAA) govern intercollegiate athletics beginning with the recruitment of high school athletes. Hundreds of pages of rules and regulations specify what is and is not permissible as coaches and others try to entice adolescents to attend certain institutions. While some of these rules and regulations have been written to protect prospective intercollegiate athletes, most were established to control the actions of zealous coaches seeking to gain advantages in the cutthroat process of recruiting blue-chip athletes. For example, there are limitations on the time for and number of contacts between coaches and high school athletes, because otherwise some coaches would continually bombard these adolescents with letters, calls to their cell phones, and text messages. Impermissible contacts continue primarily because intercollegiate athletic organizations do not allocate the personnel and other resources required to enforce their rules and regulations. Of course, this raises questions about whether coaches are morally obligated to follow the rules for recruiting, whether any actions in recruiting are justifiable as long as coaches are not caught, or if ethical recruiting can be legislated and enforced.

During the recruiting process, prospective intercollegiate athletes are permitted to take a limited number of expense-paid trips to college campuses. During these visits, coaches attempt to convince the athletes to join their teams through tours of impressive athletic facilities, promises of stardom, and fun experiences. Sometimes these campus visits get out of hand, such as when hosts, who usually are intercollegiate athletes, provide prospective recruits with alcohol and sexual encounters, as happened at the University of Colorado in 2005.

Another approach used to get the most highly skilled athletes to attend a specific institution is to provide inducements or benefits to the athlete, family members, or friends. Extra benefits have been given even though this practice violates the rules and regulations of intercollegiate athletic organizations, because as amateurs, athletes cannot receive these benefits and maintain their eligibility to compete. Although cash payments, cars, credit cards, clothing, and houses for families are not openly provided, coaches and friends of athletic programs have used creative ways to get payments to athletes, as illustrated in movies such as *Blue Chips*. The NCAA banned Southern Methodist University from competing in football (the death penalty) because of repeated rule violations and especially for giving money to athletes. Some coaches have secured the signing of a prized recruit by hiring as a member of the coaching staff the athlete's father, the athlete's interscholastic or club coach, or another significant individual to this athlete. Many question whether such hires are unauthorized inducements, even though there are no specific rules prohibiting these hires.

The recruiting process is an intensely stressful time for coaches and prospects alike because coaches are limited in the number of recruits to whom grants-in-aid can be awarded, and prospects have one chance to commit in writing to an institution. If the coach is incorrect in assessing the potential contributions of a recruit, then three possible outcomes are likely to occur. First, the coach can simply accept his or her incorrect assessment of talent and honor the grant-in-aid commitment for four years. Second, the coach can pressure the athlete to renounce his or her grant-in-aid, which enables the coach to award another grant-in-aid to some other athlete. Third, the coach can decide not to renew a grant-in-aid if it is claimed that this athlete is not skilled enough, is not putting forth the required effort or training, or some other reason the coach can state.

Once signed, the athlete also has three probable alternatives. First, if the athlete chooses to leave the team because of lack of skill, playing time, or interest, the grant-in-aid is not renewed. Second, the athlete can choose to remain on the team, which may be permitted by the coach, but often without the grant-in-aid. Third, the athlete can transfer to another institution, although sitting out a year (i.e., not playing) is required if the transfer is at the same level of competition, such as from a NCAA Division I institution to another NCAA Division I institution. In analyzing these options, differing opinions may develop. One perspective is that since intercollegiate athletics is a business, athletes should know that if they do not have the requisite skills, then whatever happens is just how the game is played. Others argue that athletes have become disposable and replaceable commodities to be used to help a team win.

Another vital aspect of the recruiting process is getting athletes admitted into colleges. Because of accusations of poorly qualified recruits who have enrolled in colleges just to play sports, the NCAA over the years has raised its requirements regarding minimal standards for admission relative to high school grades and admission test scores. Also, given that institutions varied in how effectively they monitored and enforced academic admission requirements, the NCAA, rather than institutions, qualifies through its Clearinghouse all athletes who compete through NCAA Divisions I and II member institutions.

Once recruits meet the minimal academic requirements specified by intercollegiate athletic organizations, another hurdle exists at the institutional level. Admissions staffs, especially at institutions with selective admission standards, are expected to treat all applicants equitably and to admit the class of students with the highest overall academic credentials and potential. Faculty members agree because they expect that students who are admitted have the academic preparation and abilities to succeed. But, coaches argue that once recruits, especially blue-chip athletes with the potential to make significant contributions to help win, have met the minimal qualifying standards academically as specified by the intercollegiate athletic organization, they should be admitted, regardless of institutional requirements.

This conflict between admitting the most academically qualified class of students and individuals with special athletic skills has been resolved on most campuses in favor of coaches, as they are granted at least a certain number of preferential admissions. Coaches justify this unique admission status for some of the best athletes by saying that these prospective students are essential for staying competitive within the conference or on the national level. They also argue that these athletes are being treated the same way as outstanding musicians or others with special talents.

Many faculty members counter these arguments by emphasizing that students with outstanding musical and academic abilities and potential achieve at high levels in academic programs, while athletes perform in an extracurricular activity. Preferential admissions are not unique to NCAA Division I institutions, as they occur at academically elite institutions as well as less academically elite institutions, and regional state universities (Shulman and Bowen 2001)—that is, exceptional athletic talent greatly increases the likelihood of admission. However, once admitted, these students often fail to perform up to their potential academically and many do not earn degrees (Shulman and Bowen 2001).

An oft-heard argument from faculty is that an athletic department should not be allowed to determine who some of the students admitted will be just so they can potentially win more games. In selective admission institutions, some faculty state that admitting talented athletes through preferred admissions discriminates against more highly qualified applicants who were denied admission. University administrators, athletic directors, and coaches counter by emphasizing the value of providing educational opportunities to athletes who would not be able to attend college, as well as the importance of public relations (and financial) benefits associated with winning teams and championships.

Academics

The overriding academic issues for many intercollegiate athletes are whether they are primarily attending college to play sports and whether the current operation of intercollegiate athletics impedes the likelihood of athletes earning their degrees. Young adults who realistically evaluate their skills realize that playing intercollegiate athletics is unlikely to lead to professional careers. Still, some of these athletes fail to take advantage of their grants-in-aid and educational opportunities. Some athletes choose not to attend classes or complete their assignments, usually resulting in their doing poorly and even failing their courses. An apathetic attitude toward learning may have been reinforced earlier in their lives as athletes when they perhaps were allowed to not take their schoolwork seriously and were given grades to ensure eligibility.

Since intercollegiate athletes are adults, some question whether they should be forced by their coaches to attend classes. Mandatory class attendance occurs when coaches send class checkers around campus to monitor whether athletes go to and remain in their classes. Failure to attend classes usually results in punishments like early morning running or loss of playing time. Would it be more beneficial to help these young adults appreciate their educational opportunities so they would choose to attend classes and learn?

Another issue regarding class attendance deals with the number of classes that some athletes miss due to competitions and travel to competitions. One of the arguments posited by university presidents against a football championship in the Bowl Championship Division (formerly NCAA Division I football) is that some type of playoff system would cause football players to miss too many classes. In reality, football players may be the athletes who miss the fewest number of classes because they typically play most or all of their games on Saturdays. In contrast, baseball and softball players play several games in the fall semester, begin an over-50-game regular season schedule in February, and play on several days of the week, with games and travel precluding attending numerous days of classes. While basketball players (and student managers, cheerleaders, and student athletic trainers) may miss several classes during the regular season, if basketball teams continue to win in conference and other postseason tournaments, the days of missed classes mount rapidly. It was reported that members of one men's basketball team that won the NCAA Division I championship did not attend any classes during their postseason play for an entire month. Not surprisingly, most of these athletes dropped, failed, or did poorly in their classes that semester. The lesson learned by these athletes from this experience was that basketball was much more important than their learning and making progress toward earning their degrees.

It could be argued that the number of class absences that intercollegiate athletes have is excessive because these students are denied opportunities to learn from their professors as well as classmates. Also questioned is whether it is fair to expect athletes to be serious students when their days and nights are filled with competitions, travel, rehabilitation of injuries, and practices. The NCAA specifies that athletes can spend only 20 hours a week on their sports (exclusive of travel time to games), but most athletes admit that they are involved with their sports many more hours than this in season and out of season.

Intercollegiate sports are played every day of the week, and often at times to meet the demands of ESPN or other television networks. It is hard for athletes to be prepared for and concentrate in an early morning class after playing in an away game that ended late the previous night. Are athletes being taught that their academic work is less important than their sports? Are athletes in football, and more often in basketball, learning that their academics are subservient to an institution making money off the broadcasting of their games?

Many intercollegiate athletic programs provide academic support services to athletes. The usual rationale for providing staff to advise these athletes in enrolling for courses, which most often occurs prior to courses being opened to other students, is so athletes do not have classes that conflict with team and individual practices and conditioning times. Sometimes the goal is to enroll athletes in easy courses with faculty who are more likely to give athletes good grades.

Tutoring is provided to athletes to bridge the learning gap, especially for those admitted preferentially because they had not demonstrated the past academic achievement of admitted classmates. Tutors assist athletes in completing their academic work in the limited time available to them around their obligations as athletes, such as during study hall. One issue surrounding the provision by departments of athletics of academic support services to athletes is whether there is oversight to ensure that hired tutors and study hall monitors do not complete the academic work for athletes, such as writing papers or doing other assignments for them. Because of numerous abuses, such as at the Universities of Tennessee, Georgia, and Minnesota, which led to distrust about the unethical conduct of some academic support staff members hired by departments of athletics, many institutions have moved academic support services under the auspices of chief academic officers.

Another issue in the academic sphere deals with whether or not first-year students should be allowed to compete immediately upon matriculation. First-year students enrolled in institutions that were members of the NCAA prior to the early 1970s were not eligible to play on varsity teams. Some stated that this rule existed so athletes could acclimate to the academic rigors of collegiate study and engage with other students socially. Freshman eligibility changed all this, with intercollegiate athletes immediately immersed in the demands of conditioning, practicing, and competing at the same time they are expected to transition into college academically and socially. The 20, 30, 40, or more hours per week that athletes dedicate to their sports leave limited time to succeed academically, make friends outside of their teams, and engage in other extracurricular activities. Many argue that this sport-centric world unfairly restricts the learning opportunities and all-around development of athletes and especially isolates them socially.

Given the time demands on athletes and sometimes their marginal preparation for college study, many athletes struggle academically and fail to earn their degrees. In the past, many athletes were victimized by an overemphasis on maintaining their eligibility by taking a smorgasbord of easy courses. As a result, intercollegiate athletic organizations strengthened the eligibility requirements. For example, the NCAA requires that athletes make satisfactory progress toward earning their degrees by receiving minimal passing grades in a specified number of courses each year in order to remain eligible to play. Each athlete must declare a major that leads to a degree, and each year each athlete must complete a required portion of this program of study. In addition, the NCAA has implemented a measure called the Academic Progress Rate (APR) to monitor the success or failure of athletes in making progress toward graduation. Each team is required to achieve at or above a 50 percent graduation rate, exclusive of those athletes who left the institution early for nonacademic reasons, or else face the loss of grants-in-aid that can be awarded. This APR will result in penalties to teams and institutions that permit some of their athletes to choose to focus on their sports instead of earning a degree.

The Knight Commission on Intercollegiate Athletics, many faculty, and some in the general public increasingly question whether some groups or levels of intercollegiate athletics are threatening the academic integrity of higher education. Although numerous rules and regulations exist, issues such as preferential admissions, unearned grades given to maintain eligibility, missed classes, lack of progress toward degrees, and an overemphasis on athletics to the detriment of academics persist.

The driving force behind this imbalance in most cases is the commercialized business model of intercollegiate athletics.

Commercialism

A historical way to begin to explore commercialism in intercollegiate athletics is to examine the evolution of conferences. Conferences for intercollegiate athletics began to be established more than 100 years ago among institutions with similar enrollments, missions, and geographical proximity. The geographical basis for these conferences sought to reduce the number of missed classes, which the faculty supported, and reduce costs, which benefited the athletics department. This has changed dramatically over the years.

The goal of conferences today, after extensive realignments at the highest level of competition in the NCAA, is to obtain the widest feasible geographical reach, which enables conferences to extract higher revenues from network and cable television because of the size of the potential viewing audience. Conference commissioners and athletic directors actively pursue maximal revenues. Many faculty members are less supportive of conference expansion and realignments because athletes miss more classes due to travel time to and from distant institutions.

Television, radio, and the Internet exercise considerable influence over intercollegiate athletics. Commercialism leads some directors of athletics and coaches to schedule competitions almost anywhere and any time if these contests yield greater revenues. Television has led to rule changes in sport, such as adding a number of television time-outs for broadcasting more commercials. This is important because advertising sales are the primary revenue sources for the television companies, which pay conferences and athletics departments.

There is a fear that television has become so dominant in intercollegiate athletics that institutions of higher education can no longer control its influence. For example, the current structure of the postseason football bowl games is controlled by television. Whether a specific bowl can deliver attractive teams, based on their conference affiliations and won–lost records, determines whether payouts to teams are in the thousands or millions of dollars. The clamor for determining the top football team in NCAA Division I or Bowl Championship Division will not lead to a playoff system until there is more money to be made for teams and conferences. If commissioners, who are the real powerbrokers in the conferences with the leading football teams, can develop a system that expands the revenues without having to share these with institutions not playing at their competitive level, then a Division I football champion will be determined on the field. So, is the decision about crowning a NCAA Division I football champion about really missing classes or making more money?

Another issue in intercollegiate athletics is the arms race as institutions continually seek to keep up in quantity and quality of their sport facilities for conditioning, practicing, and competing. Intercollegiate athletics is an increasingly expensive enterprise given the costs of uniforms, equipment, travel, and personnel. When institutions choose or are required by their intercollegiate athletic organizations or conferences to support a certain number of teams for male and female students, the revenues seldom cover the expenses. This problem grows when conference or national rivals build bigger and better facilities. In order not to fall behind in being able to attract the most talented athletes, other athletic departments add expensive new sport facilities. While many times funds for these athletic facilities are private donations, a concern for many institutions is that these donations detract from fund-raising efforts to support academic programs. A related concern is that state funding may be redirected into facilities used exclusively or primarily by a small percentage of the students.

This arms race has been extended to salaries for some football and basketball coaches. Claiming market factors, some athletic directors have negotiated multimillion-dollar contracts for high-profile coaches. These coaches are paid far in excess of the salaries paid to institutional presidents or the most outstanding faculty; plus, their salaries exceed those of many professional sport coaches. Justifications for these salaries include that these coaches are the most visible and successful public relations ambassadors for their institutions, are analyzed and critiqued incessantly, and their teams must win.

Because of the importance placed on winning, these coaches are usually able to command whatever extra benefits they request for their teams and financial packages that include television shows, summer sport camps, cars, and incentives and bonuses associated with winning. An ethical issue about the increasing salaries for high-profile coaches is why nonprofit educational institutions would pay coaches millions of dollars primarily because their teams win games. How are such salaries justified when other teams are being eliminated or funds, especially from state coffers, are being allocated to offset budgetary shortfalls in athletic departments?

Another commercial influence on intercollegiate athletics is corporate advertising and sponsorships. Almost everything, except for the institution's name and athletes' names, seems to have a price and can be bought by a corporation or local business. Corporate logos are visible throughout athletic facilities and on uniforms. Special events, courts and fields, facilities, and most everything else includes or can include advertisements. Athletic directors justify this commercialization of intercollegiate athletics because of rising costs. With the emphasis on winning, it is inevitable that more money will be needed for grants-in-aid, travel accommodations commensurate with the level of the institutions' teams, expanding personnel costs for administrative staffs, facilities, and coaches' salaries.

Another commercial feature in intercollegiate athletics is licensing and merchandise sales. Many athletic programs view this as an underutilized source of revenue when it is operated by institutions. Some athletic directors argue that the sale of jerseys, sweatshirts, other types of clothing, and team-related merchandise is associated most often with athletics, so the department of athletics should be the primary recipient of the revenues. Sometimes, such as at the University of Kansas, control of institutional word marks, trademarks, and mascot symbols has been transferred to athletic departments. Does this mean that intercollegiate athletics is more visible and more important than the institution?

It is agreed by most that intercollegiate athletics is a business and operates with an emphasis on profit maximization in the selling of entertainment and sometimes clothing and merchandise. Why then, ask tax-paying businesses against whom they compete for consumers, are intercollegiate athletic programs not required to pay unrelated business income taxes? According to Internal Revenue Service rules, because of the affiliation with not-for-profit educational institutions, and because intercollegiate athletic programs have been able to justify that revenues from the sale of entertainment, clothing, and merchandise have been used to directly fund their athletic programs, they have not had to pay income taxes on their business transactions. Many question whether multimillion dollar salaries for coaches and expenditures for large traveling parties during bowl trips directly benefit athletes or divert funds to administrators or other supporters of commercialized intercollegiate athletics.

Another issue facing intercollegiate athletics is gambling. Some athletes have shaved points, which occurs when gamblers promise payments to athletes for playing in ways to keep the point spread at the level of the bets placed by the gamblers. Since intercollegiate athletes are not permitted to accept pay for their play, some are vulnerable to this enticement, especially since they do not have to lose the game, just help manipulate the point spread. In addition, the point spread provided in newspapers and online makes gambling an issue for college students, including athletes.

Another area of concern affecting some intercollegiate athletes occurs when they sign with sport agents and receive benefits not permitted by the NCAA. Intercollegiate athletic organizations require that athletes maintain their amateur status, which means athletes cannot receive benefits provided by sport agents who seek to represent these athletes in negotiating contracts with professional teams. Some athletes have lost their eligibility to compete because they were told by sport agents that they could receive cash, cars, and other inducements in anticipation of lucrative professional contracts. Other athletes, such as Marcus Camby at the University of Massachusetts, have willingly received financial benefits from sport agents. Some athletes may be tempted to accept money to shave points or to accept cash and other benefits from sport agents because they feel exploited—that is, these athletes realize that athletic departments make millions of dollars because of their athletic performances. Yet, each athlete is limited to receiving a grant-in-aid.

Whether intercollegiate athletes should receive financial benefits in addition to the allowable tuition, fees, room, and board is a significant concern for some outstanding players. Because of a related lawsuit settled out of court in 2008, the NCAA allocated millions of dollars that intercollegiate athletes could access to help them pay other educational expenses. Even with the availability of this assistance, some athletes claim they are being exploited. Economists agree that the marginal revenue added by an outstanding intercollegiate football and basketball player is several hundred thousand dollars.

The issue of potentially paying football and basketball players is complex. First, where would the money come from to pay these athletes? Second, would all or only some football and basketball players be paid? Third, how much would each athlete be paid, and how would this amount be calculated? Fourth, would any other athletes be paid, and if so, how much? Fifth, if only male athletes were paid, would this violate Title IX of the 1972 Education Amendments? Sixth, would paying athletes make them employees of the institution and thus eligible for benefits such as insurance and workman's compensation?

For the millions who attend NCAA Division I football and basketball games, the growing revenues and expenses in intercollegiate athletics are usually perceived as necessary for entertaining fans. It is fun to tailgate, socialize, and party in support of favorite teams, and especially if these teams win. What many fans and most of the general public do not understand is that most athletic departments operate at a loss. As a result, millions of dollars from institutional resources are provided to athletic departments to subsidize a small percentage of the students. Is this fair? If not, should this practice be allowed to continue?

Proposed Reforms and Teaching Values in Intercollegiate Athletics

The issues and controversies associated with intercollegiate athletics have led to call for reform as they question whether the integrity of higher education is being jeopardized by an overemphasis on winning associated with recruiting, academics, and commercialism (Byers and Hammer 1995; Duderstadt 2000; Sperber 1990). The overarching suggestion has been for institutions and their presidents to reduce the commercialization of intercollegiate athletics that is interwoven with the emphasis on winning. To return to an emphasis on education first, is greater institutional oversight and control needed? Intercollegiate athletics, it is argued, should not compromise the well-being of athletes, the academic mission of the institution, or the good name of the institution to win or make money.

Some people argue that one solution would be to simply eliminate recruiting. Then, institutions would be admitting only those athletes who meet the academic standards for admission that apply to all other students. Coaches could be expected to develop the skills of players who choose to attend each institution. (And, for those individuals who really are not interested in going to college, they could join developmental or minor leagues funded by the professional leagues, as happens in other countries.) Institutions could limit grants-in-aid to tuition, fees, and books, award them to athletes only on the basis of need, and guarantee them for four years. If these changes were to be enacted, intercollegiate athletics could again be described as extracurricular activities for students, rather than part-time to full-time jobs for recruited athletes.

One way to emphasize academics, and thereby reduce the emphasis on athletics and winning, could be to require one-year residency prior to competition for freshmen and transfer students. With this change, academic eligibility to participate would be based on a student's academic performance in college and not on a standardized test score or grades from high school. Students who want to compete in athletics could be required to attain and maintain a minimum cumulative grade-point average of 2.0 and make incremental progress toward earning a degree in four years. To keep athletics from replacing academics as the reason for attending college, the schedules of all teams could be shortened and restricted to one academic term. Maybe athletes could compete only one day per week while classes are in session. Athletes could be excused from classes no more than five days per academic year for travel and competition. With athletics no longer consuming the lives of athletes, academic support services for athletes could be the same as for other students. If these changes were to be enacted, intercollegiate athletics would be much less likely to replace academics in importance, and athletes would have the time and ability to focus on learning and earning degrees.

The commercialism of intercollegiate athletics could automatically lessen if the above changes were to be implemented. For example, millions of dollars would be saved by eliminating recruiting expenses, hiring fewer coaches to recruit, reducing the amounts of grants-in-aid, eliminating athlete-only academic support services, and lowering salaries for coaches since they would no longer be expected to recruit. Directors of athletics could be expected to constrain, not expand, their budgets, and place the welfare of athletes ahead of the demands of television or needs of professional sport teams. If these changes were to be enacted, personnel in departments of athletics would be evaluated on the basis of developing athletes' sport skills, educating athletes in character, and preparing athletes for careers other than in sports, not on how much money they brought in or games won.

Conclusion

Numerous problems plague youth, interscholastic, and intercollegiate sport. The most significant culprit is the overemphasis on winning because of how it contributes directly to most of the other issues. Coaches and athletes cheat, engage in gamesmanship, and use, or condone the use of performance-enhancing drugs to gain competitive advantages to help win. When fun and the other goals of young athletes are not achieved, it is usually because of adults focusing more on winning than on providing children with character-based lessons for life. When academic rules, eligibility regulations, and ethical behaviors are violated in pursuit of victories, many interscholastic athletes are being taught that winning is more important than showing respect and responsibility. When the most important outcome is winning, some coaches and athletes in intercollegiate athletics will break recruiting and academic rules and regulations.

One reason sport is important in society is because it provides the opportunity to teach character at all levels of sport. Coaches and sport administrators can teach sportsmanship, which includes playing fair, following the letter and spirit of the rules, respecting the judgments of officials, treating opponents with respect, shaking hands at the end of the game, never running up the score, never cheating, and never taunting. Since many lessons learned in sports will last a lifetime, coaches, parents, and sport administrators have the opportunity to ensure that character development is emphasized and achieved.

When coaches and other adults teach, model, shape, and reinforce the development of character, athletes will become individuals who compete in morally responsible ways. The way to develop the values of athletes is through teaching moral values and moral reasoning and consistently reinforcing them. Athletes will follow the behaviors and actions of coaches and other adults who model moral courage and do the ethically right thing. Since people do what is measured and reinforced, athletes will be more likely to reason morally and live principled lives whenever character and other moral values are expected and rewarded.

References

Acosta, R. V., and L. J. Carpenter. 2008. "Women in Intercollegiate Sport: A Longitudinal, National Study—Thirty-One-Year Update, 1997–2008." Available at: http://www.acostacarpenter.org/2008%20Summary%20Final.pdf.

Blanchard, K., and N. V. Peale. 1988. *The Power of Ethical Management.* New York: William Morrow.

Bredemeier, B. J. L. 1995. "Divergence in Children's Moral Reasoning about Issues in Daily Life and Sport Specific Contexts." *International Journal of Sport Psychology* 26 (4): 453–463.

Byers, W., with C. Hammer. 1995. *Unsportsmanlike Conduct: Exploiting College Athletes.* Ann Arbor: University of Michigan Press.

Carpenter, L. J., and R. V. Acosta. 2005. *Title IX.* Champaign, IL: Human Kinetics.

Citizenship through Sports Alliance. 2006. 2005 Youth Sports National Report Card. *Strategies* 19 (3): 26–28.

Coakley, J. 2009. *Sports in Society: Issues and Controversies,* 10th ed. Boston: McGraw-Hill.

Duderstadt, J. J. 2000. *Intercollegiate Athletics and the American University.* Ann Arbor: University of Michigan Press.

Longman, Jere. 2001. "Pushing the Limits—a Special Report: Someday Soon, Athletic Edge May Be from Altered Genes." Available at: http://query.nytimes.com/gst/fullpage.html?res=9C01E3DF113BF932A25756 C0A9679C8B63&sec=&spon=&pagewanted=2.

National Federation of State High School Associations. "The Case for High School Activities." Available at: http://www.nfhs.org/web/2004/01/the_case_for_high_school_activities.aspx.

Rudd, A., and S. Stoll. 2004. "What Type of Character Do Athletes Possess? An Empirical Examination of College Athletes versus College Non-Athletes with the RSBH Value Judgment Inventory." *Sport Journal* 7 (2): 1–10.

Shulman, J. L., and W. G. Bowen. 2001. *The Game of Life: College Sports and Educational Values.* Princeton, NJ: Princeton University Press.

Sperber, M. 1990. *College Sports, Inc.: The Athletic Department vs. the University.* New York: Henry Holt.

3

Worldwide Perspective

The Olympic Games provide a comprehensive backdrop for understanding political, national, cultural, and ethical pressures to win in international sport. Ethical breaches have occurred because the stakes have become so high, with huge financial rewards and benefits accruing to those who win. This chapter examines amateurism, nationalism, politics, racial and sexual discrimination, bidding scandals, unethical behaviors, and the use of performance-enhancing drugs and their impact on the values espoused by leaders of the Olympic Movement and in other international sport competitions. Numerous specific examples will provide the context for explaining that some athletes, officials, and others associated with sports have chosen to behave in unethical ways to gain competitive and personal advantages.

Doping scandals have threatened international cycling as many sponsors have chosen to no longer associate with this tainted sport. Racism, sexism, gamesmanship and cheating, and the fixing of competitive contests plague some international sports. Athletes and others associated with sports have attempted to rationalize or justify their unethical behaviors as the way the games must be played to win. Others view these same actions as unprincipled and immoral. In seeking to address unethical problems, several sport organizations have enacted drug testing, legislated codes of ethics and other behavioral rules, and honored those who have served as exemplars of sportsmanship, integrity, and character in sport.

Amateurism in the Olympic Games

The English heritage of the word *amateur* carries the meaning of "lover of." An amateur describes a person who engages in an activity like sports without formal preparation and is used in contrast with the expert who possesses extensive knowledge, education, or ability. An amateur also is a person who engages in an activity like sport without receiving monetary benefits or making a living by engaging in this activity. For example, Bobby Jones has been praised for being an amateur and playing for the love of the game. Jones did not dedicate himself solely to golf or receive prize money when he won the U.S. Amateur, British Amateur, United States Open, and British Open championships in 1930.

The concept of amateurism in sports, which was modeled upon the nineteenth-century British Amateur Sport Ideal, became an essential feature of the modern Olympic Games from their beginning in 1896 until the 1970s. The myth or façade of amateurism was removed when higher levels of performance, possible only through extended physical training, were expected and significant financial benefits were accepted.

When Frenchman Pierre de Coubertin sought to reestablish the Olympic Games, he began by calling a conference in 1894 that led to the formation of the International Olympic Committee (IOC). The IOC helped organize the first Olympic Games in the modern era, which were held in Athens in 1896. One espoused goal was to provide friendly competitions among amateurs who competed socially and casually for the love of their respective sports. Even as the world changed, the IOC through the Olympic Movement tried to preserve a nineteenth-century perspective of amateurism that was founded on elitist class distinctions and masculine dominance.

Amateurism as a participation requirement for athletes was an idealistic requirement for the Olympic Games for decades. If an amateur is narrowly defined as an individual who does not dedicate extensive amounts of time and effort to skill development and has not received pay or benefits because of his or her athletic abilities, many athletes who competed in the early years of the Olympic Games were dishonest in claiming to be amateurs. Given the IOC's expectation for amateurism, many of the early Olympic athletes were upper-class individuals who enjoyed the leisure time to practice their skills, such as in private clubs, and the financial means to provide needed equipment.

As IOC president between 1952 and 1972, Avery Brundage attempted to vigorously enforce the amateurs-only requirement for athlete eligibility. To dramatically emphasize this in 1968, he led the IOC to disqualify Austrian skier Karl Schranz for receiving money from ski equipment companies. Even though most people wanted to believe that the love of the game motivated athletes to spend endless hours training and honing their skills, in reality, this level of dedication was almost impossible without their receiving financial benefits because of their athletic abilities and successes.

Despite resistance from most IOC members, by the 1970s many Olympic athletes were receiving appearance fees and other under-the-table payments; several governments were supporting athletes, such as through military appointments with assignments to train and compete in their sports, and equipment and shoe companies were also subsidizing athletes. Inevitably, the ever-increasing quest to become "swifter, higher, stronger," as stated in the Olympic Motto, resulted in a dramatic change in eligibility rules of the Olympic Games from the myth of amateurism to the reality of elite athletes who benefit financially from their achievements.

Today, each international sport federation determines the eligibility rules for athletes competing in the Olympic Games and other international competitions. For example, boxing remains open to only amateurs, while basketball players can be members of professional sport teams. The other sports are somewhere in-between these two extremes. While some Olympic committees, like the United States Olympic Committee, pay athletes for winning gold, silver, and bronze medals, most do not, possibly due to financial limitations.

Most Olympic athletes, such as those who compete in judo, badminton, and rowing, receive limited media coverage, endorsement opportunities, and financial benefits as they pursue their dreams of being the best in their respective sports and events. Although a few publicized Olympic athletes, such as swimmer Michael Phelps in the 2008 Beijing Olympic Games, are known, most people would never recognize the names of the hundreds of Olympic athletes who are not sponsored by sport equipment or apparel companies. Some athletes benefit from coaches provided by national Olympic committee or national training centers, while most athletes fund themselves or have family members who help them financially. Each athlete's training and financial circumstances are individualized depending on the wealth, political context, and sport structure of his or her nation.

While many athletes continue to embody the amateur ideal of competing for the love of the game, a comparatively smaller number of Olympic athletes enjoy fame and fortune. Television, corporations willing to invest millions of dollars in sports for sponsorship and advertising purposes, an increasing number of professional athletes, and lucrative endorsement opportunities for winners of the most prestigious events have contributed to a swelling tide of commercialism associated with the Olympic Games.

Nationalism and Politics in the Olympic Games

The Olympic Charter states that its competitions are between individuals, not nations. In reality, though, individuals are not permitted to enter the Olympic Games, only representative athletes who have been selected by national Olympic committees are. Athletes, typically dressed in team uniforms, enter the stadium during Opening Ceremonies behind their nations' flags. National anthems are played to honor the athletes who win gold medals. Nations that win the most medals or gold medals claim that these symbolize the superiority of their political systems.

IOC members for years claimed that the Olympic Games promoted international peace, friendship, and camaraderie among athletes. Yet, the IOC structured competitions, pageantry, and rewards based on national affiliation. Beginning in the 1956 Melbourne Olympic Games, athletes during the Closing Ceremonies were encouraged to enter the stadium intermingled with athletes of the world, not as representatives of their nations. Still, the rhetoric about friendship among nations seemed to ring hollow and ignore the reality that the Olympic Games had become highly politicized. Many Olympic athletes have realized that they were sometimes used to achieve purposes far afield from friendship among nations.

Nationalism became a volatile ideological clash between nations within the context of the Olympic Games in the years following World War II. Since the beginning of the modern Olympic Games, the IOC stressed that national Olympic committees should operate independent of politics and affiliations with governments. But, the IOC willingly ignored the governmental control over the Soviet Union's Olympic committee because the IOC wanted to include athletes from this huge and increasingly powerful nation in the Olympic Movement.

Despite eligibility rules that defined amateurs as athletes who did not receive financial support because of their talents and skills, the IOC in another deviation from stated policy allowed the Soviet Union to be represented in the Olympic Games by state-supported athletes. Previously, a few athletes who were in the militaries of other countries, including the United States, had spent considerable time training for the modern pentathlon in lieu of fulfilling other military duties. But, the Soviet Union was the first nation to be represented by many athletes whose military status appeared to be in name only as they dedicated themselves to sport training.

It was noteworthy that when the Soviet athletes competed for the first time in 1952, they were housed separately from other competitors, as Soviet leaders alleged concerns about the safety of their athletes. This action did not seem to adhere to the spirit of friendship and internationalism among athletes.

In another postwar situation, controversies raged about what nation should represent China and Germany in the Olympic Games. Did Nationalist China (renamed the Republic of China), the island nation that was home to the national Olympic committee, represent China? Or, was it Communist China (People's Republic of China) with its millions of people? Although athletes from the People's Republic of China competed in the 1952 Helsinki Olympic Games, the government refused to allow its athletes to compete in the 1956 Melbourne Olympic Games because the Republic of China was participating. This conflict disappeared for a while when the Communist nation withdrew from the Olympic movement and the Republic of China or Taiwan became the only representative in 1956. The People's Republic of China did not return until the 1980 Lake Placid Winter Olympic Games.

Controversy also surrounded how to deal with Germany after that nation was divided into communist and democratic sectors after World War II. In 1952, the Federal Republic of Germany (West Germany) competed, but the German Democratic Republic (East Germany) was not invited to send a team. In 1956 (Melbourne), 1960 (Rome), and 1964 (Tokyo), the IOC negotiated a unified team composed of athletes from both nations. IOC president Brundage claimed that the Olympic Games had successfully brought the two German sectors together. This supposed harmony was short-lived as politics, as characterized the China issue, always won out over athletic competitions.

As the politically charged issues of Chinese and German representation were debated within the IOC, governments that did or did not recognize one or more of the participating nations used the Olympic Games to make their case. Respect for national heritage and the rights of athletes and responsible actions seemed not as important as using the Olympic Games to advocate that one political system was superior to another.

Boycotts of the Olympic Games have been used to make political and ideological statements for years. Given that the Olympic Games had become the most significant international sports festival, some nations and individuals chose to use them to advance a cause, communicate with people throughout the world about a human rights or equity issue, and express opposition to the actions of others. A boycott, which inevitably began with the threat of preventing athletes from competing in the Olympic Games, came to be viewed as a viable approach to attempt to force changes in behaviors or concessions from other nations. Whenever boycotts actually occurred, the denial of the opportunity to test one's athletic abilities against the top athletes of the world illustrated a loss of fairness and justice that most people believed should characterize all sports.

Boycotts in the Olympic Games began in 1956 when Spain, Switzerland, and the Netherlands withdrew in protest against the 1955 Soviet invasion of Hungary. Egypt, Lebanon, and Iraq refused to participate in the 1956 Melbourne Olympic Games to protest the intervention in the Suez by France and Great Britain. Twenty-two African nations plus Guyana boycotted the 1976 Montreal Olympic Games. Even though their threat was successful in getting the IOC to ban South Africa and Rhodesia due to their practice of apartheid, these 23 nations still boycotted because the New Zealand team was allowed to participate.

(The issue here was a New Zealand rugby [a non-Olympic sport] team had competed in South Africa.) Due to the 1979 invasion of Afghanistan by Soviet troops, the United States and 64 other nations boycotted the 1980 Moscow Olympic Games. The Soviet Union and 14 Eastern Bloc nations boycotted the 1984 Los Angeles Olympic Games, possibly in retaliation. Cuba, Ethiopia, Nicaragua, and North Korea for political reasons refused to send teams to the 1988 Seoul Olympic Games.

The deadliest use of politics occurred in the 1972 Munich Olympic Games when eight Black September terrorists of the Palestine Liberation Organization killed two Israelis and took nine hostages. Wrestling coach Moshe Weinberg and weightlifter Yossef Romano fought against the kidnappers, allowing one wrestler to escape, before they were killed. After hours of tense negotiations at the airport where the kidnappers and hostages had been transported, the other Israelis were killed (weightlifter David Berger; weightlifter Ze'ev Friedman; wrestling referee Yossef Gutfreund; wrestler Eliezer Halfin; track coach Amitzur Shapira; shooting coach Kehat Shorr; wrestler Mark Slavin; fencing coach Andre Spitzer; and weightlifting judge Yacov Springer.)

The Olympic Games—and specifically these 11 victims—were used as political pawns as the terrorists sought the release of imprisoned sympathizers to their cause. IOC president Brundage suspended competitions for one day and at the Memorial Service in honor of those slain declared that the Games must go on. Brundage, whose idealistic belief that the Olympic Games were more important that just about anything, advocated that even the death of Olympians would not be allowed to forestall this international sports festival.

Many historians of the Olympic Games have questioned Brundage's decision; others applauded it. No doubt, though, the ease with which the terrorists entered the Olympic Village where the athletes were living forever changed the Olympic Games. The scope and expense of security for the athletes since 1972 vividly shows that the Olympic Games are no longer innocent sporting pastimes. The reality is that the Olympic Games operate on a massive international and televised stage. So, the Olympic Movement will likely suffer through subsequent political conflicts, such as caused by boycotts, terrorism, and demonstrations, as the Olympic Games are used to protest and advance national and political agendas.

Racism and Human Rights in the Olympic Games

The international dimension of the Olympic Games provides it with unusual influence that at times governments have been unable or unwilling to wield in addressing human rights issues. For example, the Olympic Movement and IOC members at times have focused attention on discriminatory practices and the lack of human rights that have adversely affected potential Olympians. Notable among these violations has been the South African practice of apartheid, and thus this nation's refusal to permit integrated sports.

The South African practice of apartheid eventually led the IOC to revoke recognition of the South African National Olympic Committee in 1970. Only after governmental changes in that nation led to the end of apartheid was South Africa readmitted into the Olympic family in 1991. A racially mixed team represented South Africa in the 1992 Barcelona Olympic Games.

When Germany was awarded the 1936 Berlin Olympic Games, Adolf Hitler's regime promised that Jewish athletes would be allowed on its team. Nonetheless, the persecution of Jews and other groups persisted and worsened as history has revealed. In 2001, evidence surfaced that Iraqi athletes had been tortured by Uday Hussein, who was president of the Iraqi National Olympic Committee. Thousands of individuals in Atlanta and Beijing were displaced from their homes to make way for construction of the sports venues for those games. Many individuals claimed they were not fairly compensated.

Since Beijing was awarded the 2008 Olympic Games, that nation and the IOC have endured a firestorm of criticism because of the perceptions that the People's Republic of China engaged in unjust human rights practices. This nation's commercial relationship with Sudan, where hundreds of thousands have died in Darfur, has helped fuel the allegation that the People's Republic of China has emphasized economic advancement over human rights. It also has been alleged that children were abused in factories making souvenirs for the Olympic Games. Even though promises were made regarding human rights issues that would be addressed during the bidding process for awarding the 2008 Olympic Games, numerous protesters during the Olympic Torch Relay questioned whether these promises were used to obtain the bid, not effect change.

Racism in International Sports

The United Nations (UN) General Assembly in 1977 adopted an International Declaration against Apartheid in Sports because of racism that denied athletes competitive opportunities, especially in South Africa. Since prejudice and discrimination had continued to plague sports, in 1985, the UN held an International Convention against Apartheid in Sports, which called for the establishment of a Commission against Apartheid in Sports. The UN in its declaration of 2005 as the International Year of Sport and Physical Education continued to work to counter racism in sport through peaceful competitions and play. This year-long initiative promoted the belief that the values potentially learned through sport are universal and advanced the belief that sport could serve as a global language in the elimination of discrimination and racism.

To illustrate the adverse effects of racism, one overt situation involving Basil D'Oliveira, who was born in Cape Town, South Africa, will be provided. He was prohibited from playing first-class cricket in that nation because he was classified as colored due to apartheid. After playing nonwhite cricket in his homeland, he migrated to England and became a British citizen. After playing in international test matches for England, the Marylebone Cricket Club (MCC), which at the time governed cricket, was pressured by South African white political leaders not to select D'Oliveira to play in the 1968–1969 test matches against South Africa. A public outcry against this discriminatory decision led to the MCC adding him to England's team. As a result, South African representatives cancelled the tour matches.

Racism has for years plagued international football, or soccer, as athletes of different colors, ethnicities, and religions have been subjected to the prejudice of athletes, coaches, officials, and spectators. The term *hooliganism* describes the unruly, rowdy, destructive, abusive, and sometimes racist behaviors of international soccer fans. Numerous incidents of racist taunts from fans have victimized black athletes when they have played internationally, especially in Brazil, Spain, Italy, Germany, and Eastern Europe. Based on prejudicial attitudes, some have claimed that black soccer players were not as skilled as their white counterparts. Even the renowned Brazilian star Pelé had to endure racially based taunting and other discriminatory abuse.

The International Federation of Association Football (FIFA), which has more members than either the IOC or the UN, governs international soccer, which is the most popular sport in the world. FIFA has clearly stated in its disciplinary code that players, coaches, and officials guilty of making disparaging, discriminatory, or denigrating statements, or engaging in actions directed toward another person's race, color, language, religion, or ethnic origin would be suspended and fined. Also, teams can be penalized if their fans engage in racist behaviors, and spectators can be banned. The FIFA's Code of Ethics specifically condemns racism.

In an attempt to address the issue of racism, in 1999 several associations and players' unions formed Football against Racism in Europe (FARE). Through organizations in over 30 European countries, FARE seeks to eliminate racism among fans, players, coaches, and officials at grassroots, national, and transnational levels.

In 2008, the Council of Europe of the International Sport and Culture Association, in support of the campaign for "All Different All Equal," held an international seminar that examined the issue of discrimination and racism in soccer. One outcome of that dialogue was to urge organizational leaders to establish and enforce policies to fight violence and racism in sport because of their cancerous effects on society in general and players specifically. The attendees advocated that sport has the potential to serve as a powerful tool to facilitate the acceptance of all people, regardless of race, ethnicity, religion, gender, or ability.

Athletes in numerous sports have had to deal with overt and subtle racism. The following three examples illustrate this. Althea Gibson, who was from the United States, was excluded from tournaments throughout the world due to the bigotry of the white tennis establishment that controlled the exclusive country clubs at which these events were held. Not until 1951 did she became the first African American invited to the Wimbledon Championships in England, thus opening the door forever to tennis players of all races and ethnicities. Before Tiger Woods became the top golfer in the world, he had to endure racist comments from individuals who were reluctant to accept him into their exclusive and white-dominated clubs. The first African American auto racing driver in Formula One, Englishman Lewis Hamilton, had to endure insults, jeers, and other racial abuse while racing in Spain in 2008. Many athletes, coaches, and officials have experienced abuse due to racism and prejudice, including taunts, insults, and disparate treatment. They persevered and demonstrated the strength of character to display sportsmanship and respect, even though they were not the beneficiaries of similar treatment.

In response to racism in its sport, in 2006 the International Cricket Council adopted an antiracism code that included a standard of conduct that sought to eliminate discriminatory behaviors from this sport. This code included a statement of the expectations for spectators and encouraged the use of clear wording on tickets and signs in venues to emphasize these expectations. This code also required the use of public announcements at international matches that condemned racist chants and other abusive or offensive behaviors. Offenders of this code would be removed from the venues, banned from attending future matches, and subjected to prosecution. This code might serve as an international model for players, coaches, officials, and fans in their respectful and responsible treatment of athletes of all races, ethnicities, religions, and cultures.

Females in the Olympic Games

Pierre de Coubertin and other initial IOC members believed the Olympic Games should provide opportunities for highly skilled males to display their athletic prowess. They did not believe that females should be competitive athletes. While females were excluded from the first modern Olympic Games in Athens in 1896, they were permitted to participate in the 1900 Paris Olympic Games. According to IOC records for these Games (International Olympic Committee 2008a), 22 females competed in five sports. Most of these female Olympians competed in the individual, leisurely sports of golf and tennis while wearing Victorian-style clothing appropriate to their gender. Females also were permitted to compete alongside males in sailing, croquet, and equestrian.

In the 1912 Stockholm Olympic Games, females began competing in swimming and diving. Not until the 1928 Amsterdam Olympic Games did the IOC add gymnastics and a few track-and-field events for females, with the 800 meters the longest distance run. Not until the 1972 Munich Olympic Games were females allowed to run a longer (1500-meter) race. The women's marathon was added in the 1984 Los Angeles Olympic Games. The first team sport for women was volleyball in the 1964 Tokyo Olympic Games. Other team sports added for females were basketball and team handball in 1976 (Montreal), field hockey in 1980 (Moscow), softball and soccer in 1996 (Atlanta), and ice hockey in 1998 (Nagano). As these team sports and other individual sports and events were provided for females, their participation numbers increased. Even so, females lagged behind males in competitive opportunities. For example, in the 2004 Athens Olympic Games, 40.7 percent (4,329) of the athletes were females compared with 6,296 males (International Olympic Committee 2008b); in the 2006 Turin Winter Olympic Games, there were 960 females and 1,548 males, or 38.2 percent were female athletes (International Olympic Committee 2008c).

The resistance toward females in the Olympic Games and the gradual expansion of sports and events were reflective of societal attitudes about the role of females—that is, numerous sports were perceived by some to be too aggressive or were thought to be inappropriate for females. Or, this reluctance to grant full acceptance to females may have reflected prejudicial or sexist attitudes of the all-male IOC that females were not welcome in many Olympic sports. The male control over the Olympic Games has been accused of being discriminatory and unfair, unjust, and disrespectful toward females. Not until 1981 were the first women, Pirjo Haeggman of Finland and Flor Isava-Fonseca of Venezuela, selected for IOC membership. In 2008, 15 of the 111 members of the IOC are females (International Olympic Committee 2008d).

Another historical issue regarding females in the Olympic Games that raised ethical concerns dealt with sex testing, which was used to guarantee that only females competed against females because of gender-specific physiological abilities. Stella Walsh (Stanislawa Walasiewicz), a Polish sprinter raised in the

United States who won the gold medal in the 100-meter sprint for Poland in the 1932 Los Angeles Olympic Games, was later accused of being a male. Hermann Ratjen, a German high jumper who competed as a female in the 1936 Berlin Olympic Games, was revealed to be a male in 1955. Tamara Press and Irina Press, who won five track-and-field gold medals for the Soviet Union in 1960 (Rome) and 1964 (Tokyo), ended their careers when sex testing was introduced. It was alleged that the Press sisters were male imposters.

Sex testing began in 1966 at the European Track and Field Championships in Budapest. Since the female athletes were required to parade naked in front of physicians, five world-class athletes chose not to compete in these championships. In the 1968 Mexico City Olympic Games, sex testing was initiated in an attempt to prevent males with inherent physiological advantages from masquerading as females, and thus cheating to try to win. While preventing the deceit of male imposters, sex testing was viewed by many females in the Olympic Games as degrading, sexist, and an invasion of privacy. It is noteworthy that the only female athlete in the Olympic Games between 1968 and 1996 not subjected to sex testing was Princess Anne of Great Britain, who competed in equestrian events in the 1976 Montreal Olympic Games.

One of the controversies surrounding sex testing was that some females were unfairly disqualified from the Olympic Games and other international competitions even though they were females. Misdiagnoses were associated with genetic conditions and an individual's chromosomes. According to physicians, there was compelling scientific evidence that chromosome-based sex testing could be functionally and ethically inconsistent.

Because of these problems, as well as the fact that sex testing has emotionally traumatized and socially stigmatized some female athletes, the IOC stopped the practice of sex testing for all female Olympians in 1999. As recently as the 2008 Beijing Olympic Games, though, if the gender of any female athlete was questioned, she has had to submit to a blood test to verify her eligibility.

Sexism in International Sports

Sexist treatment of females persists in many nations due to disparities in the number of sport opportunities and associated support structures, inadequacy of funding, stereotypical and cultural expectations about the roles of women, and lack of media coverage. Discriminatory practices against females begin at youth and continue to deter many females from reaching their potential in international sports. One contributing factor to these inequalities is that primarily males make sport policies by controlling governing organizations. Broadcasters, reporters, directors, and other media personnel remain primarily males.

Islamic fundamentalists in some Muslim countries have barred females from sports, unless they are dressed in head-to-toe clothing that uncover only their hands and faces. Muslim countries, such as Afghanistan, Algeria, Iran, Iraq, Kuwait, Pakistan, Qatar, Saudi Arabia, and the United Arab Emirates, historically have prohibited or strongly discouraged females from sport competitions. Those Muslim female athletes who have chosen to train and compete often have been subjected to jeering, obscenities, and other abuse. In Indonesia, the most populous Muslim nation in the world, and other countries that are predominately Muslim in Asia, however, female athletes enjoy the freedom to compete in sports of their choice without requirements about their clothing.

The Council of Europe, which was founded in 1949, seeks to promote human rights and democratic principles. In 1992 in its European Sports Charter, this council stated that each individual should be guaranteed opportunities in sports, and it advocated for the protection and development of the ethical basis of sport. Discrimination was specifically prohibited. While progress had been made, worldwide equality of opportunity for females in sport has not yet been achieved.

Bidding Scandals in the Olympic Games

Given the significant time and financial investment required to develop bids for hosting the Olympic Games, unsuccessful aspirants sometimes have hinted at the possibility that votes of IOC members who select the host cities may have been influenced by factors other than the quality of the bids, such as money. Some people involved with Salt Lake City's previous unsuccessful bid process for the Winter Olympic Games seemed to believe that the only way to be selected as the host city was to spend thousands of dollars in courting and entertaining IOC members to secure their votes. In 1998, bribery and corruption among individuals associated with the 2002 Salt Lake City Winter Olympic Games Organizing Committee were exposed. The resulting scandal revealed that representatives of this committee had given cash, scholarships, lavish gifts, and other improper benefits to several members of the IOC and their families. In 1999, four IOC members resigned, one who had been implicated died, and the IOC voted to exclude six of its members for inappropriate conduct, including breaking the Olympic Oath and harming the reputation of the Olympic Movement.

In the wake of this scandal, additional allegations were made and some evidence was provided that IOC members had accepted bribes for their votes during past bidding processes. The allegations broadened to include that vote buying had been a common practice in the successful bids of Atlanta (1996), Nagano (1998), and Sydney (2000), as well as Salt Lake City (2002). Some critics accused the IOC of fostering a corrupt bidding process because IOC members were invited to prospective host cities and treated lavishly. Over the years, the IOC had done nothing to prevent the likelihood of influence on the votes of IOC members, possibly because its members had enjoyed receiving these benefits.

In attempting to overcome the smear to its image in the aftermath of the Salt Lake City fiasco, the IOC established tighter ethics rules, including barring members from visiting any of the bid cities. The IOC restricted members from receiving gifts from bidding cities as well as added other reforms to the selection process. The IOC also changed the life terms of its members to eight-year renewable terms along with a mandatory retirement age of 70 years old and changed the nomination process for potential IOC members.

Most dramatic of the reforms may have been the change in the representational composition of the IOC. In the past, IOC members had been considered representatives of the IOC to countries of the world. While no incumbent IOC member would be excluded, over time the IOC in the future will be composed of 115 members, including 15 Olympic athletes elected by their peers at the time of the Olympic Games, 15 representatives of national Olympic committees, 15 representatives of international sport federations, and 70 other members who would bring unique abilities and experiences. Through these reforms, the IOC hoped to regain its status as a principled group of sport leaders who serve as guardians of the integrity of the premier international sports festival.

The Olympic Games have withstood dramatic societal changes throughout their more than 100-year history. Once obscure, the Olympic Games are now televised throughout the world. The revenues from television support the operations of the IOC, international sport federations, national Olympic committees, and the host cities' organizing committees, all of which are increasingly dependent on these funds. Females enjoy increasing opportunities to compete in more sports and events, rather than being relegated to the sidelines to cheer. The Olympic Games, once open to only amateurs, are primarily competitions among professional athletes. National Olympic committees pay athletes who win medals as they vie for bragging rights and associated political capital. Many athletes who win gold medals in the Olympic Games enjoy significant monetary rewards, including endorsements and celebrity status. Because of the allure of the financial benefits, some competitors choose to do whatever it takes to win. Playing by the letter and spirit of the rules is sometimes ignored and violated while in pursuit of victories.

Unethical Behavior among Officials in the Olympic Games

Officials in the Olympic Games are selected by the international sport federations for each sport, such as the International Basketball Federation, International Swimming Federation, and International Skating Union. Officials are expected to adhere to the highest ethical standards, with a representative official repeating this commitment during the Opening Ceremonies. Despite these expectations, there have been numerous problems with perceived and actual cheating by officials in the Olympic Games. Whenever cheating has occurred, athletes who have trained for years and made huge financial and personal sacrifices have been denied the right to achieve the honor and recognition that their performances merited.

The sports most affected by judging controversies and unethical behaviors have been those that require considerable subjectivity, such as dealing with artistic merit in skating events or when points are added or subtracted in boxing and gymnastics. Sometimes Cold War politics or sentiments opposing an athlete's national origin have robbed rightful winners of the recognition of a gold medal or the self-esteem of being the best—that is, athletes are cheated by powerful officials representing international sport federations who are behaving unethically. A few examples are provided to illustrate how athletes have been harmed by unethical officials.

The men's basketball gold medal game in the 1972 Munich Olympic Games ended in controversy surrounding the actions of officials on and off the court. After the team from the United States took a one-point lead on a free throw, the Soviet team had only three seconds left in the game to attempt to score. Whether due to mistakes by the court officials, clock problems, or inappropriate interference by the Secretary General of the International Basketball Federation, the Soviet team after two failed attempts successfully scored on the third try. The protest filed on behalf of the U.S. team was denied as the five-member Jury of Appeal, which voted along ideological lines between Communist and non-Communist countries. While the Soviet team members received gold medals, the U.S. team members refused to accept the silver medals because they believed they had been cheated.

In the 2002 Salt Lake City Winter Olympic Games, a French judge admitted to having been pressured to vote for the Russian pair in ice skating, rather than the Canadian pair that almost everyone else agreed had performed in a superior way. Initially, the International Skating Union (ISU) refused to take any action to rectify the injustice done to Jamie Salé and David Pelletier. Only after being pressured by IOC president Jacques Rogge, were ISU officials willing to admit that unethical behavior had cheated the Canadian pair. Salé and Pelletier were awarded gold medals.

Numerous other examples of questionable judging in skating events have occurred, yet the ISU has continued to allow national sport federations in skating to appoint judges. As a result, some of these officials became beholden to national organizations and were more likely to succumb to pressure from their leaders to assign certain ratings to selected skaters. While there have been some changes in the scoring systems in skating events, it could be argued that dropping high and low marks was dealing with the aftermath, rather than the source, of the problem of biased judges.

In gymnastics, Pound (2004) suggested that the Soviets, through their control of the International Gymnastics Federation, were able to devise a scoring approach that favored their gymnasts over the Romania team. He argued that this strategy enabled the Soviets to win the team competition in the 1976 Montreal Olympic Games, even though Romanian Nadia Comaneci and her teammates performed superbly.

Pound (2004) also described an example of unethical behavior in the 1988 Seoul Olympic Games, which he described as the most flagrant example of collusion and unethical behavior of boxing judges. He based this claim on evidence that documented the bribes some boxing judges were paid to unfairly deliver the gold medal to Korean Park Si-Hun, who was outboxed in the finals of the light middleweight class by Roy Jones Jr. of the United States.

Conflict of interest threatens the integrity of the Olympic Games when officials in positions of authority over the outcome of competitions appear to favor athletes from their own countries (Pound 2004). In the 1992 Barcelona Olympic Games, Judith McGowan, who was the lead referee in synchronized swimming, was in the position of rectifying an immediately acknowledged scoring mistake made by a judge. With the beneficiary of the mistake an athlete from the United States who received the gold medal, McGowan, also from the United States, alleged no conflict of interest in allowing an incorrect score to remain. In response to a protest from the Canadian delegation on behalf of the rightful winner, McGowan reviewed her own decision and again ruled in favor of her nation's athlete. Only after significant pressure was applied, including the threat of an appeal to the Court of Arbitration for Sport, did the International Swimming Federation finally acknowledge the injustice done to Sylvie Fréchette. But, it took over a year to rectify the abuse of power and harm done to this athlete, and finally award her a gold medal.

Numerous other examples could be provided to illustrate how officials entrusted with upholding the integrity of Olympic competitions have failed in their duties. Athletes' dreams have been shattered whenever arbitrary and capricious actions of officials cheated and stole from athletes their probable once-in-a-lifetime opportunity to stand atop the victory stand as the champions of the world. Through no fault of their own, these athletes were victimized by officials who for political reasons, financial influence, or other personal benefits acted dishonestly, disrespectfully, unfairly, and irresponsibly.

Use of Performance-Enhancing Drugs by Athletes in the Olympic Games

The Olympic Oath specifies that athletes must abide by the rules and show the spirit of sportsmanship. To publicly reinforce this commitment, an athlete from the host nation, on behalf of all athletes, recites the Olympic Oath during the Opening Ceremonies. Despite what the Olympic Oath states, many Olympic athletes have chosen to violate the rules in numerous ways to increase their chances of winning. Apparently, these athletes have convinced themselves that their training and abilities do not give them the extra second, meter, or skill needed to excel over other competitors, so they need to enhance their performances through drugs and other rule-breaking methods. In addition to cheating in violation of the Olympic Oath, these athletes have stolen from their opponents an equitable opportunity to win.

Amphetamines, steroids, and other drugs and substances were used by athletes to gain competitive advantages in the Olympic Games long before there were any written prohibitions. However, most athletes and others interested in the purity of sports emphasized that the use of performance-enhancing drugs was cheating—that is, sports stopped being competitions among athletes with an equal opportunity to win, but, rather, gave unfair advantages to those athletes who chose to artificially or chemically enhance their performances.

In 1928, the International Amateur Athletic Federation (IAAF), which governs athletics (track and field) competitions, banned the use of stimulating substances. Even as other international sport federations followed with similar bans, drug use continued in the absence of drug tests. In the 1960 Rome Olympic Games, Danish cyclist Knud Enemark Jensen, who had taken an overdose of amphetamines, collapsed during his race and died shortly thereafter. In response, the IOC established a medical commission and published its first list of prohibited substances. Drug tests were introduced at the 1968 Grenoble Winter Olympic Games and the 1968 Mexico City Olympic Games.

Ethical questions surfaced, however, as some athletes argued that drug tests were invasions of privacy, and thus violated their rights. Others claimed that submitting to drug tests characterized all athletes as cheats and, therefore, they were assumed to be tainted with drugs unless they could prove their innocence. Conversely, the IOC emphasized that use by some athletes of performance-enhancing drugs had forced the IOC to implement drug tests in order to identify and penalize those athletes who compromised the integrity of the Games through doping.

A large number of athletes from the German Democratic Republic (GDR), especially females, became medalists beginning in the 1976 Montreal Olympic Games. Numerous questions were raised when this small nation's athletes won 40 gold medals and 11 out of 13 gold medals in women's swimming.

While steroid use in the Olympic Games had been banned since 1974, not until 1984 did the IOC begin requiring drug tests for steroids. (Testing for steroids began in 1983 at the Pan American Games.) After the fall of the Berlin Wall in 1989, it was learned that many of the GDR's athletes had been given performance-enhancing steroids without their knowledge or permission. In 1998, in a noteworthy act of sportsmanship, one swimmer from that nation, Carola Nitschke, who had been given steroids beginning at age 13, returned her medals and asked that her name be removed from the record books. The IOC honored her request.

Canadian Ben Johnson's victory in world record time in the 100-meter sprint in the 1988 Seoul Olympic Games was short-lived when he tested positive for use of an anabolic steroid. He was disgraced with the loss of his medal and world record, as well as banishment from competition for two years. Johnson and many other track-and-field athletes have for years denied the use of performance-enhancing drugs, even after failing drug tests.

The Chinese swimming team used anabolic steroids and human growth hormones for years, which enabled it to become a world power in this sport. Positive drugs tests in other championships of more than 40 Chinese swimmers since 1990, however, decimated subsequent Olympic teams. In the 1996 Atlanta Olympic Games, Michelle Smith representing Ireland won three gold medals and one bronze medal in swimming. Suspicions were raised, however, since her improvement as a swimmer had been too remarkable to believe possible without perform-ance-enhancing drugs. After avoiding taking several drug tests, Smith was finally tested in 1998. When the test revealed a high alcohol level that was believed to have been used as a masking agent used to hide the presence of performance-enhancing drugs, she was suspended from competition for four years.

Blood doping has been a part of the rampant doping in and tainted image of cross-country skiing for years. In the 2002 Salt Lake City Winter Olympic Games, Austrian cross-country skiers Marc Mayer and Achim Walcher were disqualified for using blood transfusions, and two team officials who adminis-tered these transfusions were banned for the next two Winter Games. Spain's Johann Muehlegg and Russian medalists Olga Danilova and Larissa Lazutina also tested positive for a drug that boosted the production of red blood cells that carry oxygen to the muscles.

Despite these examples of disqualified athletes and for-feited medals, the extent of doping among Olympic athletes is not known. It has been suggested that many top athletes are willing to risk their physical well-being and reputations in order to earn positions on their national teams and possibly win Olympic medals, even though they may get caught and punished for using performance-enhancing drugs.

In 1999, the IOC convened a World Conference on Doping in response to doping scandals in international sports. The Lau-sanne Declaration on Doping in Sport, which was developed at this conference, called for the establishment of an international organization to fight doping. The World Anti-Doping Agency (WADA), which was fully operational by the 2000 Sydney Olympic Games, has as its purpose to promote and enforce the fight against doping in sports. WADA developed and implemented the World Anti-Doping Code and rules for the international harmonization of anti-doping policies, testing, therapeutic use exceptions, and a list of prohibited substances and methods. This code standardizes minimum and maximum sanctions for doping violations, with the first serious violation carrying a two-year suspension and a second serious violation a lifetime sanction.

Still, some athletes who have tested positive for banned substances have returned to compete in the Olympic Games and win medals. So in 2008, the IOC passed a rule that athletes would be banned for the following Olympic Games if they were suspended for at least six months during the four years prior to the Games for testing positive for banned substances. The IOC enacted this new rule to strengthen its efforts to keep the use of performance-enhancing drugs out of the Olympic Games. This rule will be applied for the first time in the 2010 Vancouver Winter Olympic Games.

Many people have stressed that athletes, along with their trainers and pharmacists, may be years ahead of the most sophisticated drug tests that the World Anti-Doping Agency has implemented—that is, many athletes believe that they can use performance-enhancing drugs to help them succeed with little risk of getting caught. Seemingly, for these athletes, competing is not about playing by the rules, but rather only about winning by doing whatever it takes chemically.

As the Paralympic Games, elite sporting events for athletes from six disability groups, have risen in stature with an increased emphasis on winning, drug tests have revealed that some of these athletes also have used performance-enhancing drugs. In the 1992 Barcelona Paralympic Games, five athletes tested positive for banned substances. That number increased to 14 athletes in the 2000 Sydney Games. In the 2002 Salt Lake City Winter Paralympic Games, Thomas Oelsner, a German Nordic skier, was stripped of his gold medal in the standing biathlon after testing positive for doping.

Individuals who win medals in the Olympic Games and Paralympic Games have reached the pinnacle of their sports. Their achievements have been the results of years of training and sacrifice. However, when they have violated the rules or benefited from unethical behaviors to gain unfair advantages, they have cheated their opponents as well as their sports. Their unprincipled actions have resoundingly declared that the only thing that matters is winning and self-advancement. Cheaters have failed to display the integrity that the leaders of the Olympic Movement believed should characterize the Olympic Games. Discriminatory practices, political and nationalistic ploys that manipulate athletes, and the use of performance-enhancing drugs have no place within peaceful, friendly, respectful, and fair competitions among the best athletes of the world.

Doping Scandals in International Cycling

The use of performance-enhancing drugs and methods is not unique to the Olympic Games, as it now threatens the integrity of all sports. The World Conference on Doping was called by the IOC in 1999 partially in response to doping scandals in cycling. A triggering event occurred in 1998 when Willy Voet, an employee of the Festina racing team, was caught with a carload of performance-enhancing drugs, including erythropoietin (EPO), human growth hormones, testosterone, and amphetamines. The Tour de France expelled the Festina team from the race, with several of the Festina riders admitting to having used performance-enhancing drugs.

Doping has plagued the Tour de France almost since its beginning in 1903. In seeking an advantage or to cope with this grueling 21-stage race, riders, especially since the 1960s, have used alcohol, cocaine, and amphetamines. It was amphetamines that contributed to the death of England's Tom Simpson in the 1967 Tour. In more recent years, steroids, human growth hormones, and blood doping have been used by numerous cyclists.

On the day before the start of the 2006 Tour de France, news broke of the Operation Puerto drug bust that accused a Spanish physician, Eufemiano Fuentes, and others of administering performance-enhancing drugs to over 200 athletes, many of whom were cyclists. Tour favorites Jan Ullrich, who had won the 1997 Tour and was an Olympic gold medalist in 2000, Ivan Basso, and Oscar Sevilla, were implicated in this scandal. These riders and others were suspended by their teams for allegations of using performance-enhancing drugs. Now retired, Ullrich has repeatedly denied doping, even though he paid a six-figure fine in hopes of clearing his name and reputation. Although Floyd Landis of the United States won the 2006 Tour de France, he was stripped of the victory because his level of testosterone exceeded the allowed limit despite his numerous denials of doping.

Many cyclists have used blood doping, which cannot be detected by any existing drug test, to gain advantages in international cycling. The process for blood doping involves athletes removing some of their own blood, which results in their bodies developing replacement red blood cells. Close in time to competitions, these athletes are reinfused with their own blood, thus increasing the blood's oxygen-carrying capacity and muscular endurance. Many retired cyclists, including Germany's Jorg Jaksche, have admitted to blood doping, even though it is not permitted in international cycling. The 2007 Tour had just begun when the prerace favorite, Alexandr Vinokourov of Kazakhstan, was found to have engaged in blood doping.

Some cyclists and other athletes who use performance-enhancing drugs also use substances to hide their cheating. For example, in 2002, Italy's Stefano Garzelli tested positive for a diuretic used to mask the presence of other drugs. In 2007, Bjarne Riis, who won the 1996 Tour de France, admitted that he had used EPO regularly between 1993 and 1998. These and other doping scandals in the Tour and throughout professional cycling have so seriously undermined the credibility of this sport that numerous team and event sponsors have withdrawn their financial support because they do not want to be associated with this tainted sport.

While most people rail against the use of performance-enhancing drugs in sports, not everyone categorizes their use as bad or unethical. Some people advocate that if an athlete chooses to use performance-enhancing drugs and accepts the penalties if caught for violating the rules, this athlete should be allowed to use these drugs. Another argument suggests that knowing where to draw the line between therapeutic use of drugs and drugs used for performance enhancement has become increasingly blurred. It also has been proposed that instead of banning or penalizing the use of performance-enhancing drugs, drug use should be permitted and these drugs made available equally to all athletes. This, they argue, would be fairer than having competitions between athletes who have access to better pharmacists or trainers, and those without these drugs.

Gamesmanship and Cheating in International Sports

Those who cheat do so intentionally and apparently do not feel bound by the same rules that they expect others to follow. Following are a few examples of cheating, including one that occurred in the 2000 Sydney Paralympic Games. The basketball team representing Spain in these Games was disqualified after winning the gold medal when it was discovered that most of the players did not have the alleged disabilities that qualified them for these competitions.

The World Cup finals between the United States and China in 1999 was one of the most highly attended and significant women's sporting events ever. Those in attendance saw the U.S. goalkeeper Briana Scurry intentionally move forward in violation of the rules before the Chinese player Liu Ying contacted the ball on her penalty kick. The U.S. team's championship, won due to Ying's missed shot deflected by Scurry, was tarnished by cheating, as Scurry openly admitted that she used this strategy to gain an unfair advantage.

More and more soccer players are faking injuries and rolling around on the ground as they attempt to mislead officials to get them to stop or delay games. For example, in the 2002 World Cup, Brazilian player Rivaldo faked an injury that was so obvious that he was fined for cheating. But, most of those faking injuries are not penalized, which has led to an increase in this gamesmanship ploy.

Another benefit derived from faking injuries is the unwritten rule in soccer that when a player is injured, the team in possession of the ball will kick it out-of-bounds. But, if the injury is deceptive, rather than real, it can result in a stoppage of play to the benefit of the team of the athlete who is faking the injury. In addition, when play is restarted, the ball is supposed to be passed back to the team that deliberately hit it out. But, since there is no rule requiring this, it opens the door for players to take unfair advantage of those who previously showed good sportsmanship. Either of these tactics potentially can determine the outcomes of games.

The code of conduct of cricket is based on gentlemanly behavior and proper etiquette, as players are taught at an early age to display sportsmanship and civility toward competitors. In the midst of highly competitive matches where winning is paramount, however, players sometimes engage in *sledging*. This term is used to describe swearing at opponents or intentionally saying abusive and offensive words to competitors in order to negatively affect their play.

These are just a few examples of how athletes have chosen to use gamesmanship and have cheated to help them gain advantages. These choices seem to prioritize winning over playing fairly or displaying sportsmanship.

Gambling and Fixing Outcomes in International Sports

Gambling and fixing the outcomes of events threaten the integrity of sports. In 1915, a British football betting scandal occurred when Manchester United was trying to prevent relegation (forced movement to a lower level of competition because of a poor win-loss record). Its opponent was Liverpool, which was not in jeopardy of relegation or fighting for top honors. So, a Football League First Division match was fixed in Manchester United's favor, as players from both sides wagered on the result. Manchester United players Sandy Turnbull, Arthur Whalley, and Enoch West, and Liverpool players Jackie Sheldon (who was the plot's ringleader), Tom Miller, Bob Purcell, and Tom Fairfoul were banned from soccer for life. The bans of four men were lifted in 1919 in recognition of their service to the country during World War I (except Turnbull, who was killed during the war; West, who claimed his innocence, was not reinstated until 1945).

In 1964, another British betting scandal in soccer involved eight professional players who subsequently were jailed for fixing matches. The instigator, Jimmy Gauld, approached other players to entice them to bet on the outcome of fixed matches. David Layne, Peter Swan, and Tony Kay bet against their side in a match in 1962. In 1964, Gauld sold his story to a British tabloid and incriminated these three players. His taped conversations subsequently were used to convict all four players. Six other players, Brian Philips, Sammy Chapman, Ronald Howells, Ken Thomson, Richard Beattie, and Jack Fountain, also received jail sentences for their involvement. All 10 of these players were banned from soccer for life.

In 1993, Marseille, which historically has been the most successful soccer club in France, won the title in that nation's top league and in the United Europe Football Association Champions League. Because the Marseille chairman, Bernard Tapie, subsequently was found guilty of financial irregularities and match-fixing, the club was stripped of both titles and relegated from the top competitive league.

German soccer referee Robert Hoyzer in 2005 confessed to fixing the outcome of matches and was sentenced to prison for fraud. Hoyzer also received a lifetime ban from officiating by the German Football Association. Croatian gambler Ante Sapina, who operated the organized crime syndicate behind this massive scandal, was sentenced to prison as well. Although Hoyzer alleged that other referees and some players had received money for their participation in this match-fixing scandal, only referee Dominik Marks, who denied involvement, received a suspended sentence.

In 1994, Andres Escobar, a defender on the Colombian team, was murdered after he returned home from the FIFA World Cup. His own-goal (i.e., a player accidently causes the ball to go into his own side's goal) was responsible for the difference in a 2–1 loss to the U.S. team. There was speculation that members of the Medellin drug cartel had bet a significant amount of money on Colombia to win and blamed Escobar for the loss.

Bookmaking (i.e., accepting bets and paying winnings depending on the outcome of the sporting event) in many European nations is regulated, but not illegal. Many international tennis tournaments are played in nations where gambling is socially acceptable and part of the cultural fabric. Since only one player in a game where unforced errors occur regularly is needed to determine the outcome of a match, international tennis may be a likely victim for fixing outcomes and gambling manipulators. Proximal to events as prestigious as Wimbledon and the Davis Cup, anyone, even while matches are being played, can place a bet on the overall outcome, winner of each set, or result of a specific rally. In 2007 and 2008, Italian tennis players Alession di Mauro, Giorgio Galimberti, Potito Starace, and Daniele Bracciali were suspended and fined by the Association of Tennis Professionals (ATP) for betting on tennis matches (although they were not involved in any of the matches).

In 2007, the ATP developed anticorruption rules that seek to eliminate wagering from international tennis. These rules require players to report within 48 hours any attempts to influence the outcome of matches. Rule violations will lead to bans, disqualifications, and fines. These penalties could help dissuade players from tanking, through which they put forth minimal effort in order to lose the match.

While other specific incidences of unethical behaviors in international sports could be provided, these are sufficient to illustrate the existence of the intentional rule-breaking and lack of sportsmanship and fair play displayed by some. Most individuals actively involved with sports want to preserve the integrity of their games. This may be because they believe in the potential of sport to develop character, understand the impact that sport potentially can have on societal values, or at least do not wish to erode public confidence. One way that sport organizations have attempted to address threats to the integrity of sports is through legislating expectations for ethical conduct.

Codes of Ethics

In 1999, the IOC Ethics Commission was created as Rule 22 of the Olympic Charter. This commission was charged with guarding the ethical principles of the Olympic Movement, as described in the Olympic Charter and Code of Ethics. To help encourage greater autonomy, no more than four of the nine members of the IOC Ethics Commission may be IOC members. This Code of Ethics governs the ethical behaviors of IOC members, international sport federations, national Olympic committees, organizing committees of host cities, athletes, and others associated with the Olympic Games such as officials and delegation leaders. It was the Code of Ethics that IOC members violated by accepting financial benefits in exchange for votes for cities bidding to host the Olympic Games. It is the Code of Ethics, as well as the World Anti-Doping Code, that Olympic athletes violate when they choose to use performance-enhancing drugs. The IOC Ethics Commission has the authority to issue sanctions, including permanent or temporary ineligibility and disqualification, for noncompliance with this code.

In 2004, FIFA approved a Code of Ethics, developed by its Commission for Ethics and Fair Play. This code, which seeks to safeguard the integrity and reputation of soccer throughout the world, governs the behaviors of athletes, coaches, officials, and others associated with soccer. Revised in 2006, this code called for the establishment of an independent Ethics Committee to investigate immoral and unethical methods and practices like illegal betting, match fixing, bribery, and conflicts of interest. FIFA representatives stated that rigorous enforcement and exclusion of offending athletes, players' agents, coaches, officials, and administrators were needed. Discrimination on the basis of culture, ethnicity, gender, race, politics, or language is specifically banned, as is gambling.

In 1998, the International Tennis Federation developed a Code of Ethics for Coaches in response to coaches in several countries who had acted unethically toward the players they were coaching. This code, developed in conjunction with male and female professional players, provides for reporting mechanisms and disciplinary action against offenders.

The International Association of Athletics Federations (IAAF) promotes ethical values among track-and-field athletes and officials. Its Code of Ethics specifically emphasizes equality, dignity, fair play, anti-doping, and friendly and loyal cooperation and understanding among everyone associated with the IAAF and its operations.

These examples of the codes of ethics developed and enforced by international sport organizations have responded to an increase in unprincipled actions by athletes and others associated with these sports. The need to specify expectations and sanctions for unprincipled actions in sports indicates that the cultures in many sports have changed. While around-the-clock televised and online coverage of sports has contributed to the notoriety of unethical actions, the media are not causing these problems. For many individuals, cheating has replaced sportsmanship as the accepted norm in sports. A win-at-all-cost mentality could describe those athletes, coaches, and trainers who espouse the idea that "if you are not cheating to win, you are not trying hard enough."

Examples of Sportsmanship in the Olympic Games

This chapter will conclude with three examples drawn from the Olympic Games. In the midst of the highest level of sport competition, these athletes put aside their goals of being the best because they chose to do what they believed was right. While not seeking fame or fortune as they displayed the epitome of the true spirit of sportsmanship during the Olympic Games, each one subsequently was awarded the Pierre de Coubertin medal by the IOC.

The first recipient of this medal was German Lutz Long who suggested to Jesse Owens in the 1936 Berlin Olympic Games to begin his leap in the long jump farther back to prevent the likelihood of disqualifying himself by fouling a third time. Long, in helping his chief competitor who went on to defeat him for the gold medal, risked the ire of Adolf Hitler but won the admiration of Owens and others.

At the 1964 Innsbruck Winter Olympic Games, Italian Eugenio Monti and his teammate were expected to win the gold medal in the two-man bobsled. They were in first place with the fastest time when Monti learned that the British team of Tony Nash Jr. and Robin Dixon discovered a broken axle bolt just prior to their final run. In a remarkable display of sportsmanship, Monti removed the axle bolt from his sled and gave it to Nash and Dixon, who had an outstanding run and won the gold medal. When asked about his action, Monti replied that the axle bolt had not won the gold medal, but rather the skill and performance of Nash and Dixon had. Monti truly respected the spirit of competition more than winning.

In the 1988 Seoul Olympic Games, Canadian Finn class sailor Lawrence Lemieux was sailing in second place in the fifth of the seven-event race when due to dangerous winds, the Singapore team of Joseph Cahn and Shaw Her Siew sailing in the 470 class were thrown into the water. With the capsized and injured men in peril, Lemieux immediately left his race and sailed to rescue them. Lemieux was honored for his sportsmanship, self-sacrifice, and courage.

References

Barney, R. K., S. R. Wenn, and S. G. Martyn. 2002. *Selling the Five Rings: The International Olympic Committee and the Rise of Olympic Commercialism*. Salt Lake City: University of Utah Press.

Espy, R. 1979. *The Politics of the Olympic Games.* Berkeley: University of California Press.

Guttmann, A. 1984. *The Games Must Go On: Avery Brundage and the Olympic Movement.* New York: Columbia University Press.

Hoberman, J. M. 1986. *The Olympic Crisis: Sport, Politics and the Moral Order.* New Rochelle, NY: Aristide D. Caratzas.

International Olympic Committee. 2008a. Available at: http://www.olympic.org/uk/games/index_uk.asp.

International Olympic Committee. 2008b. Available at: http://www. olympic.org/uk/games/past/index_uk.asp?OLGT=1&OLGY=2004.

International Olympic Committee. 2008c. Available at: http://www. olympic.org/uk/games/past/index_uk.asp?OLGT=2&OLGY=2006.

International Olympic Committee. 2008d. Available at: http://www. olympic.org/uk/organisation/ioc/members/index_uk.asp.

Pound, R. W. 2004. *Inside the Olympics: A Behind-the-Scenes Look at the Politics, the Scandals, and the Glory of the Games.* Etobicoke, Canada: J. Wiley and Sons.

Schneider, A. J., and H. Fan. 2007. *Doping in Sport: Global Ethical Issues.* London: Routledge.

Simson, V., and A. Jennings. 1992. *The Lords of the Rings: Power, Money, and Drugs in the Modern Olympics.* London: Simon and Schuster.

Voet, W. 2001. *Breaking the Chain. Drugs and Cycling; The True Story.* London: Yellow Jersey.

4

Chronology

This book examines sport ethics in the modern era, operationally defined as a period of about 125 years. This time period is chosen to include the entire history of the modern Olympic Games, from 1896 through 2008, and developments in all levels of amateur sports in the United States. A few examples of professional athletes are included because they illustrate significant unethical and ethical behaviors. Most examples come from the popular team sports of baseball, basketball, and football, but also include sports like cycling, figure skating, and track and field. The breadth of these examples of unethical behaviors in sport include academic misconduct, cheating, gambling, lying, recruiting violations, use of performance-enhancing drugs, and violence.

In examining the history of sport from an ethical perspective, two contrasting types of incidents are especially relevant to consider. First, what have been times when athletes and others involved with sports have made choices and acted in ways that most people would categorize as unethical? That is, when these individuals gambled, were violent, cheated, lied, or took performance-enhancing drugs, did they adversely affect how the games were played and perceived by fans and other participants? Second, have there been times when athletes have demonstrated sportsmanship, fair play, and other praiseworthy actions? That is, did these individuals enhance their reputations because their actions showed that striving to win and championship performances can be congruent with ethical behaviors? Following are some examples of unethical and ethical actions in sport that provide evidence of individuals demonstrating or failing to demonstrate principled behaviors.

Examples of Unethical Behaviors in Sport

1880s   Many college baseball players, in the absence of eligibility rules, play on resort teams and local teams during the summer months and receive money. Baseball players being paid while subsequently playing intercollegiate baseball remains an unresolved issue for years. Even after colleges establish rules precluding students from retaining their eligibility if they have been paid to play, for years many students use assumed names and are paid to play baseball during the summer.

1887   Owners in the National League of Professional Baseball Clubs make a "gentleman's agreement" to exclude African Americans from their teams. This racial discrimination pervades organized professional baseball until Branch Rickey signs Jackie Robinson to a contract in 1945, and he begins playing for the Brooklyn Dodgers in 1947.

1890s   Intercollegiate football, which is played without helmets and protective pads, becomes increasingly brutal. Teams use mass formation plays, like the flying wedge, hit opponents with their fists, and intentionally inflict physical harm, sometimes with blows to the head that cause deaths, until the level of violence results in calls for reform in the rules. In 1906, the Intercollegiate Athletic Association of the United States (changed to NCAA in 1910) is established and begins to change the rules, such as by legalizing the forward pass. Gradually over the years, rules in football eliminate some of the brutality, and eligibility rules prevent the use of nonstudent players. Other associated problems with football in the 1890s through 1920s are gambling, drunkenness, and riotous behaviors by students and other fans.

1919   Concerns about gambling threaten the integrity of professional baseball from its earliest years, but not until eight Chicago White Sox players accept money from gamblers to fix the outcome of the World Series against the Cincinnati Reds does Major League Baseball take a firm stand in trying to eliminate this problem. Even though the court acquits Eddie Cicotte, Oscar Felsch, Arnold Gandil, Joe Jackson, Fred McMullin, Charles Risberg, Buck Weaver, and Claude Williams from criminal charges in 1921, Major League Baseball's new commissioner, Kenesaw Mountain Landis, bans these players from professional baseball for life.

1920s   When professional football begins with the establishment of the American Professional Football Association (name is changed to the National Football League in 1922), it is minimally regulated. In addition to the poorly paid players jumping from team to team for more money, college students using assumed names are enticed to play for pay. College officials, in attempting to enforce amateurism, ban these athletes from intercollegiate teams if their actions become known. During this decade, the leading college football powers bring in significant revenues and build massive stadiums, while the players must fund their own college expenses, although some receive under-the-table payments. Major controversies and even the breaking off of relationships between institutions characterize a decade in which football becomes commercialized while operating under the guise of amateurism.

1929   The Carnegie Foundation publishes its examination of intercollegiate athletics, which identifies commercialism and the loss of educational values as key problems. The authors, based on their interviews with individuals associated with athletics, especially football, and visits to over 100 institutions, identify the institutions that recruit and pay players. Even though the NCAA has few rules about academic eligibility and compensation, intercollegiate athletics is allegedly open only to amateurs.

1930s When physical education professionals oppose competitive sports for elementary and middle school-aged children, based on their developmental needs, others disagree and begin to organize competitive sports programs for boys. Among these are Pop Warner Football, which Joe Tomlin begins in 1930, and Little League Baseball, which Carl Stoltz starts in 1939. Many of the thousands of local and national youth sport programs begun over subsequent years experience the ethical problems described in Chapters 1 and 2.

1948 The NCAA, in an attempt to prevent the awarding of financial aid based on athletic skill, passes the Principles for the Conduct of Intercollegiate Athletics (called the Sanity Code). Even though several intercollegiate athletic programs refuse to stop their practice of making financial awards to athletes, NCAA members fail to expel them and enforce this code. As a result, the NCAA establishes policies in 1956–1957 to govern recruiting and awarding of scholarships to athletes.

1951 Bookmakers and gamblers pay 33 basketball players from seven colleges, including City College of New York (winner of the 1950 National Invitational Tournament [NIT] and the 1950 NCAA championship) and the University of Kentucky, to shave points in 49 games. (Point-shaving occurs when gamblers pay athletes to manipulate the difference in the projected scores of two teams to enable the gamblers to win on their bets.) Most of the players receive suspended sentences, while the fixers and gamblers serve time in prison. City College of New York de-emphasizes basketball. The Southeastern Conference bans the University of Kentucky, winner of the NCAA basketball championship in 1948, 1949, and 1951, from conference play, and other institutions decide not to play the team, thus cancelling its 1952–1953 season. The National Basketball Association (NBA) bans all of the players involved from playing in its league.

Following an administrative Honor Code investigation, 29 West Point cadets in the class of 1952 and 54 cadets in the class of 1953 admit their knowledge of or participation in a cheating ring. This investigation proves that numerous football players and other athletes provide information and copies of some common examinations to other cadets. The United States Military Academy dismisses the guilty cadets.

1956   Brawls and brutality characterize the semifinal water polo match between the Soviet Union and Hungary in the Melbourne Olympic Games. Intense animosity exists between these two teams following the invasion of Hungary four weeks prior to the Games by Soviet troops to suppress an anti-Communist uprising. Officials call off the game with Hungary leading 4–0. Hungary goes on to win the gold medal.

1961   Gamblers and fixers Aaron Wagman and Joseph Hacken entice 37 players from 22 colleges to alter the point spreads in 44 basketball games. The players who fixed games play for Brooklyn College, Columbia University, La Salle University, Mississippi State University, New York University, North Carolina State University, Seaton Hall University, St. Joseph's University, St. John's University, the University of North Carolina, and the University of Tennessee, among others. In addition, some evidence points to Jack Molinas's paying numerous other players to fix games. All of the players escape convictions.

1977   During a NBA game, the Los Angeles Lakers' Kermit Washington punches the Houston Rockets' Rudy Tomjanovich. This life-threatening blow detaches Tomjanovich's face from his skull, causing blood and spinal fluid to leak into his skull capsule. Washington receives a 60-day suspension without pay for this violent incident.

1979   Gamblers, with connections to organized crime, and Ernie Cobb, Rick Kuhn, and Jim Sweeney, Boston College basketball players, consort to shave points in nine games. One player (Kuhn) and the gamblers receive prison terms for their conviction of conspiracy to commit sports bribery in this point-shaving scheme.

1980   Rosie Ruiz appears to finish as the first female runner in the Boston Marathon. The Boston Athletic Association strips Ruiz of the title for cheating, because she shows no fatigue, she fails to recall landmarks along the course, and there is no video evidence that she actually runs in the marathon.

1986   The court, due to a mistrial, drops charges for shaving points against five Tulane University basketball players. These players, who were alleged to have received money and cocaine for fixing the outcome of games, include John "Hot Rod" Williams, who subsequently plays 13 seasons in the NBA. Tulane cancels its basketball program (which resumes in the 1989–1990 season).

        Jan Kemp, an English teacher, receives an award of over $2.5 million (later reduced to $1.1 million) for lost wages, mental anguish, and punitive damages from the University of Georgia. The court decides that the University of Georgia wrongfully fires Kemp because of her accusation that the institution preferentially treats and passes student-athletes in its developmental studies program. Her lawsuit details the practice of enrolling and keeping eligible athletes who can barely read and write.

1987   While on NCAA probation for rule violations, representatives of Southern Methodist University (SMU) give money to numerous football players. SMU's football program receives the "death penalty," the harshest penalty ever imposed by the NCAA Infractions Committee, for its persistent rule violations and deceit. The penalties include cancellation of the 1987 football season, banishment from bowl games and television for two years, and loss of scholarships. SMU, which cannot play home games in 1988, chooses not to field a team that season.

1988   The University of Kentucky forces the resignations of coach Eddie Sutton and director of athletics Cliff Hagan after numerous recruiting violations occur in the basketball program. In two recruiting violations, the father of high school prospect Chris Mills receives a package containing $1,000 from assistant coach Dwane Casey, and Eric Manuel receives improper assistance on his college entrance exam. The NCAA bans Manuel from its competitions, but he subsequently plays for Hiwassee College, a National Association of Intercollegiate Athletics (NAIA) institution. Mills goes on to play at the University of Arizona and then 10 seasons in the NBA. The NCAA places Kentucky on probation for three years, bans it from the NCAA tournament for two years, and strips it of its two wins in the 1988 NCAA tournament.

Ben Johnson wins the 100-meter dash in the Seoul Olympic Games. After Johnson tests positive for the use of performance-enhancing drugs, he loses this gold medal and the world record he set.

1989   Commissioner Bart Giamatti bans Pete Rose, who holds the Major League Baseball (MLB) record for most hits, from baseball for life for gambling on baseball. The evidence in a 225-page investigative report shows that Rose bets thousands of dollars daily on baseball games, even while managing the Cincinnati Reds. After years of denial, in 2004, Rose admits in his autobiography to gambling on baseball games.

1993   Monica Seles, the top-ranked female professional tennis player, defeats Germany's Steffi Graf to win the Australian Open in January. During a changeover in sides of the court during her quarterfinal tennis match in a tournament in Hamburg, Germany, in April, Guenter Parche, a deranged fan of Graf, runs out of the crowd and plunges a steak knife between Seles's shoulder blades. While Seles recovers physically within a few weeks, she struggles with the psychological scars of the brutal attack. Due to Parche's psychological problems, he avoids imprisonment and receives a two-year suspended sentence. More than two years later, Seles returns to competition, but she never regains the number one ranking.

1994   Stevin Smith and Isaac Burton Jr., Arizona State basketball players, accept bribes to shave points. In 1999, for their conspiracy to commit sports bribery, they receive prison sentences of one year and two months, respectively.

Shane Stant executes the plan of Shawn Eckardt, Derrick Smith, and Tonya Harding's ex-husband, Jeff Gillooly, to club the knee of rival skater Nancy Kerrigan at the United States Olympic Trials. Without Kerrigan competing, Harding wins this competition and qualifies for the Lillehammer Winter Olympic Games. Harding finishes eighth in the Olympic Games, but then pleads guilty to conspiracy to hinder prosecution of the attack. The United States Figure Skating Association bans Harding from competitive figure skating for life.

1995   A federal court indicts Kenneth Lee and Dewey Williams, Northwestern University basketball players, for fixing the outcome of three games. They receive money to shave points in three games from their bookie, former Notre Dame kicker Kevin Pendergast. In 1998, these two players receive convictions for committing sports bribery and are sentenced to one month in prison, while the bookie serves two months in prison.

The court finds, after a highly publicized and lengthy criminal trial, O. J. Simpson, the 1968 Heisman trophy winner at the University of Southern California and NFL All-Pro running back for the Buffalo Bills, not guilty of the murder of his ex-wife Nicole Brown Simpson and her friend Ronald Goldman. In a much-less known civil trial in 1997, the court finds Simpson liable for the wrongful death of Goldman and the battery of Brown and awards a judgment of $33.5 million to the families of Brown and Goldman. In 2007 Simpson and three other men enter a hotel room and take sports memorabilia that Simpson claims has been stolen from him. Simpson is convicted of kidnapping and robbery and sentenced to a minimum of nine years in prison.

1996   After Jim Harrick coaches the University of California at Los Angeles (UCLA) men's basketball team to the 1995 NCAA men's basketball championship, UCLA fires him for lying on an expense report. The University of Rhode Island (URI) hires Harrick as its basketball coach in 1997. Christine King, a secretary in the basketball office, alleges that Harrick harasses her, changes players' grades, has term papers written for players, and gives players improper benefits. URI settles a lawsuit with King for $45,000. After moving to the University of Georgia in 1999, Harrick subsequently resigns under pressure in 2003 due to academic improprieties, including the travesty of grades given to basketball players by his son, Jim Harrick Jr., who is an assistant coach.

Mike Cito, a high school football player, sharpens the edges of his helmet, which results in players from the opposing team getting cut. Cito receives a year-long ban from competition against any school in New Mexico and expulsion from the Albuquerque private school he attends.

1997   The National Basketball Association (NBA) commissioner, David Stern, suspends Dennis Rodman for 11 games and fines him for kicking a cameraman during a Minnesota Timberwolves game. Some people assume that the severity of these penalties relates to Rodman's previous behavior problems, such as head-butting referee Ted Bernhardt during one game and his profanity-laced tirade against officials after another game.

Marcus Camby, an All-American basketball player at the University of Massachusetts, acknowledges taking thousands of dollars in cash and gifts from sport agents while playing in college. John Lounsbury and Wesley Spears, the two agents, give Camby these gifts because they want him to sign with them when he turns professional. The NCAA strips the University of Massachusetts of its 1996 tournament victories and requires the return of the money it receives for advancing to the national semifinals.

Golden State Warriors' Latrell Sprewell chokes, punches, and threatens his coach, P. J. Carlesimo, alleging that the coach disrespected him. Initially banned for a year by NBA commissioner Stern, arbitrator John Feerick reduces Sprewell's suspension to 68 games and the $6.4 million Sprewell loses during the suspension. The two seasons on Sprewell's contract remain.

1999   Tony Limon throws an elbow during a high school basketball game that breaks the nose of an opposing player and receives a five-year prison sentence for the assault. This criminal case is highly unusual since an altercation in a school sport seldom results in a court conviction or even a lawsuit. Limon claims that his coach, Gary Durbon, encourages violence and rough and physical play, allegations that the coach denies.

The International Olympic Committee (IOC) expels six of its members and a seventh member resigns for receiving improper benefits, such as cash, tuition payments, medical treatment, and lavish gifts in exchange for their votes in the 2002 Salt Lake City Winter Olympic Games bidding scandal. With this admission of improprieties among these and other IOC members, the IOC changes the selection process for future host cities.

United States goalkeeper Briana Scurry violates the rules for penalty kicks when she moves forward to cut off the angle as Chinese player Liu Ying hits her penalty kick. This quick move to gain an advantage outside the rules helps the U.S. women's soccer team win the World Cup.

The NCAA penalizes the University of Minnesota with probation for four years and reduces grants-in-aid, official visits, and evaluation opportunities due to serious academic fraud. With the full knowledge and support of the men's basketball coach, Clem Haskins, a team tutor writes hundreds of papers for numerous basketball players over a five-year period. These violations involve extra benefits, academic eligibility, unethical conduct, and lack of institutional control. Coach Haskins resigns, and the NCAA show cause requirement applies to him, which means that no NCAA institution can hire him to coach for a designated period of time without permission of the NCAA Infractions Committee.

2000   Thomas Junta beats to death another father in a fight after their sons participate in a youth hockey practice in Massachusetts. Junta receives a prison sentence of six to ten years for killing Michael Costin.

The Boston Bruins' Marty McSorley hits the Vancouver Canucks' Donald Brashear in the head with his stick during a National Hockey League (NHL) game. Brashear suffers a serious concussion and is unconscious and convulsing due to McSorley's actions. In a criminal case, a Canadian court finds McSorley guilty of assault with a weapon, but he serves no prison time. NHL commissioner Gary Bettman suspends McSorley for a full year.

Orlando Lago, a Police Athletic League assistant coach and volunteer coach at South Broward High School in Hollywood, Florida, punches umpire Tom Dziedzinski because Lago is not happy when Dziedzinski calls a player out for attempting to steal third base. Lago receives 10 years probation for the aggravated battery of breaking Dziedzinski's jaw.

2001   Danny Almonte pitches his Bronx, New York, team to third place in the Little League World Series. An investigation reveals that his father, Felipe Almonte, and the team's coach, Rolando Paulino, are aware that Danny is actually 14 years old despite a birth certificate that alleges that he meets the Little League requirement of being no older than 12. While Danny is cleared of any wrongdoing, his father and coach receive a lifetime ban from Little League Baseball for cheating.

2002   Ed Martin pleads guilty to conspiracy to launder money and admits he gave $616,000 to University of Michigan players Chris Webber, Robert Traylor, Maurice Taylor, and Louis Bullock. The institution forfeits all games in the 1992–1993, 1995–1996, 1996–1997, 1997–1998, and 1998–1999 seasons, including the 1992 and 1993 Final Four games, repays the NCAA about $450,000 received for postseason play, and takes down the banners for participating in the 1992 and 1993 Final Fours, 1997 NIT title, and 1998 Big Ten Conference tournament title. Chris Webber initially lies to a grand jury, but then pleads guilty to criminal contempt for lying about accepting money from Martin. He is sentenced to 300 hours of community service and pays a $100,000 fine.

Judge Marie-Reine Le Gougne admits to being pressured by the French skating organization to vote for the Russian figure skating pair in the Salt Lake City Winter Olympic Games. The high ratings help the Russian pair win the gold medal and are in exchange for favorable ratings for the French ice dancing team. The IOC awards a second gold medal to the Canadian pair that initially receives a silver medal. Le Gougne receives a suspension for her misconduct.

2003 Carlton Dotson shoots his teammate and friend Patrick Dennehy during a target practice outing. While Dotson claims self-defense and mental problems, in 2005 he receives a 35-year prison sentence. Dennehy's disappearance, until his body is found six weeks later, and the circumstances surrounding this murder trigger an investigation of the Baylor University basketball program. Coach Dave Bliss tells his players to lie to investigators and impugn Dennehy's character as Bliss attempts to cover up wrongdoings, such as payments to players and unreported positive drug tests. Baylor administrators penalize this program with restrictions on recruiting and grants-in-aid. The NCAA adds penalties of the elimination of nonconference games in 2005–2006 and an extension in probationary years. Bliss receives a 10-year "show-cause" order from the NCAA for his unethical conduct.

2004 Tim Montgomery, Olympic gold medalist in the 4x100 meter relay, admits to using human growth hormone and The Clear (tetrahydrogestrinone), an anabolic steroid, supplied by Victor Conte, founder and owner of the Bay Area Laboratory Co-Operative (BALCO). This use of banned substances erases Montgomery's world record in the 100-meter dash set at the IAAF Grand Prix final in 2002. In 2008, Montgomery receives a 46-month prison sentence for a multi-million-dollar bank fraud and money-laundering scheme. He also faces charges for dealing heroin.

In a NBA game between the Indiana Pacers and Detroit Pistons, Pacer Ron Artest goes into the stands and shoves a fan who he mistakenly believes throws a beer cup at him. Nine fans receive injuries during the brawl that breaks out. The NBA suspends nine players for a total of 146 games, with Artest receiving the longest suspension of the remainder of the 2004–2005 NBA season.

2005   Jeffrey Robertson, whose son plays on the Canton High School football team in Canton, Texas, shoots and critically wounds Coach Gary Joe Kinne at the school. Due to previous confrontations, including shoving and verbally abusing the coaches at a football team picnic, Robertson is barred from the school and football games. Robertson, who may have been unhappy with his son's playing time or treatment by the coaches or other players, receives a conviction for assault with a deadly weapon and 20-year sentence.

Coach Mark Downs offers to pay an eight-year-old $25 to hit an autistic teammate in the face with a ball so this boy will not be able to play in a baseball playoff game. The court finds Downs guilty of corruption of minors and criminal solicitation to commit simple assault and sentences him to a 1- to 6-year term.

Mark Ricard hits coach John Crovo six times with an aluminum bat after Crovo suspends Ricard's daughter for missing a high school softball game to attend a prom. This public mugging occurs at Sacred Heart Academy, an all-girls, private Catholic High School in Connecticut, where a sign near the field lists expectations for spectators, including showing respect for coaches.

2006   Epiphanny Prince scores 113 points for her Murry Bergtraum High School basketball team in New York City in its 137–32 rout of Louis Brandeis High School. After the game, the opposing coach complains that Prince's coach encourages her to make as many shots as she can to set the record, instead of substituting lesser-skilled teammates. The media applauds Prince's achievements, rather than questioning whether or not the coach's action shows sportsmanship.

The International Cycling Union strips Floyd Landis of the Tour de France crown after he tests positive for an abnormally high testosterone level and finds him guilty of doping. Landis denies the findings of repeated tests of other urine samples, alleging improprieties in the testing protocol. Landis receives a two-year ban from cycling.

Mitch Cozad, backup punter at the University of Northern Colorado, stabs Rafael Mendoza's kicking leg in an attempt to take over his position as punter for the team. The ambush on Mendoza leaves a deep gash, but he returns to the team and punting. Convicted of second-degree assault, Cozad receives a seven-year prison sentence.

Zinedine Zidane receives a red card disqualification in the World Cup finals after he headbutts Italian defender Marco Materazzi. Zidane claims he struck Materazzi because of insulting comments from Materazzi about Zidane's mother and sister, an accusation that Materazzi denies. FIFA, soccer's world governing body, suspends and fines both players.

Miami University (Miami) and Florida International University (FIU) football players engage in a bench-clearing brawl that leads to the ejection of several players. After reviewing a video of the brawl, the conferences and institutions suspend 18 FIU and 13 Miami players from their teams' next games.

2007   Michael Crawley, an assistant youth football coach at Cudahy Middle School in Cudahy, Wisconsin, throws a 12-year-old player to the ground and threatens to kill him. Specifically, after Ryan Mullarney blocks Crawley's son, who goes to the ground and appears injured, Coach Crawley grabs Mullarney by the face mask and throws him to the ground while hurling profanities at him. Crawley is sentenced to 24 days in jail and placed on 8 months' probation after pleading guilty to charges of battery and disorderly conduct.

NBA referee Tim Donaghy provides information to gamblers, bets on NBA games, and may have affected the outcome of games through his officiating calls during his 13 seasons as a NBA official. Donaghy, who admits betting on more than 100 NBA games he officiated, receives a 15-month sentence in federal prison for wire fraud and transmitting wagering information through interstate commerce.

Marion Jones, gold medalist in track in the Olympic Games, admits using steroids. She pleads guilty to lying to federal prosecutors about the use of performance-enhancing drugs and lying to investigators about her association with a check-fraud scheme. The IOC strips Jones of three gold and two bronze medals won in the 2000 Sydney Olympic Games. Jones serves a 6-month prison sentence, must complete 800 hours of community service, and is placed on probation for 2 years.

In the first game of the NFL season, Bill Belichick directs his staff to videotape the defensive signals of the New York Jets. Commissioner Roger Goodell punishes Belichick with a $500,000 fine and the New England Patriots with a $250,000 fine and loss of a first-round pick in the 2008 draft. Belichick's taping of opponents' signals, which violates NFL rules, begins with his hiring as head coach with the Patriots in 2000.

2008   Some University of Oregon basketball fans resent that Oregon native Kevin Love spurns his father's alma mater and chooses to attend the University of California–Los Angeles (UCLA) in 2007. When his team plays at Oregon, fans send cell phone messages threatening to kill him. When members of Love's family come to the game, they are pelted with cups, obscene gestures, and profane insults. Love responds to the abuse by leading his team to victory with an outstanding performance.

The Mitchell Report, commissioned by MLB, cites the names of players associated with taking performance-enhancing drugs. Among the players who admit to using steroids, human growth hormones, or other performance-enhancing drugs are Jose Canseco, Ken Caminiti, and Jason Giambi.

Former University of Oklahoma and Indiana University basketball coach Kelvin Sampson resigns with a $750,000 buyout. Even though Sampson breaks NCAA recruiting rules for making excessive contacts with potential recruits while at the University of Oklahoma, Indiana University hires him in 2007. The NCAA alleges that since coming to Indiana, Sampson commits major recruiting violations and gives false and misleading information to investigators.

Are there more incidents of unethical behavior in sports today, or does the media simply report and emphasize them? It could be argued that there is a greater prevalence of cheating, violence, use of performance-enhancing drugs, and other unethical behaviors at all levels of sport in recent years. It is more likely that the intensity of competitions and rewards for winning have contributed to a cheating culture in sport. Not all is bad, however, as the following positive role models for sportsmanship show.

Examples of Ethical Behaviors in Sport

1925   During the U.S. Open, golfer Bobby Jones barely touches his ball as he addresses it, but it moves slightly. No one else sees this, including his playing partner, Walter Hagen. Because Jones sees the ball move, he assesses himself a one-stroke penalty. That stroke puts him into a playoff, which he loses to Willie Macfarlane. Rather than ignoring the rules in order to claim a victory, Jones states that following the rules is the honorable thing to do.

1936   During the long jump competition in the Berlin Olympic Games, German jumper Lutz Long suggests to Jesse Owens, who faults in his first two attempts, to move his take-off point back to avoid a third fault that would disqualify him. Owens accepts this stunning act of sportsmanship, as Adolf Hitler watches, and completes a successful jump. Owens goes on to win the gold medal, defeating his honorable rival.

1940   Dartmouth University outplays nationally ranked Cornell University until Cornell scores a touchdown on a fifth down, which is mistakenly awarded on the next-to-last play of the game. The game ends with the score Cornell 7 and Dartmouth 3. After reviewing data and pictures from the game the next day, the official admits his mistake in allowing a fifth down to be played. Upon learning this, the president of Cornell sends a telegram to the president of Dartmouth, awarding the Dartmouth team the victory.

1947   Brooklyn Dodger Pee Wee Reese stands beside and puts his arm around Jackie Robinson, his African American teammate, as Robinson is mercilessly taunted by racial epithets and slurs by Cincinnati Reds' players during a game. Reese's acceptance of Robinson is revealed when he shakes Robinson's hand in welcoming his new teammate to spring training, declines to sign a petition refusing to take the field with Robinson, and helps smooth the acceptance of Robinson into MLB by befriending him. Reese's support of Robinson stands in dramatic contrast to the widespread physical and psychological abuse and death threats to which Robinson is subjected as he integrates professional baseball in the modern era.

1964   Eugenio Monti and his teammate expect to win the gold medal in the two-man bobsled in the Innsbruck Winter Olympic Games after recording the fastest time thus far. Then Monti learns that the British team of Tony Nash Jr. and Robin Dixon discover a broken axle bolt just prior to their final run. Monti removes the axle bolt from his sled and gives it to Nash and Dixon, who have an outstanding run and win the gold medal. For showing the true meaning of sportsmanship, Monti receives the Pierre De Coubertin medal given by the IOC.

1969   Jack Nicklaus, after sinking his putt, concedes Tony Jacklin's two-foot putt, resulting in the Ryder Cup ending in a tie between the United States team and the European team.

1994   Pete Sampras's illness prior to the final match of the 1994 Lipton tennis tournament appears to give the victory to Andre Agassi. In a gesture of sportsmanship,

Agassi suggests waiting to see, if given time, when Sampras will be able to play the match. Sampras wins the delayed match.

1998   The unranked University of Texas football team defeats a highly ranked University of Nebraska team, ending that team's 47-game home-game winning streak. As the Texas players leave the field, the capacity crowd gives them a standing ovation. Texas coach Mack Brown praises this display of sportsmanship.

2006   Norway's cross-country ski coach Bjornar Hakensmoen gives Canadian Sara Renner his left pole when her ski pole breaks during the sprint relay final in the Turin Winter Olympic Games. Renner and her teammate Beckie Scott go on to win the silver medal. Hakensmoen states that his action reflects Norway's belief in fair play as he is reacting like any good sportsman should. Others suggest Hakensmoen demonstrates the Olympic ideal of sportsmanship.

Framingham State University's soccer team needs to win its game against Bridgewater State College to win the Massachusetts State College Athletic Conference regular-season title and advance to the postseason tournament. Even though Framingham's shot for a goal fails to enter the back of the goal, the official awards a point. Coach Tucker Reynolds tells his team to allow Bridgewater to score a goal to tie the game because it is the right and fair thing to do under the circumstances. Bridgewater wins the game 3–2. The players leave the game with something more valuable than a victory as they demonstrate the essence of sportsmanship.

2007   Hayley Milbourn finishes her round at the Interscholastic Athletic Association of Maryland Golf Championships only to discover that she has been playing with someone else's ball. Even though Milbourn is the two-time reigning champion, shoots the best score, and no one else notices her mistake, she reports the violation of the rules. She says that she cannot accept a trophy she does not deserve because of the rule violation.

2008   With two teammates on base, senior Sara Tucholsky of Western Oregon University hits her first home run as a high school or college softball player. In her triumphant home run jog, she misses first base. As she turns around to tag the base, she collapses with a knee injury, forcing her to crawl back to the base in pain. If her coach replaces her with a pinch runner, she gets credit only for a single. While Tucholsky's teammates cannot assist her around the bases, Central Washington University (CWU) players Mallory Holtman and Liz Wallace do just that, even though it means that CWU is giving up a run. In a remarkable display of empathy and sportsmanship, Holtman and Wallace carry Tucholsky around the bases, stopping at each base so Tucholsky can touch each base with her uninjured leg. Even though this home run helps eliminate CWU from the playoffs, Holtman states that it is the right thing to do because Tucholsky deserves a home run for hitting the ball over the fence.

In addition to these examples of ethical conduct, several national sport associations honor outstanding sportsmanship through awards and recognitions. A few descriptions of these programs emphasize how important it is to reinforce sportsmanship and have role models for playing fair. It also is important to illustrate how athletes and coaches can be successful while playing within the letter and spirit of the rules.

1991   The Institute for International Sport (IIS) begins National Sportsmanship Day on the first Tuesday in March to promote thoughtful discussions and activities by athletes, parents, coaches, and administrators about how sports can serve as a positive force in society. Beginning in 1994, *USA Today* enhances the growth of National Sportsmanship Day with the sponsorship of a national essay contest. Beginning in 2006, the IIS annually recognizes educational institutions that make an exceptional commitment to a culture of sportsmanship among athletes and other students with recognition as All-American Sportsmanship Schools.

1999 The Citizenship Through Sport Alliance begins its National Sportsmanship Awards to recognize athletes and others involved with sport. Honorees include outstanding individuals from the National Collegiate Athletic Association, Major League Baseball, National Association of Intercollegiate Athletics, National Basketball Association, National Federation of State High School Associations, National Football League, National Hockey League, National Junior College Athletic Association, United States Olympic Committee, Women's National Basketball Association, National Association of Collegiate Directors of Athletics, and National Association for Sport and Physical Education.

2005 The National Council on Youth Sport (NCYS) promotes organized youth sports that develop positive attributes, including healthier lifestyles, self-esteem, fair play, and good citizenship. NCYS, through its STRIVE awards program, begins to recognize coaches, administrators, officials, and volunteers who teach, model, and reinforce respect, initiative, values, and excellence.

In addition, numerous sportsmanship awards have been established to recognize unsung sportsmen and sportswomen who serve as positive role models for others. Following are descriptions of a few of the national awards that reinforce that sport can and does teach life lessons.

1930 The Amateur Athletic Union (AAU) establishes the Sullivan Award, which it presents to the outstanding amateur athlete in the United States. In addition, the recipient must demonstrate leadership, character, sportsmanship, and the ideals of amateurism.

1999 The NCAA Sportsmanship Award begins to recognize male and female athletes who show sportsmanship, civility, fairness, honesty, respect, responsibility, and unselfishness.

2005 The NAIA initiates the Coach of Character Award, which recognizes a coach who makes character integral to intercollegiate athletics.

2006   The NAIA establishes the Dr. LeRoy Walker Champions of Character Award to honor an athlete who excels in academics and athletics, including showing a commitment to the Champions of Character core values of respect, responsibility, integrity, servant leadership, and sportsmanship.

In addition to these illustrative awards programs, numerous youth sport organizations, schools and colleges, and conferences recognize the sportsmanship, fair play, and ethical behaviors of children, adolescents, and young adults through annual awards. These awards symbolize that sports can be valued because of what they can help teach. For example, athletes of all ages can be competitive and strive diligently to win, while at the same time showing respect for their opponents and the officials.

Are sportsmanship and fair play important? Most sport organizations must believe they are because in recent years they have established codes of ethics or conduct for players, coaches, parents, and officials to strengthen the commitment of everyone to build character through sport and to reduce incidents of unethical behaviors.

1999   Representative sports leaders develop the Arizona Sports Summit Accord that emphasizes sportsmanship, character, and ethical conduct in sports at all levels. This statement of principles enjoys the support of many amateur sport programs in the United States.

2001   The Coaches Council of the National Association for Sport and Physical Education establishes a Code of Conduct for holding coaches at all levels of sport accountable. Numerous other sport organizations, such as the National Youth Sports Coaches Association, National High School Athletic Coaches Association, and United States Olympic Committee, provide codes of ethics or conduct.

Sports can help athletes learn that behaving honorably means not taking advantage of opponents, officials, or loopholes in the rules. When coaches and parents consistently teach, model, and reinforce that acting in ethical ways is more important than the outcome on the scoreboard, athletes will keep winning in perspective. Sport, especially at the youth and interscholastic levels, can build character as long as that goal remains foremost in the minds of all involved. Having the role models described in the second section of this chapter can certainly help athletes realize that ethical behaviors can be a part of sport.

5

Biographical Sketches

This chapter provides biographical sketches of some of the
outstanding individuals who have helped shape the ethical
culture of sport. These athletes, coaches, sport administrators, and educators have modeled sportsmanship, fair play, and
moral values. These individuals have demonstrated that sport
can teach character, athletes can behave ethically and be successful while keeping winning in perspective, and "how the
game is played" is much more important than the outcome on
the scoreboard.

Arthur Robert Ashe Jr. (July 10, 1943–February 6, 1993)

Ashe was born to Arthur Sr. and Mattie Ashe in Richmond, Virginia, where Ashe learned tennis as a young boy in the segregated South. After graduating first in his class at Sumner High
School in St. Louis, Ashe graduated from UCLA in 1966 with a
degree in business administration. In 1963, he became the first
African American on the U.S. Davis Cup team, his first of 10
teams. In 1965, Ashe won the NCAA singles tennis title and
helped UCLA win the NCAA team championship. He won
three major tournament singles titles—the U.S. Open (1968),
Australian Open (1970), and Wimbledon (1975)—and was
inducted into the International Tennis Hall of Fame in 1985.
In 1969, Ashe cofounded the National Junior Tennis League,
which focused on teaching children tennis while emphasizing

academics, self-discipline, and learning life skills. Repeatedly denied a visa to travel to South Africa (finally granted in 1973), Ashe became an activist against apartheid. Due to a heart attack in 1979 and two heart surgeries, Ashe retired from competitive tennis but did not slow down. He captained five U.S. Davis Cup teams; his teams won in 1981 and 1982. Through a blood transfusion in 1983, Ashe contracted the human immunodeficiency virus. In 1988, Ashe published a three-volume book, *A Hard Road to Glory*, which detailed the history of African Americans in sports, to fill a void in the literature. In his memoir, *Days of Grace*, Ashe discussed how his contracting acquired immune deficiency syndrome (AIDS) provided him the opportunity to establish the Arthur Ashe Foundation for the Defeat of AIDS. Ashe's sportsmanship, professional courtesy, and graciousness on and off the court, dedication to equity and humanitarian causes, and boundless spirit left a remarkable legacy.

Margaret Ann (Peggy) Kirk Bell (October 28, 1921–)

Bell, the daughter of Bob and Grace Kirk, attended Sargent College in Boston and graduated from Rollins College with a degree in physical education. At age 17, Bell, who was an all-around athlete growing up in Findlay, Ohio, started playing golf. As an amateur golfer, she won three Ohio Amateurs, the North and South Women's Amateur Golf Championship and the Titleholders in 1949, and was a member of the U.S. Curtis Cup team in 1950. Also in 1950, Bell became a charter member of the Ladies Professional Golf Association (LPGA). She and her husband bought (with others), expanded, and operated Pine Needles Lodge and Golf Club in Southern Pines, North Carolina, which hosted the U.S. Women's Open in 1996, 2001, and 2007. Bell wrote two instructional books, *Golf Magazine's Winning Pointers from the Pros*, with Gene Sarazen, and *A Woman's Way to Better Golf*, as well as an autobiography, *The Gift of Golf: My Life with a Wonderful Game*, with Lee Pace. A gracious person with an engaging personality, Bell made each one of her thousands of students feel special. Bell received the LPGA Teacher of the Year Award in 1961, in part because of her demonstration of professionalism throughout her career, and was the first woman inducted into the World Golf Teachers Hall of Fame (2004). In 1990, she received the Bob Jones Award from the United States Golf Association in recognition of her distinguished sportsmanship in golf. A pioneer in the development of the golf school and a tireless promoter of the game she loves, Bell received the 2007 Professional Golf Association First Lady of Golf Award.

William (Bill) Warren Bradley (July 28, 1943–)

Bradley was born in Crystal City, Missouri, to Warren and Susie (Crowe) Bradley. He was an Eagle Scout and later received the Distinguished Eagle Scout Award from the Boy Scouts of America. An outstanding student academically and All-American basketball player at Crystal City High School, Bradley spurned numerous grant-in-aid offers to attend Princeton University. Bradley was a three-time All-American, the 1965 National Player of the Year, and captain of the basketball team that won the gold medal in the 1964 Tokyo Olympic Games. In 1965, he was the first basketball player chosen to receive the Sullivan Award presented to the top amateur athlete in the United States. After completing his studies as a Rhodes Scholar at Oxford University, Bradley joined the New York Knicks. During his 10-year career, the Knicks won NBA Championships in 1970 and 1973. He was inducted into the Naismith Memorial Basketball Hall of Fame in 1983. In 1979, Bradley began his first of three terms as a United States Senator from New Jersey. As a Senator, he was known for policy reforms, such as in child support, children's health, campaign finance, and federal budget cuts. After choosing not to run for reelection in 1996, Bradley became an unsuccessful presidential candidate for the Democratic nomination in 2000. In his 2000 best-selling book, *Values of the Game*, Bradley described the values he holds dear, including respect, responsibility, courage, discipline, passion, resilience, and teamwork. While Bradley explained the role of these values to basketball in this book, more importantly, he emphasized their application to life. Even though Bradley played basketball during a different era, his principles and values remain timeless.

Avery Brundage (September 28, 1887–May 8, 1975)

Brundage was born in Detroit, to Charles and Amelia (Lloyd) Brundage and graduated from Chicago English High School. In 1909, he received a degree in civil engineering from the University of Illinois. Brundage represented the United States in the pentathlon, decathlon, and discus in the 1912 Stockholm Olympic Games, finishing 6th, 14th, and 22nd, respectively. His lucrative construction business enabled Brundage to dedicate more than 40 years to administrating and preserving amateur sports. He served as president of the Amateur Athletic Union (AAU; 1928–1935), president of the United States Olympic Committee (USOC; 1929–1953), and president of the International Olympic Committee (IOC; 1952–1972). Brundage opposed the proposed United States boycott of the 1936 Berlin Olympic Games. He vigorously opposed professionalism in the Olympic Games as he tried to prevent increasing violations of amateurism by governmental and commercially funded athletes. He adamantly opposed using the Olympic Games for political reasons. When Tommie Smith, gold medalist, and John Carlos, bronze medalist, raised their black-gloved fists as a Black Power symbol during the national anthem and medal ceremony at the 200-meter race in the 1968 Mexico Olympic Games, Brundage convinced the IOC to expel them from the Olympic Village and suspended them from the Olympic team. Brundage resumed the 1972 Munich Olympic Games after one day of mourning and a memorial service for the 11 Israeli athletes who had been killed in the Palestinian terrorist attack. He was an Olympic purist who passionately believed in and consistently enforced the moral superiority of amateur sport competition. Some have argued that Brundage was a Nazi sympathizer in opposing a boycott in 1936, or maybe he believed that athletics should never be embroiled with politics. Brundage withstood accusations of being a Communist stooge, but he still welcomed the Soviet Union to the Olympic family in the 1950s in the midst of the Cold War. He campaigned against commercialism in the Olympic Games and would be distressed that professional athletes now compete in the Olympic Games. His refusal to let terrorists stop the Games reaffirmed his adamancy that athletics should rise above all else.

Walter Byers (March 13, 1922–)

Byers became the first executive director of the NCAA in 1951 and served until his retirement in 1987. Through leadership, integrity, dedication, energy, and vision, he built the NCAA into a formidable organization. His tenure as executive director spanned from the point-shaving scandal at the University of Kentucky to the death penalty assessed against Southern Methodist University for paying football players and other violations. When the NCAA changed its rules to permit giving financial aid based on athletic skill in 1956, Byers insisted on the use of the term *student-athlete* in an attempt to focus on a balance between academics and sports. He was expected to prevent people and institutions from violating NCAA recruiting, academic, and operational rules (and penalizing those who did through a new enforcement process), while generating millions of dollars annually for member institutions. Byers saw coaches' salaries increase from a few thousand to millions of dollars. He discusses in his book, *Unsportsmanlike Conduct: Exploiting College Athletes*, that players who were responsible for bringing in the ticket and television revenues should receive some pay, not be limited to the NCAA-allowed grant of tuition, fees, room, and board. Depending on who is asked, Byers either eagerly welcomed female athletes into the NCAA fold in the early 1980s, or wrested control from the Association for Intercollegiate Athletics for Women. The NCAA under Byers lost control over televised football in 1984 in an antitrust lawsuit as the major football-playing conferences and teams were no longer willing to share the revenues. He led the NCAA in trying to reign in academic abuses by increasing standards and requirements, such as requiring minimum grade-point averages and standardized admission test scores. Byers's impact was significant as he shaped the growth of intercollegiate athletics from an extracurricular activity for college males to a commercialized business involving recruited male and female athletes.

Ken Carter (ca. 1959–)

Carter, who was born in Fernwood, Mississippi, was a record-setting basketball player at Richmond (California) High School in the 1970s. He attended George Fox University in Oregon on a scholarship but did not graduate. After returning to coach at his high school alma mater, he sent a firm message to his team in 1999 that academic achievement was much more important than winning basketball games. When 15 out of 45 of the freshmen, junior varsity, and varsity players failed to honor their contracts to attend class, sit in the front row, turn in their assignments, and earn minimum grades, he locked them out of the gymnasium. Despite the varsity's 13–0 record, Carter forfeited two games and would not allow his players to return to the gym until, by spending their former practice and playing time studying, they got serious about their academic work. Carter was undeterred by the criticism he received from parents and others because he wanted the boys to learn that broken dreams of playing professional basketball, prison, and death were their likely fates without an education. The boys must have learned what Carter was trying to teach them since all 15 of the former low-performing students attended college. Carter believed that sport could teach how to compete on the court and also how to become productive citizens throughout life. Carter wanted to be sure that this lesson was learned by the boys on his team. After leaving coaching in 2002, he established the Coach Carter Foundation, which provides educational and mentoring programs for minority youth.

Roberto Clemente (August 18, 1934–December 31, 1972)

Clemente was born in Carolina, Puerto Rico, to Melchor and Luisa (Walker) Clemente. He graduated from Vizcarondo High School, while playing baseball on local teams. Between 1955 and 1972 as a Pittsburgh Pirate, Clemente was a 12-time All-Star, won 12 Gold Gloves for his stellar play and strong arm in right field, won four batting titles, amassed 3,000 hits, was the National League's MVP in 1966, and helped the Pirates win the 1960 and 1971 World Series. In 1973 (posthumously), he was inducted into the National Baseball Hall of Fame, the first Latin American to be selected. Clemente's humanitarianism was greatly admired as he was actively involved with charity work, such as delivering food and baseball equipment to Latin American countries. Clemente's life ended in an airplane crash while attempting to deliver aid to earthquake victims in Nicaragua. MLB honors the player who best demonstrates Clemente's sportsmanship and service with the Roberto Clemente Award. Clemente became a baseball legend, hero throughout Latin America, and cultural icon through his drive and character. Posthumously, he was awarded the Congressional Gold Medal (1973) and Presidential Medal of Freedom (2003). Other players have honored him by calling him a great human being on and off the field.

Anita Luceete DeFrantz (October 4, 1952–)

Born in Philadelphia, DeFrantz is the daughter of Anita and Robert DeFrantz. While attending Connecticut College on an academic scholarship, DeFrantz was introduced to rowing. Three years later, she won a bronze medal in the women's eight at the 1976 Montreal Olympic Games. After receiving a bachelor's degree in philosophy from Connecticut College, DeFrantz continued rowing while earning a law degree from the University of Pennsylvania. She was a plaintiff in a lawsuit challenging President Jimmy Carter's decision that the United States would boycott the 1980 Moscow Olympic Games. While serving as vice president of the 1984 Los Angeles Games Organizing Committee, she helped convince 43 African nations not to boycott. She has served as president and member of the board of directors of the Amateur Athletic Foundation in Los Angeles (now the LA84 Foundation) since it was established in 1984. Formed to manage Southern California's multimillion-dollar share of the surplus from the Los Angeles Olympic Games, this foundation awards grants to youth sport organizations and manages a sport resource center and library. In 1986, DeFrantz was the fifth woman appointed to the International Olympic Committee, as well as the first African American and American woman. Through her service with several organizations, DeFrantz remains a passionate advocate for athletes, children, women, and minorities.

Jean Driscoll (November 18, 1966–)

Born in Milwaukee, Driscoll is the daughter of James and Angela Driscoll, a utility worker and a nurse, respectively. She was born with spina bifida, a birth defect characterized by an incomplete closure of the spine, Driscoll did not let that limit her even when she became confined to a wheelchair as a teenager. Recruited to play wheelchair basketball at the University of Illinois, she began to compete in track races while earning a bachelor's degree in speech communication. She later received a master's degree in rehabilitation administration from the University of Illinois. Driscoll became an eight-time winner of the Boston Marathon as a wheelchair racer and won 12 track medals in the 1988, 1992, 1996, and 2000 Paralympic Games. Driscoll has been a global advocate for Wheels for the World, which restores wheelchairs and provides them to potential athletes in third-world countries. She has worked with the American Association of Adapted Sports Programs to provide sport opportunities to school students with physical and visual challenges. The Women's Sports Foundation named her Sportswoman of the Year in 1991 and awarded her the Wilma Rudolph Courage Award in 2006. Driscoll's autobiography, *Determined to Win*, describes her determination to overcome physical limitations and succeed in life.

Joe Dumars III (May 24, 1963–)

Dumars was born to Ophelia and Joe Dumars in Shreveport, Louisiana. He attended Natchitoches Central High School and McNeese State University. Dumars played guard for 14 years with the Detroit Pistons (1985–1999). He made the All-Defensive First Team in 1989, 1990, 1992, and 1993, was a six-time NBA All-Star, and won two NBA Championships (1989 and 1990), earning the Finals' Most Valuable Player (MVP) in 1989. In 1999, Dumars returned to the Pistons as Vice President of Player Personnel. Then, when he was President of Basketball Operations, he acquired the team that won the 2004 NBA Championship. Dumars received the J. Walter Kennedy Citizenship Award for exemplary community service in 1994 and was inducted into the Naismith Memorial Basketball Hall of Fame in 2006. Despite starring on a team known as the "Bad Boys," Dumars exemplified ethical behavior, fair play, and integrity. In 1996, he won the first NBA Sportsmanship Award, which was later named in his honor because of his class, character, sportsmanship, and leadership.

Anthony (Tony) Kevin Dungy (October 6, 1955–)

Born in Jackson, Michigan, the son of Wilbur and CleoMae Dungy, Dungy was encouraged to emphasize academics since both of his parents were teachers. Dungy graduated from Parkside High School and the University of Minnesota, starring as quarterback. He played for the Pittsburgh Steelers as a defensive back in 1977 and 1978, helping to win the 1978 Super Bowl, and the San Francisco 49ers in 1979. After 16 years as an assistant coach with the University of Minnesota, Pittsburgh Steelers, Kansas City Chiefs, and Minnesota Vikings, Dungy got his first head-coaching position with the Tampa Bay Buccaneers in 1996. Dungy brought his successful Tampa 2 defense to the Indianapolis Colts in 2002. In seven seasons, he led the Colts to a 85–27 regular-season record, five American Football Conference South titles, and a 29–17 victory over the Chicago Bears in the 2007 Super Bowl, becoming the first African American head coach to win the Super Bowl. Dungy has been an active contributor to community organizations and projects that benefit children and families. In 2007, Dungy was appointed to the President's Council on Service and Civic Participation, a representative group that seeks to promote the spirit of service. Dungy believes that coaches are teachers who prioritize faith and family ahead of football and who do not scream at or demean their players. His coaching philosophy resonates throughout his 2007 best-selling book, *Quiet Strength*, in which Dungy proves that football coaches can be successful without having to be vulgar and verbally abusive. Dungy stresses that every member of the team, from the highest paid to the least skilled player, is important to the team, so he is dedicated to the development and importance of each player.

Joe Ehrmann (March 29, 1949–)

Ehrmann was an All-American football player at Syracuse University, as well as a lacrosse player. He played defensive tackle for 13 seasons in the NFL and United States Football League. After his retirement from professional football, Ehrmann cofounded Building Men and Women for Others, which seeks to transform the culture of sport so it teaches social responsibility to players, coaches, and parents. He serves as an assistant coach at Gilman School in Baltimore, where he teaches life lessons to his football players. Specifically, he teaches boys to replace the standard criteria for masculinity of athletic ability, sexual conquest, and economic success with the importance of building relationships with others and committing to causes bigger than themselves. An inspirational and dynamic speaker, Ehrmann teaches a code of conduct that includes accepting individual responsibility, leading courageously, displaying teamwork, and standing up against abuse and other types of oppression. He has received numerous honors, including the Frederick Douglas National Man of the Year Award and *Baltimore Business Journal's* Renaissance Person of the Decade.

Fred Engh (August 13, 1935–)

Engh is the son of Lynn and Rosealma Engh and was born in Johnstown, Pennsylvania. Engh, who holds a bachelor's degree in physical education from the University of Maryland, in 1981 founded and currently serves as President and Chief Executive Officer (CEO) of the National Alliance for Youth Sports (NAYS). This organization offers educational programs for volunteer coaches, parents, and administrators to enhance youth sport programs. The services provided by the NAYS include Recommendations for Communities, which were developed through the National Summit on Raising Community Standards in Children's Sports, National Standards for Youth Sports, and associations for coaches, parents, and youth sport administrators so they can work collaboratively for the benefit of youth. Engh wrote *Why Johnny Hates Sports*, an examination of the state of youth sports, as a platform for advocating for character development of youth through sports.

Henry Louis (Lou) Gehrig (June 19, 1903–June 2, 1941)

Gehrig, born in New York City, was the son of German immigrants Christina and Heinrich Gehrig. To honor his mother's wishes, he enrolled at Columbia University (on a football grant) to pursue a degree in engineering. His impressive hitting talents diverted him to the New York Yankees in 1923. After Gehrig replaced Wally Pipp at first base in 1925, he played 2,130 consecutive games, earning him the nickname the "Iron Horse." Gehrig hit 493 home runs (including 23 grand slams), had 2,721 hits, averaged 147 RBIs (runs batted in) a season, and achieved a lifetime batting average of .340. He set an American League record 184 RBIs in 1931, won the 1934 Triple Crown (meaning he led the league in home runs, RBIs, and batting average), and was the 1936 American League MVP. His .361 batting average in seven World Series helped lead the Yankees to six World Series titles. When Gehrig was afflicted with amyotrophic lateral sclerosis, a progressive neurological disease that came to be known as Lou Gehrig's disease, his consecutive game streak and career ended in 1939. Gehrig was inducted into the National Baseball Hall of Fame later that year. A consummate gentleman, who never complained that teammate Babe Ruth sought out and received most of the publicity, Gehrig became an authentic American hero. He became legendary in baseball because of his reserved personality, humility, kind heart, winning attitude, honesty, and overall character.

Grant Henry Hill (October 5, 1972–)

Hill, the son of Janet and Calvin Hill, was born in Dallas, where his father starred as a running back for the Dallas Cowboys. Hill was a 1990 All-American at South Lakes High School in Reston, Virginia. A graduate of Duke University, Hill helped Duke win the NCAA men's basketball championships in 1991 and 1992 and advance to the finals in 1994. He won a gold medal in the 1996 Atlanta Olympic Games as a member of the U.S. basketball team. An exceptional offensive and defensive player, Hill has played for the Detroit Pistons (1994–2000), where he earned the NBA Rookie of the Year Award (along with Jason Kidd), Orlando Magic (2000–2007), and Phoenix Suns (2007–present) in the NBA. Despite career-threatening injuries, each time Hill successfully returned to the court through diligent effort. In 2005, he received the NBA Sportsmanship Award in recognition of his ethical behavior, fair play, integrity, and distinguished contributions. In 2008, Hill became the only player to receive the NBA Sportsmanship Award a second time. An All-Star in seven seasons, Hill's talents in scoring, rebounding, and assists have been impressive. Maybe more impressive has been his strong work ethic, humble and gracious personality, and outstanding sportsmanship. Hill embraces being a role model for academic achievement, emphasis on family, high moral code, and philanthropic contributions. Influenced strongly by his parents, he has established himself as a person of integrity, character, grace, and leadership.

Michael Terrence (Terry) Holland
(April 2, 1942–)

Born in Clinton, North Carolina, Holland played basketball at Davidson College under Coach Charles "Lefty" Driesell and graduated with a degree in economics in 1964. After serving as an assistant coach for five seasons, Holland succeeded Driesell as head coach in 1969. In 1974, Holland became the men's basketball coach at the University of Virginia and in 24 seasons led his teams to a record of 326–173. He has served as athletic director at Davidson College (1990–1995), the University of Virginia (1995–2001), and since 2004 at East Carolina University. Holland's legacy as a coach and administrator has been to win with class. As a coach and Southern gentleman, Holland had a reputation for integrity, honesty, and reliability, as he emphasized academics, held his players to high standards, and mentored young professionals. Politely, he has spoken his mind as an athletic administrator, including about reforms needed in intercollegiate athletics. Holland has proposed changing game times to reduce missed class time for athletes, recruiting only athletes who as students meet institutional academic requirements, and making freshmen ineligible to help them get established academically.

Robert (Bobby) Tyre Jones Jr. (March 17, 1902–December 18, 1971)

Jones was born in Atlanta, the only son of Robert and Clara (Thomas) Jones. In 1922, he earned a mechanical engineering degree from Georgia Institute of Technology, where he played on the golf team, followed by a degree in English literature from Harvard University in 1924. After one year in law school at Emory University, Jones passed the bar exam. Bobby Jones played golf on a part-time basis, was always an amateur, retired from competition at the age of 28, and yet was one of the greatest golfers ever. After winning the Georgia State Amateur Championship at age 14, Jones played exhibition matches during World War I to raise money for war relief. After winning his first of four U.S. Opens in 1923, he captured a total of 13 major championships out of 21 attempts. In 1930, Jones became the only golfer ever to win the U.S. Open, U.S. Amateur, the British Open, and the British Amateur in the same year. In five Walker Cup competitions representing the United States, Jones won nine of ten matches. In 1930, he received the first Sullivan Award given by the Amateur Athletic Union to the outstanding amateur athlete in the United States. Jones exemplified sportsmanship and fair play. In the 1925 U.S. Open, for example, he called a penalty stroke on himself for slightly moving the ball prior to his shot. The United States Golf Association's sportsmanship award is named the Bob Jones Award. Although a lawyer, and never a professional player, Jones became a professional in golf by accepting fees, making instructional films, and writing instructional books. He also wrote three biographical books: *Golf Is My Game, Bobby Jones on Golf,* and *Down the Fairway: The Golf Life and Play of Robert R. Jones, Jr.* He helped develop the first set of matched golf clubs, codesigned the Augusta National golf course, and founded and popularized the Masters tournament. Jones, who was respected for his humility, talent as a player, writer, teacher, and golf course designer, and for being a gentleman, was inducted into the inaugural class of the World Golf Hall of Fame in 1974.

Johann Olav Koss (October 29, 1968–)

Born in Drammen, Norway, Koss won gold and silver medals in the 1992 Albertville Winter Olympic Games and three gold medals in the 1,500-meter, 5,000-meter, and 10,000-meter speed skating events in the 1994 Lillehammer Winter Olympic Games. Skating in his native Norway, Koss set new world records in winning all three of these events in 1994. After his retirement from competition, Koss completed undergraduate medical training at the University of Queensland in Australia, and then an executive MBA at the University of Toronto, Canada. In 1994, he was named a United Nations Children's Fund International Goodwill Ambassador, and from 1998–2002 served as a member of the Athlete's Commission of the IOC. Koss founded and serves as CEO of Right to Play (formerly Olympic Aid), which uses sports and play to develop children and youth in more than 20 underprivileged and disadvantaged countries. Right to Play seeks to make a difference through sport in the lives of children by teaching commitment, communication, conflict resolution, fair play, integrity, respect, self-esteem, and teamwork.

Michael (Mike) William Krzyzewski (February 13, 1947–)

Krzyzewski was born in Chicago to Polish immigrants William and Emily Krzyzewski. He attended Weber High School and in 1969 graduated from the United States Military Academy (USMA). After completing his five-year military commitment, he served as a graduate assistant to his former college coach, Bobby Knight, at Indiana University. After serving as head coach at USMA (1975–1980), Krzyzewski moved to Duke University. Through the 2008–2009 season, his Duke teams recorded a 760–215 record, reached 10 Final Fours, won 3 NCAA National Championships, and captured 11 Atlantic

Coast Conference (ACC) tournament championships. He was inducted into the Naismith Memorial Basketball Hall of Fame in 2001. As the national basketball coach, Krzyzewski coached the U.S. men's team to a gold medal at the 2008 Beijing Olympic Games. He established the Emily Krzyzewski Family LIFE Center, a community center that serves economically disadvantaged children and their families. In addition to his service activities, Krzyzewski demonstrates a commitment to high academic standards and is recognized for the academic achievement of his players, with almost every player earning his degree. Krzyzewski has shared his coaching philosophy, strategies for teaching and motivating players, and especially his emphasis on leadership and application of principles for life in *Leading with the Heart: Coach K's Successful Strategies for Basketball, Business, and Life* and *Beyond Basketball: Coach K's Keywords for Success.* Among these key words or concepts for Krzyzewski are commitment, integrity, respect, and selflessness, which he has modeled for his players.

Richard Lapchick (July 16, 1945–)

Lapchick is the son of Bobbie (Sarubbi) and Joe Lapchick, a former center for the Original Celtics and legendary coach for St. John's University and the New York Knicks. Lapchick serves as Director of the Institute for Diversity and Ethics in Sport and DeVos Sport Business Management Program at the University of Central Florida. Lapchick, who was born in Yonkers, New York, earned a BA from St. John's University and PhD from the University of Denver. Lapchick, an activist for human rights and racial equality, for many years has published the Racial and Gender Report Cards, which are studies of racial and gender hiring practices and trends of major professional and amateur sport organizations in the United States. He helped establish the Center for the Study of Sport in Society at Northeastern University, which emphasizes education for athletes of all ages and violence prevention through its award-winning Project TEAMWORK initiative. Lapchick founded and serves as president of the National Consortium for Academics and Sport. Through this consortium, athletes at more than 200 colleges and universities return to college and earn their degrees while providing community service to millions of youth in the areas of race relations, conflict resolution skills, prevention of gender violence, and avoidance of drugs and alcohol. Lapchick's concern for intercollegiate and professional sports encompasses ethical issues associated with academic exploitation of athletes, use of performance-enhancing drugs, violence, and gambling. Lapchick has written 13 books, more than 450 articles, and numerous columns, and given over 2,700 public speeches on topics related to these pivotal issues. Considered an expert on sport and social issues and advocate for social change, Lapchick has been recognized for his many contributions with numerous humanitarian and service awards.

Dale Bryan Murphy (March 12, 1956–)

Murphy, who was born in Portland, Oregon, graduated from Woodrow Wilson High School and attended Brigham Young University. He was drafted by the Atlanta Braves, with whom he debuted in MLB in 1976 as a catcher. He moved to the outfield, where he won five consecutive Gold Gloves from 1982 to 1986. He appeared in seven All-Star Games and won consecutive National League MVP awards in 1982 and 1983. He concluded his professional career with the Philadelphia Phillies and then Colorado Rockies in 1993. One of the "Athletes Who Care" named by *Sports Illustrated* as one of the Sportsmen and Sportswomen of the Year in 1987, Murphy has worked with the Make-a-Wish Foundation, March of Dimes, American Heart Association, and Operation Kids. His book *The Scouting Report on Professional Athletics* discusses how a professional athlete should balance his playing career, family, and giving to others. *The Scouting Report for Youth Athletes* provides information for young athletes, coaches, and parents with an emphasis on using sport to teach honesty, dedication, and sportsmanship. Murphy has established the iWontCheat foundation to promote ethics among young athletes, with a special emphasis on not cheating in sports, the classroom, or life. His honors include induction into the World Sports Humanitarian Hall of Fame (1995) and the Roberto Clemente Award (1988), which is given annually to the MLB player for his character and charitable contributions.

Dikembe Mutombo (June 25, 1966–)

Dikembe Mutombo Mpolondo Mukamba Jean-Jacques Wamu-tombo was born to Biamba Marie Mutombo in Kinshasa in the Democratic Republic of the Congo. Mutombo came to George-town University on a United States Agency for International Development (USAID) scholarship planning to become a doctor, even though at the time he spoke little English. Coach John Thompson recruited the seven-foot-two-inch Mutombo to play basketball and helped him become a superlative shot blocker. During his 17 seasons in the NBA, Mutombo played with the Denver Nuggets, Atlanta Hawks, Philadelphia 76ers, New Jersey Nets, New York Knicks, Chicago Bulls (off-season only), and Houston Rockets, and won the NBA Defensive Player of the Year Award four times. A well-known humanitarian, he established the Dikembe Mutombo Foundation in 1997 to improve living conditions in the Democratic Republic of the Congo. Personally and through his foundation, Mutombo donated millions of dollars to the construction of the first modern hospital in Kinshasa in nearly 40 years. Mutombo has won numerous awards for his humanitarian service, including the J. Walter Kennedy Award in 2001 given by the NBA for his outstanding service and dedication to the community.

James Naismith (November 6, 1861–November 28, 1939)

Naismith was the son of Scottish immigrants Margaret (Young) and John Naismith in Almonte, Ontario, Canada. He lost his parents to typhoid fever at the age of nine and was raised by his uncle from whom he learned lessons in honesty, initiative, reliability, and self-reliance. Naismith graduated from Almonte High School in 1883, but only after dropping out and working for four years. He earned a bachelor's degree in physical education from McGill University in Montreal, a theology degree from Presbyterian College of Theology, and a medical degree from Gross Medical College in Denver. While teaching at the YMCA Training School in 1891, Naismith developed basketball. Naismith in his book, *Basketball: Its Origin and Development*, which was published posthumously in 1941, explained that basketball developed initiative, cooperation, self-confidence, self-control, and sportsmanship. Amos Alonzo Stagg, the famous University of Chicago football coach and friend from the YMCA Training School, recommended Naismith to the University of Kansas as an all-around athlete, medical doctor, and Presbyterian minister who did not smoke, drink, or cuss. For 39 years beginning in 1898, Naismith served as Director of Physical Education and campus chaplain, started intramurals, and established a basketball team (he believed people played basketball, not coached it). Naismith used sports to develop men morally, spiritually, and physically. He used his ministerial preparation to teach moral lessons; his medical education to measure, heal, and care for students' bodies; and his physical education expertise to teach sports and emphasize sportsmanship. Naismith threw up the ceremonial first ball for the inaugural game of basketball in the 1936 Berlin Olympic Games. In 1959, he was the first inductee into the Naismith Memorial Basketball Hall of Fame.

Alan Cedric Page (August 7, 1945–)

Page was born in Canton, Ohio, the son of Georgiana (Umbles) and Howard Page. He was a star in several sports, especially football, at Central Catholic High School. Page graduated as an Academic All-American from the University of Notre Dame in 1967, was a member of the 1966 national championship team, and was named an All-American. Page earned his JD in 1978 from the University of Minnesota while playing professional football for the Minnesota Vikings and Chicago Bears. A six-time All-Pro, in 1971, Page was the NFL Defensive Player of the Year and NFL Most Valuable Player. After his retirement, he practiced law before being elected (1992) an associate justice of the Minnesota Supreme Court. His numerous honors have included induction into the College Football Hall of Fame (1993) and Professional Football Hall of Fame (1988) and receipt of the Theodore Roosevelt Award (2004), given by the NCAA for his outstanding citizenship, achievements, and contributions. Motivated partially by having NFL teammates who could not read, Page became an advocate of education and has stressed that academic preparation is more important than sports. Page has emphasized that athletics can and should teach life lessons, including hard work, dealing with success and failure, and sportsmanship. For more than 20 years, the Page Education Foundation has provided grants to more than 2,000 ethnic minority students to help them attend college. In exchange for this financial assistance, the Page Scholars have provided over 200,000 hours of community service as role models and mentors for children.

Jack (Jackie) Roosevelt Robinson (January 31, 1919–October 24, 1972)

Robinson was born in Cairo, Georgia, to Jerry and Mallie Robinson. After his sharecropper father left, his mother moved her family to Pasadena, California, in search of a better life. Robinson was a football, basketball, track, and baseball star while attending Muir Technical High School, Pasadena Junior College, and UCLA. After serving in a segregated Army during World War II, Robinson played for the Kansas City Monarchs in the Negro Leagues. He was scouted by the Brooklyn Dodgers because General Manager Branch Rickey was looking for an African American with exceptional courage, character, and self-control whom he wanted to give the opportunity to break the color barrier in MLB. Rickey, in signing Robinson, required Robinson to endure racial slurs, vindictive epithets, attempts to injure him, and death threats without retaliation. On April 15, 1947, Robinson became the first African American MLB player in the modern era as he withstood merciless attacks without fighting back to help ensure the acceptance of African Americans in MLB. In tribute to his accomplishments on and off the field, on the 50th anniversary of his debut, MLB retired Robinson's number 42. His baseball achievements include the Rookie of the Year Award in 1947; National League MVP in 1949; member of six World Series teams, including winning the World Series in 1955; and induction into the National Baseball Hall of Fame in 1962. He also received (posthumously) the Presidential Medal of Freedom in 1984 and Congressional Gold Medal in 2003. The MLB Rookie of the Year Award is named the Jackie Robinson Award in his honor.

Arthur (Art) Joseph Rooney Sr. (January 27, 1901–August 25, 1988)

Rooney was born the son of Irish immigrants Daniel and Margaret (Murray) Rooney in Coulterville, a suburb of Pittsburgh. He graduated from Duquesne Prep and attended Duquesne University. Rooney purchased a NFL franchise and founded the Pittsburgh Pirates in 1933 (he changed the team's name to Steelers in 1940). The Steelers had perennial losing records until the 1970s when his team won Super Bowls in 1975, 1976, 1979, and 1980. Rooney showed respect for every person as he became Pittsburgh's most beloved figure—people talked almost reverentially about Rooney and what he did for the city. Many described Rooney as a man with class who made people feel important by genuinely caring about each person. For more than 40 years, Rooney served as a guiding light, became one of the league's leaders, and was highly respected by other owners for his wisdom and professionalism. Among his many honors was induction into the Professional Football Hall of Fame in 1964.

Wilma Glodean Rudolph (June 23, 1940–November 12, 1994)

Rudolph was born in Clarkville, Tennessee, to Ed, a railroad porter and handyman, and Blanche, who did cooking, laundry, and housecleaning for wealthy white families. In addition to having to overcome the prejudice of limited educational and financial opportunities in the segregated South, Rudolph was born prematurely weighing only 4.5 pounds, experienced several childhood illness, including double pneumonia and scarlet fever, and suffered from polio. Her mother and several older siblings provided physical therapy exercises in nursing Rudolph's left leg so she could walk with and eventually without a brace. While playing basketball in high school, Rudolph came to the attention of Ed Temple, the track and field coach at Tennessee State University, who invited her to attend a summer sport camp. Making the most of this opportunity, Rudolph become an Olympian at age 16 and won a bronze medal in the 4x100-meter relay in the 1956 Melbourne Olympic Games.

While still in high school, Rudolph had her first child. After joining the Tennessee State track team, Rudolph won gold medals in the 100 meters, 200 meters, and 4x100-meter relay in the 1960 Rome Olympic Games, thus becoming the first female to win three gold medals in track and field in a single Olympics. After earning her bachelor's degree in elementary education, Rudolph was a teacher and track coach. The Wilma Rudolph Foundation, which she established in 1981, assists young athletes with free coaching and instruction to help them succeed when faced with difficult circumstances. The Wilma Rudolph Courage Award is presented annually by the Women's Sports Foundation to a female athlete who courageously overcomes adversity and serves as an inspirational model for others. In addition to the many honors she received for her athletic achievements, Rudolph won the Sullivan Award for her leadership, character, and sportsmanship.

Dean Edwards Smith (February 28, 1931–)

Born in Emporia, Kansas, Smith was the son of Alfred, a teacher and coach, and Vesta (Edwards) Smith, also a teacher. At Topeka High School, Smith was a football quarterback, baseball catcher, and all-state basketball player. While attending the University of Kansas on an academic scholarship, Smith played on Coach Forrest "Phog" Allen's basketball team that won the NCAA championship in 1952. After serving as an assistant coach at the University of Kansas, United States Air Force Academy, and the University of North Carolina at Chapel Hill, Smith became North Carolina's head coach in 1961. When he retired in 1997, his teams had won 879 games and the NCAA men's basketball championships in 1982 and 1993. Smith coached the United States men's basketball team to a gold medal in the 1976 Montreal Olympic Games. The Naismith Memorial Basketball Hall of Fame inducted him in 1982, and the National Collegiate Basketball Hall of Fame recognized him in its founding class in 2006. Smith emphasized integrity and character and expected his players to behave appropriately on and off the court. He was respected for complying with NCAA, conference, and institutional rules, and for emphasizing education, with almost all of his players earning their degrees. His recruitment of Charlie Scott, as North Carolina's first African

American grant-in-aid basketball player, helped promote deseg-regation and equal treatment in local businesses and on cam-pus. Smith's coaching approach could be summed up with "Playing Hard, Playing Together, and Playing Smart" as he described in his book, *The Carolina Way: Leadership Lessons from a Life in Coaching*. While his teams won consistently, Smith was regarded as a coach who did not cheat to win. He stressed that positive lessons learned in basketball would prepare the young men who played on his teams for making significant contribu-tions later in their lives.

Dawn Michelle Staley (May 4, 1970–)

Born in Philadelphia and raised by her mother, Estelle Staley, Dawn Staley was *USA Today*'s national player of the year as a senior in high school. She became a three-time All-American and two-time National Player of the Year at the University of Virginia. Staley played professionally for two seasons in Europe, three seasons in the former American Basketball League, and eight seasons in the Women's National Basketball Association (WNBA). Staley was a five-time WNBA All-Star and two-time winner of the WNBA's Kim Perrot Sportsmanship Award. In 1996, she established the Dawn Staley Foundation dedicated to working with at-risk youth and serving charitable and community causes. In 2007, the WNBA created the Dawn Staley Community Leadership Award in her honor because of her dedication to giving to the community and her spirit of gen-erosity and character. Staley helped lead the United States women's basketball team to gold medals in the 1996, 2000, and 2004 Olympic Games and was honored by being chosen as the flag bearer in the Opening Ceremonies for the United States in 2004. After eight successful years coaching at Temple Univer-sity, Staley became the women's basketball coach at the Univer-sity of South Carolina in 2008.

Sharon Kay Stoll (December 16, 1946–)

Stoll was born in Wadsworth, Ohio, to Carl and Hazel Stoll, who were partners in Y&S Crop Service. She attended Tuslaw

High School, and earned her bachelor's degree from the College of the Ozarks. She holds a master's degree and PhD in sport philosophy from Kent State University. Stoll, who is recognized as a passionate advocate for and expert on character development, directs the Center of ETHICS at the University of Idaho, directs Winning with Character, and lectures nationally on moral education, moral reasoning, and moral development. She has served as a consultant to the United States Military Academy, U.S. Navy, U.S. Air Force, President's Commission of the NCAA, National Youth Sport Coaches Association, and National Federation of State High School Associations. She has evaluated moral development in sport and developed and taught intervention techniques to enhance the moral reasoning of high school, college, and professional athletes. In two of her books, *Who Says It's Cheating? Anybody's Sport Ethics Book* and *Sport Ethics: Applications for Fair Play*, Stoll emphasizes that competitive sport can potentially teach moral reasoning and build character. She has been featured in the national electronic and print media as an influential sport educator.

Charlene Vivian (Stoner) Stringer (March 16, 1948–)

Born in Edenborn, Pennsylvania, Stringer credited her parents Buddy, a coal miner, and Thelma, a housewife, as her great inspirations. She earned bachelor's and master's degrees in health and physical education from Slippery Rock University. Stringer was the first women's coach to take teams from three different institutions—Cheney University of Pennsylvania, the University of Iowa, and Rutgers University—to the NCAA Final Four. She has coached these teams to over 800 wins, the third most victories in college women's basketball, and received numerous Coach of the Year recognitions. In 1993, Stringer was honored with the Carol Eckman Award given by the Women's Basketball Coaches Association to the coach who demonstrates spirit, courage, integrity, commitment, leadership, and service to women's basketball. She was inducted into the Women's Basketball Hall of Fame in 2001. The U.S. Sports Academy honored her in 2002 by naming its annual women's coaching award as the C. Vivian Stringer Medallion Award of Sport for Women's

Coaching. In her inspirational autobiography, *Standing Tall: A Memoir of Tragedy and Triumph*, published in 2008, Stringer describes the challenges of her life, including her daughter's special needs due to contracting childhood meningitis, her husband's sudden death from a heart attack, and surviving breast cancer.

Jim Thompson (February 20, 1949–)

The son of William and Marjorie (Score) Thompson, a farmer and an elementary school teacher, respectively, Jim Thompson has a bachelor's degree in elementary education from the University of North Dakota, a master's degree in public affairs from the University of Oregon, and a master's degree in business administration from Stanford University. Thompson founded (1998) and serves as Executive Director of the Positive Coaching Alliance (PCA), which works to transform the culture of youth sports and helps develop character in young athletes. The message of the PCA has been delivered nationally to thousands of sport administrators, parents, and athletes. Thompson is tireless in his efforts to help coaches enrich the positive experiences of young athletes so they will learn life lessons while enjoying their sport experiences. Thompson is the author of *The Double-Goal Coach: Positive Coaching Tools for Honoring the Game and Developing Winners in Sports and Life*; *Positive Coaching: Building Character and Self-Esteem through Sports*; and *Shooting in the Dark: Tales of Coaching and Leadership*, which provide concrete strategies for achieving the goals of the PCA.

LeRoy Walker (June 4, 1918–)

The youngest of 11 children, Walker was born in Atlanta and grew up in Harlem, New York City. Walker displayed outstanding academic and athletic skills in football and basketball at Benedict College, graduating in 1940. He immediately earned his master's degree from Columbia University and later his doctorate from New York University. Walker coached and taught at Benedict College, Bishop College, and Prairie View A&M University, before going to North Carolina Central University where he spent the majority of his career. As a track-and-field coach, he coached numerous All-Americans, national champions, and Olympians. Prior to becoming the United States' first African American Olympic track-and-field coach in 1976, he coached Olympic teams from Ethiopia, Israel, Jamaica, Kenya, and Trinidad-Tobago. He shared some of his expertise in track and field in two books, *Championship Techniques in Track and Field* and *Track and Field: A Guide for the Serious Coach and Athlete.* Walker was a member of the United States Olympic Committee (USOC) Board of Directors and then served as USOC treasurer (1986–1992) and president (1992–1996). His many honors and recognitions include induction into the National Track and Field Hall of Fame (1983) and U.S. Olympic Hall of Fame (1987). Walker, who dedicated much of his life to the advancement of track and field nationally and internationally, always did so with grace and humility while honoring others. Throughout his long and distinguished career, he has served as a role model of respect, responsibility, and justice.

Hazel Virginia (Hotchkiss) Wightman (December 20, 1886–December 5, 1974)

Wightman was born in Healdsburg, California, where she played tennis to strengthen herself physically. In 1911, she graduated from the University of California at Berkeley. Between 1909 and 1911, Wightman swept the U.S. tennis championships in singles, women's doubles, and mixed doubles. During her long career, she won 43 adult U.S. titles, the last at age 68, and a total of 16 U.S. championship titles. Wightman won gold medals in women's doubles (with Helen Wills Moody) and mixed doubles (with Dick Williams) at the 1924 Paris Olympic Games. She helped organize the Ladies International Tennis Challenge between British and American teams in 1923, played on five teams, and served as captain for 13 years. The winner of these annual competitions (the last one was in 1989) received the Wightman Cup, a sterling silver vase Wightman donated as the trophy. She was called the "Queen Mother of American Tennis" because of her lifelong participation in, achievements in, and promotion of women's tennis. Wightman, the mother of five, taught tennis to many young people, without charge, wrote a short instructional book, *Better Tennis*, and welcomed aspiring champions into her home when they traveled to Boston to play in tournaments. In 1940, a group of New England women initiated the Service Bowl Award, a trophy given in her honor to the player who annually made notable contributions to sportsmanship, fellowship, and service to tennis. Wightman was the first recipient, as well as a 1946 recipient after this award became a national honor given by the United States Tennis Association. Wightman was inducted into the International Tennis Hall of Fame in 1957. "Lady Tennis" aptly symbolized her unparalleled reputation for sportsmanship as well as her grace and manners on and off the court.

John Wooden (October 14, 1910–)

Wooden was born in Hall, Indiana, to Roxie and Joshua Wooden. He led his Martinsville High School team to three consecutive state championship finals, winning the title in 1927. He earned three-time All-American honors at Purdue University, graduating in 1932 with a degree in English. While teaching and coaching in high school, Wooden played professional basketball in the National Basketball League. Following service in the Navy during World War II, Wooden earned his master's degree from Indiana State University. From 1946 to 1948, Wooden served as basketball coach and athletic director at Indiana State. Then during 27 seasons as UCLA's coach, beginning in 1948, his teams amassed a 620–147 record, including 10 NCAA championships, an 88-game winning streak, and four 30–0 seasons. Wooden's honors include induction into the Naismith Memorial Basketball Hall of Fame as a player (1960) and coach (1973), induction into the National Collegiate Basketball Hall of Fame in its founding class (2006), and the Presidential Medal of Freedom (2003), the nation's highest civilian honor. Long retired, Wooden remains a highly respected teacher of the game of basketball and life lessons. In his first book, *Practical Modern Basketball*, Wooden shared some of his tactical coaching strategies. His autobiographical book, *They Call Me Coach*, provided insights into the values that made Wooden a remarkable person and highly successful coach. He wrote about the importance of effort and achieving individual potential and shared numerous maxims and philosophical building blocks in *Wooden: A Lifetime of Observations and Reflections*

On and Off the Court. Wooden taught and modeled the virtues and characteristics of character in his highly acclaimed Pyramid of Success. This one-page model describes the characteristics of individuals who will be successful in life and basketball if they act in accordance with the values that Wooden identified. He believed that his legacy in coaching was revealed through the successes of his players, not on the court, but in their lives.

These brief biographies vividly illustrate how the lives and contributions of athletes and coaches can serve as exemplary role models for those who follow their paths. In addition to these remarkable individuals, there are many others who daily positively impact the lives of youth, adolescents, and adults inside and outside of sports.

6

Data and Documents

This chapter provides facts, statistics, and documents that will help readers contextualize significant events, issues, and challenges as they impact the operation of sports on an ethical or unethical basis. While the information and data will illustrate historical and current practices, the documents will provide guidance about how unfair or non-sportsmanship behaviors could be replaced by values-based actions and displays of character. One goal of providing this information is to broaden the perspective about how each level of sport has not, but potentially could have, succeeded in developing the values it claims result from sport participation. Another goal is to provide the context for continuing ethical problems that have not yet been resolved, but that need to be addressed if sport is to overcome cheating, an overemphasis on winning, the use of performance-enhancing drugs, discriminatory treatment of females and ethnic minorities, and gamesmanship. The information and data are provided in a chronological manner, beginning with youth sports through the Olympic Games, along with sections addressing some ethical issues associated with females and African Americans in sports.

Youth Sport

Children play because it is fun. They enjoy exploring the world around them and discovering and expanding their abilities to move. They mimic the activities of adults as they learn to throw, catch, and kick balls. Since parents want to provide safe play spaces, they increasingly have organized sport opportunities for their children. As early as age three, children are enrolled in organized classes, programs, and teams in figure skating, gymnastics, ice hockey, soccer, and other sports. Despite questions from educators and physicians about whether young children are developmentally ready for competitive sports at early ages, many children at early ages engage in structured practices each week almost year round. So, it should not be surprising when ethical problems begin to impact sport participants from a young age, especially with an adult-imposed emphasis on winning. Table 6.1 lists several of the ethical challenges facing youth sport, as well as proposes what could be the rights of youth sport athletes. It could be argued that these rights represent morally reasoned ways to address each of the challenges.

While youth sport has been praised by parents and youth sport coaches for teaching character and life lessons to children, sometimes positive values are not learned. Instead, myths persist because adults want to believe things that have not been proved to be true, as illustrated in Table 6.2.

Honor the Game

Ethical problems associated with youth sports, as illustrated through these myths, have led to the formation of numerous organizations dedicated to address the last truth listed, which is to help youth sports teach positive values. For example, the Positive Coaching Alliance (PCA) has established national partnerships with organizations like Little League Baseball, Pop Warner (football), and the American Youth Soccer Association with the goal of transforming youth sports. One effective strategy advocated by the PCA is entitled Honor the Game. Document 6.1 describes this initiative, which provides a framework for how youth athletes, youth sport coaches, and parents can demonstrate their commitment to using sport to teach character and life lessons.

> Many people talk about "sportsmanship," or what it means to be a "good sport." What does it mean to you to be a good sport? Answers to this question vary widely. Sadly, PCA has even heard stories of coaches telling their teams that if they win the Sportsmanship Award at a tournament, they will spend the entire following week conditioning! Why might a coach say this? Unfortunately, many coaches equate being a good sport with being soft or weak.

TABLE 6.1
**Ethical Challenges Facing Youth Sports Contrasted with the Ethical
Rights of Youth Sport Athletes**

Ethical Challenges Facing Youth Sports	Ethical Rights of Youth Sport Athletes
1. Coaches and parents taking the fun out of youth sports by putting too much pressure on young athletes.	1. The right to have fun playing.
2. Coaches and parents sending the message that winning is the important thing as shown by rewarding winning more than anything else.	2. The right to receive positive reinforcement for showing effort, playing hard, and doing one's best.
3. Adults allowing anyone to coach youth in sports.	3. The right to have qualified coaches whose abilities have been certified and who have cleared criminal background checks.
4. Coaches and parents insisting that a young athlete dedicate himself or herself to playing only one sport year-round.	4. The right to play or not play any sport and to have time off from sports.
5. Coaches and parents expecting young athletes to be tough and play through injuries.	5. The right to have injuries evaluated properly, to be given any needed medical care, and to allow injuries to heal before being expected to play.
6. Coaches arguing with officials when they do not agree with a call and allowing young athletes to argue with officials about calls.	6. The right to have coaches and parents model showing respect to officials and the right to be expected to show respect to officials.
7. A parent demanding that a coach should give a child more playing time or that this coach should play a child in a certain position.	7. The right to play various positions, against balanced competition, and for approximately the same amount of time as all other players.
8. Coaches focusing on developing the skills and advancement of the best athletes.	8. The right to play at a level commensurate with his or her ability with the dual goals of seeking to win and learning life lessons.
9. Coaches modeling their actions after professional and collegiate models along with having unrealistic performance expectations of young athletes.	9. The right to learn basic skills and fundamental strategies in developmentally appropriate ways and to receive positive coaching.
10. Coaches teaching and encouraging young athletes to intentionally violate game rules and taunt opponents in order to gain competitive advantages.	10. The right to play sports according to the rules without fear of violence or harm and to receive respect from opponents coupled with the responsibility to play by the rules and show respect to opponents.

Source: Author.

PCA believes the time has come to unite behind a powerful new term, "Honoring the Game." Coaches, parents, and athletes need to realize that an Honoring the Game perspective needs to replace the common win-at-all-cost perspective. If a coach and his or her team have to dishonor the game to win it, what is this victory really worth, and what sort of message is this sending young athletes.

If Honoring the Game is to become the youth sports standard, it needs a clear definition. At PCA we say that Honoring the Game

TABLE 6.2
Myths and Truths in Youth Sports

Myths	Truths
Myth . . . The best athletes are those who work the hardest.	The truth is . . . The elite often have innate, natural advantages.
Myth . . . Early, focused skills training makes a Tiger roar.	The truth is . . . In golf, sometimes; in most sports, no.
Myth . . . America is the world's athletics superpower.	The truth is . . . We're the fattest nation—and it all starts in preschool.
Myth . . . Organized competition breeds success.	The truth is . . . Unstructured play is often more valuable.
Myth . . . Children want to win.	The truth is . . . They do, but it means far more to adults.
Myth . . . Athletic scholarships support amateurism.	The truth is . . . The lure of a payoff turns peewees into mini-pros.
Myth . . . The poor benefit the most from college sports.	The truth is . . . Rich kids are far likelier to get roster spots.
Myth . . . Grade-school travel teams identify future stars.	The truth is . . . They reward early bloomers, leaving the rest behind.
Myth . . . No national body coordinates grassroots sports.	The truth is . . . The U.S. Olympic Committee is supposed to.
Myth . . . Children inevitably find their best sport.	The truth is . . . Most are never exposed to sports they might excel at.
Myth . . . Money is pouring into youth sports.	The truth is . . . It is, but not in the communities that need it most.
Myth . . . Media coverage drives up participation.	The truth is . . . Kids play a game—then they become fans.
Myth . . . Grassroots hoops has gotten too professional.	The truth is . . . The problem is it lacks a professional approach.
Myth . . . Playing sports builds character.	The truth is . . . It depends on who runs, and who surrounds, the team.

Source: Farrey, T. *Game on: The All-American Race to Make Champions of our Children,* 2008. (Used by permission)

goes to the "ROOTS" of positive play. Each letter in ROOTS stands for an important part of the game that we must respect. The R stands for Rules. The first O is for Opponents. The next O is for Officials. T is for Teammates, and the S is for Self.

R is for Rules

Rules allow us to keep the game fair. If we win by ignoring or violating the rules, what is the value of our victory? PCA believes that honoring the letter AND the spirit of the rule is important.

O is for Opponents

Without an opponent, there would be no competition. Rather than demeaning a strong opponent, we need to honor strong opponents because they challenge us to do our best. Athletes can be both fierce and friendly during the same competition (in one moment giving everything to get to a loose ball, and in the next moment helping an opponent up). Coaches showing respect for opposing coaches and players sets the tone for the rest of the team.

O is for Officials

Respecting officials, even when we disagree with their calls, may be the toughest part of Honoring the Game. We must remember that officials are not perfect (just like coaches, athletes and parents!). Take time to think about how to best approach an official when you want to discuss a call. What strategies do you have to keep yourself in control when you start to get upset with officials' calls? We must remember that the loss of officials (and finding enough in the first place) is a major problem in most youth sports organizations, and we can confront this problem by consistently respecting officials.

T is for Teammates

It's easy for young athletes to think solely about their own performance, but we want athletes to realize that being part of a team requires thinking about and respecting one's teammates. This respect needs to carry beyond the field/gym/track/pool into the classroom and social settings. Athletes need to be reminded that their conduct away from practices and games will reflect back on their teammates and the league, club, or school.

S is for Self

Athletes should be encouraged to live up to their own highest personal standard of Honoring the Game, even when their opponents are not. Athletes' respect for themselves and their own standards must come first.

Having this definition of Honoring the Game (HTG) is a start. To make Honoring the Game the youth sports standard, coaches, leaders, and parents need to **discuss** HTG with their athletes. Coaches need to **practice** it with their athletes (i.e. have players officiate at practice). And perhaps most importantly, all adults in the youth sports setting (coaches, leaders, parents, officials, and fans) need to **model** it. If these adults Honor the Game, the athletes will too.

Source: Positive Coaching Alliance (1001 N. Rengstorff Ave., Suite 100, Mountain View, CA 94043), Honor the Game, 2008, Available at http://www.positivecoach.org/subcontent.aspx?SecId=163 (Used by permission)

Children will not learn how to honor the game if they are not actively involved with sports. Today, most schools fail to meet the physical activity and fitness as well as sport skill instructional needs of children because physical education programs have been eliminated due to budgetary constraints or pressures to increase the amount of the school day dedicated to instruction in reading, mathematics, or other subjects. According to the National Center for Health Statistics, 16 percent (over 9 million) children and teens ages 6 to 19, based on 1999–2002 data, are overweight. The prevalence of being overweight for children ages 6 to 11 has increased over 100 percent, and for adolescents 12 to 19 has increased over 200 percent since 1980. While viewing television, playing video games, and surfing the Internet may be contributing factors, so, too, are super-sized fast foods, concern about safe play spaces, and the reduction in school physical education and sport programs.

Since most children do not participate in daily physical education, parents and interested citizens have continued to expand the number of youth sport programs. While many of these programs advocate for children having fun while learning sport skills in developmentally appropriate ways and times, other children are subjected to highly competitive sport teams when their bodies, psychological development, and emotional maturity are not ready for the pressures of winning and performing as miniature professionals. Yet, national championships, beginning at very young ages and continuing for older children, abound in numerous sports as listed in Table 6.3.

An ethical concern is that seeking victories in order to qualify for and succeed in these national championships, in programs modeled after professional sports with fully uniformed children playing with all the trappings of commercialized sport, may be teaching lessons other than character building. Except for winners pictured with their trophies, every other team or athlete in qualifying events and these championships ends the season having lost on the scoreboard. The pressures from coaches, who have dedicated huge amounts of time and emotional energy, and parents, who have spent large sums of money and made huge psychological investments, may be teaching these young athletes that the only thing that really matters is winning. Also, when children play in national championships at an early age, it is not surprising that some parents begin to envision their children as potential superstars. It is important to note that many of these competitors, as well as those who compete in national championships in their older years, often do not persist in sports, choosing instead to drop out of them.

TABLE 6.3
Examples of National Championships for Young Athletes

Age Group	Gender	Sponsoring Organization	National Championship
6 years and under	Boys; girls	Callaway Golf (a golf equipment company)	Callaway Junior World Golf Championship
8 years and under	Boys; girls	Amateur Athletic Union	Amateur Athletic Union Basketball National Championships
8 years and under	Boys; girls	United States Tennis Association	U.S. Open Junior Tennis Championships
8–11 years with weight limits	Boys	Pop Warner Football	Junior Pee Wee Pop Warner Super Bowl
8–11 years	Girls	Pop Warner Cheer and Dance	Junior Pee Wee Cheer and Dance Championships
9 years and under	Boys; girls	Amateur Athletic Union	Amateur Athletic Union Junior Olympic Swimming Meet
9 years and under	Boys; girls	US Club Soccer	Youth World Series
9 years and under	Boys; girls	Youth Basketball of America	Youth Basketball of America National Championships
9–12 years	Boys; girls	Little League	Little League Baseball World Series
9–12 years	Girls	Little League	Little League Softball World Series
10 years and under	Girls	Amateur Athletic Union	Amateur Athletic Union Girls Junior National Volleyball Championships
10 years and under	Boys; girls	Babe Ruth League	Cal Ripken Baseball 10-Year-Old World Series

Source: Author.

Interscholastic Sports

When young athletes drop out of sports, they are deprived of potential physical, psychological, emotional, and social benefits. Instead of what many individuals claim is an overemphasis on only the most successful players, should opportunities for individuals of all skill levels be provided? One way to decrease the increased prevalence of overweight and obese youth could be to provide more sport opportunities that are characterized more by fun and learning life lessons than on competitions among the most highly skilled. Often the world of sports is viewed as a pyramid, with fewer and fewer people playing sports as they age and the demand for higher skilled performances increases. Maybe a way to address the ethical dilemma of sport excluding people could be to broaden and widen the base by providing lifelong participation opportunities in sport along with allowing those with advanced skills to continue to compete at their level in high school, college, and professionally. This alternative approach to sport opportunities is illustrated in Figure 6.1. If this approach were to be implemented, more children, adolescents, and adults would have opportunities to play sports at levels commensurate with their skill levels.

Figure 6.1
Model for Increased Participation in Sports

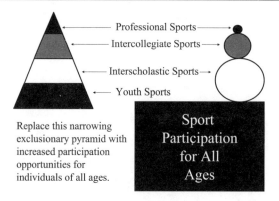

Professional Sports

Intercollegiate Sports

Interscholastic Sports

Youth Sports

Replace this narrowing exclusionary pyramid with increased participation opportunities for individuals of all ages.

Sport Participation for All Ages

Source: Author.

Extracurricular Physical Activity Programs

Document 6.2 supports this concept by stating that intramural as well as interscholastic sports should be financially supported so more school-aged adolescents could participate in sports.

Extracurricular physical activity programs provide students with additional opportunities to be active and to use the skills taught in physical education class. They also offer important social and psychological benefits: Studies have found that participation in extracurricular activities is negatively associated with tobacco and other drug use and positively associated with good conduct, academic achievement, and staying in school.

Extracurricular opportunities to engage in physical activity may be interscholastic or intramural. Interscholastic sports programs consist of team or individual competition between schools, and intramural programs consist of sports and recreational activities, both competitive and non-competitive, among students within one school. At present, interscholastic sports programs, which serve only a small portion of the student body, are more commonly available than intramural programs.

In keeping with a more inclusive approach to promoting physical activity, all schools should offer quality intramural programs that feature a diverse selection of competitive and non-competitive, structured and unstructured activities that meet the needs, interests, and abilities of all students. In addition to team sports, intramural programs could include physical activity clubs (e.g., dance, hiking, yoga). Because they can be designed for students with a wide range of abilities, intramural programs may be beneficial for the large group of students who have not participated much in physical activity: boys and girls who lack the skills or confidence to play interscholastic sports or who dislike competitive sports altogether. Whereas interscholastic sports emphasize competition and winning, intramurals emphasize participation and enjoyment without pressure. However, to promote physical activity among young people, high schools should continue to offer interscholastic sports programs.

Source: Wechsler, H., A. B. Devereaux, M. Davis and J. Collins, Using the School Environment to Promote Physical Activity and Healthy Eating, *Preventive Medicine* 2000, 31: S121-S137, as quoted in Appendix 8 of the U.S. Department of Health and Human Services, *Healthy People 2010: Understanding and Improving Health*, 2000.

Historically, interscholastic sports were almost exclusively provided only for boys. Although occasionally girls attending non-city or rural schools were allowed to play on basketball teams, it was believed by most educators and accepted by most parents that females were not interested in sports or did not possess sport skills. Societal attitudes through the 1960s reinforced the traditional perspective that boys played sports and girls cheered for them. Girls, however, seldom had opportunities to learn sport skills, maybe through the lack of parental encouragement, sports equipment, instructional programs, or teams on which to play. Some have argued that this limitation of females in sports was unfair.

When the federal government passed the Education Amendments in 1972 (P. L. 92-318), educational opportunities for females in schools began to expand. Title IX in Section 1681 of this legislation, as amended by section 3 of P. L. 93-568 in 1975, prohibits discrimination on the basis of sex in any federally funded education program or activity. It states, "No person in the United States shall, on the basis of sex, be excluded from participation in, be denied the benefits of, or be subjected to discrimination under any education program or activity receiving Federal financial assistance ..." Although these 37 words do not specifically mention athletics or sports, this law has forever changed the world of sports in the United States for females.

P. L. 93-568 describes the reach of nondiscrimination on the basis of sex in educational programs or activities receiving financial assistance. Section 106.41 on athletics states that

> no person shall, on the basis of sex, be excluded from participation in, be denied the benefits of, be treated differently from another person or otherwise be discriminated against in any interscholastic, intercollegiate, club or intramural athletics offered by a recipient, and no recipient shall provide any such athletics separately on such basis.

While broadly disallowing disparate treatment in all educational programs and services, this federal law specifically requires equal opportunity in interscholastic sports. Figure 6.2 illustrates how this law and changing societal attitudes toward females participating in sport have resulted in an over 925 percent increase in girls playing interscholastic sports in the year since the passage of the 1972 Education Amendments. It also should be noted that over this same time period, participation opportunities for boys increased 17.8 percent.

With over 7 million adolescents playing interscholastic sports, it is not surprising that many of these athletes and their parents believe they will receive grants-in-aid to pay for a college

Figure 6.2
Participation Numbers by Gender in Interscholastic Sports

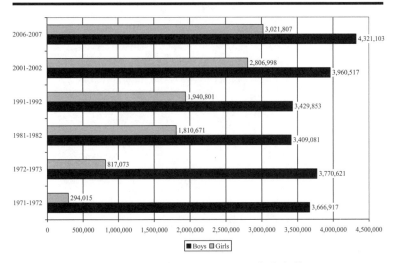

Source: National Federation of State High School Associations, 2006–07 High School Athletics Participation Survey, p. 47, 2007. (Copyright NFSH 2008; Used by permission)

education based on their athletic abilities. Oftentimes, this expectation is accompanied by pressures to win, playing only one sport year-round, overuse injuries, and burnout leading to their dropping out of sports. As Table 6.4 describes, the likelihood of receiving a grant-in-aid is quite small. Some athletes will get the opportunity to play intercollegiate sports. Few will play professionally. (Note that the data in Table 6.4 include only athletes in National Collegiate Athletic Association [NCAA] institutions and thus do not include athletes who play in National Association of Intercollegiate Athletics [NAIA] and National Junior College Athletic Association [NJCAA] institutions.)

Arizona Sports Summit Accord

Since the last time that many individuals will play organized sports is in high school, coaches, parents, and educators should take advantage of the opportunity to teach character and other positive values through sport. Depending on the leadership of interscholastic sports, these values may be taught, or different lessons may be learned. Given the numerous examples of ethical misbehaviors in interscholastic sports, many in sport have stated that there was the need to raise the

TABLE 6.4
Estimated Probability of Competing in Athletics beyond the
High School Interscholastic Level

Student-Athletes	Men's Basketball	Women's Basketball	Football	Baseball	Men's Ice Hockey	Men's Soccer
High School Student Athletes	546,335	452,929	1,071,775	470,671	36,263	358,935
High School Senior Student Athletes	156,096	129,408	306,221	134,477	10,361	102,553
NCAA Student Athletes	16,571	15,096	61,252	28,767	3,973	19,793
NCAA Freshman Roster Positions	4,735	4,313	17,501	8,219	1,135	5,655
NCAA Senior Student Athletes	3,682	3,355	13,612	6,393	883	4,398
NCAA Student Athletes Drafted	44	32	250	600	33	76
Percent High School to NCAA	3.0%	3.3%	5.7%	6.1%	11.0%	5.5%
Percent NCAA to Professional	1.2%	1.0%	1.8%	9.4%	3.7%	1.7%
Percent High School to Professional	0.03%	0.02%	0.08%	0.45%	0.32%	0.07%

Source: National Collegiate Athletic Association, Estimated Probability of Competing in Athletics beyond the High School Interscholastic Level, 2007. (Used by permission)

consciousness of sport administrators, coaches, athletes, parents, and the general public about these problems. So, in 1999, the Josephson Institute Center for Sports Ethics brought together 50 influential leaders in sports. This group issued the Arizona Sports Summit Accord, provided in Document 6.3, which calls for a greater emphasis on building character and behaving ethically in sports.

Preamble

At its best, athletic competition can hold intrinsic value for our society. It is a symbol of a great ideal: pursuing victory with honor.

The love of sports is deeply embedded in our national consciousness. The values of millions of participants and spectators are directly and dramatically influenced by the values conveyed by organized sports. Thus, sports are a major social force that shapes the quality and character of the American culture.

In the belief that the impact of sports can and should enhance the character and uplift the ethics of the nation, we seek to establish a framework of principles and a common language of values that can be adopted and practiced widely.

It is therefore agreed:

1. The essential elements of character-building and ethics in sports are embodied in the concept of sportsmanship and six core principles: trustworthiness, respect, responsibility, fairness, caring, and citizenship. The highest potential of sports is achieved when competition reflects these "Six Pillars of Character."
2. It is the duty of sports leadership—including coaches, athletic administrators, program directors, and officials—to promote sportsmanship and foster good character by teaching, enforcing, advocating, and modeling these ethical principles.
3. To promote sportsmanship and foster the development of good character, sports programs must be conducted in a manner that enhances the mental, social, and moral development of athletes and teaches them positive life skills that will help them become personally successful and socially responsible.
4. Participation in athletic programs is a privilege, not a right. To earn that privilege, athletes must conduct themselves, on and off the field, as positive role models who exemplify good character.
5. Sports programs should establish standards for participation by adopting codes of conduct for coaches, athletes, parents, spectators, and other groups who impact the quality of athletic programs.
6. All sports participants must consistently demonstrate and demand scrupulous integrity and observe and enforce the spirit as well as the letter of the rules.
7. The importance of character, ethics, and sportsmanship should be emphasized in all communications relating to the recruitment of athletes, including promotional and descriptive materials.
8. In recruiting, educational institutions must specifically determine that the athlete is seriously committed to getting an education and has or will develop the academic skills and character to succeed.
9. The highest administrative officer of organizations that offer sports programs must maintain ultimate responsibility for the quality and integrity of those programs. Such officers must assure that education and character-development responsibilities are not compromised to achieve sports performance goals and that the academic, emotional, physical, and moral well-being of athletes is always placed above desires and pressures to win.
10. The faculties of educational institutions must be directly involved in and committed to the academic success of student-athletes and the character-building goals of the institution.
11. Everyone involved in athletic competition has a duty to treat the traditions of the sport and other participants with respect. Coaches have a special responsibility to model respectful behavior and the duty to demand that their athletes refrain from

disrespectful conduct including verbal abuse of opponents and officials, profane or belligerent trash-talking, taunting, and unseemly celebrations.

12. The leadership of sports programs at all levels must ensure that coaches, whether paid or voluntary, are competent to coach. Minimal competence may be attained by training or experience. It includes basic knowledge of 1) the character-building aspects of sports, including techniques and methods of teaching and reinforcing the core values comprising sportsmanship and good character, 2) first-aid principles and the physical capacities and limitations of the age group coached, and 3) coaching principles and the rules and strategies of the sport.

13. Because of the powerful potential of sports as a vehicle for positive personal growth, a broad spectrum of sports experiences should be made available to all of our diverse communities.

14. To safeguard the health of athletes and the integrity of the sport, athletic programs must discourage the use of alcohol and tobacco and demand compliance with all laws and regulations, including those relating to gambling and the use of drugs.

15. Although economic relationships between sports programs and corporate entities are often mutually beneficial, institutions and organizations that offer athletic programs must safeguard the integrity of their programs. Commercial relationships should be continually monitored to ensure against inappropriate exploitation of the organization's name or reputation and undue interference or influence of commercial interests. In addition, sports programs must be prudent, avoiding undue financial dependency on particular companies or sponsors.

16. The profession of coaching is a profession of teaching. In addition to teaching the mental and physical dimensions of their sport, coaches, through words and example, must also strive to build the character of their athletes by teaching them to be trustworthy, respectful, responsible, fair, caring, and good citizens.

Source: Josephson Institute (9841 Airport Blvd., #300, Los Angeles, CA 90045), Arizona Sports Summit Accord, 1999. Available at http://josephson institute.org/sports/resources/accord/accord-intercollegiate.html (Used by permission)

Before discussing intercollegiate sports, the next section examines females in sport. This interlude in the sequential presentation of data and documents seems appropriate since federal legislation and participation opportunities have most dramatically impacted females at the scholastic and collegiate levels.

Females in Sports

Females of all ages have historically been excluded from sports. Traditional and societal roles and domestic responsibilities as wives and mothers limited their participation in sport. Until recent decades, physicians, women physical educators, and many women warned that females' physical and emotional makeup predisposed them to less vigorous and competitive physical exertion. Also, most sports were developed, governed, and participated in by males, who usually dismissed females as incapable of matching their stronger and faster athletic achievements. It was also perceived that most females were simply not interested in competing in sports. But, as the events and individuals described in Table 6.5 illustrate, significant changes occurred as females no longer accepted discriminatory exclusion and sought opportunities to achieve their athletic potential.

When the Association for Intercollegiate Athletics for Women (AIAW) was established, it offered women an educational model for intercollegiate athletics that differed from that of the NCAA. The policies of the AIAW sought to prevent or control abuses that afflicted men's athletics, such as ethical problems dealing with academics, recruiting, and commercialism. This different approach, however, met its demise when the NCAA began to offer national championships for females. The financial incentives offered to NCAA institutions were so substantial that athletic directors and presidents chose to abandon the AIAW, leading to its demise in 1982. As a result, almost all women's and men's intercollegiate athletic programs operate following the men's model, with the same ethical problems that the women's model attempted to prevent.

It is important to analyze the significance of Title IX of the 1972 Education Amendments to intercollegiate athletics. Given considerable uncertainty about the breadth of its application and the resistance from many males (especially football coaches) to extend equal opportunity to females in intercollegiate athletics, the federal government in 1979 issued a clarifying policy interpretation. The original legislation and this policy interpretation make it clear that intercollegiate athletic programs must provide equal opportunity to all students in three broad categories, as specified in Table 6.6.

TABLE 6.5

Significant Events Affecting the Exclusion and Inclusion of Females in Sports

Date	Noteworthy Event	Effect or Implication
1850	Amelia Bloomer popularizes wearing loose-fitting pants worn under a skirt (these became known as bloomers).	Bloomers become the costume worn by females in gymnasiums, which frees them to play basketball and other sports in the late 1800s and early 1900s.
1874	Tennis, which is first introduced in the United States by a female, gains societal acceptance as a sport for females because it can be played in Victorian-style clothing and at a leisurely pace.	In 1884, the first women's singles tennis championship is contested at the All-England Lawn Tennis Club at Wimbledon. In 1887, the first women's national tennis championship is held in the United States.
1892	Senda Berenson teaches the new game of basketball to Smith College students and modifies the rules to restrict players to one-third of the court to protect them from overexertion.	Basketball becomes the most popular sport for college women and schoolgirls. Basketball as played by most females remains a half-court game until 1938. Most colleges begin to play the game full court until 1970.
1896	Stanford plays the University of California in the first women's intercollegiate basketball game.	Only a few institutions offer athletic teams for females in basketball or any other sport for several decades because competitive sports are perceived as too physically and emotionally demanding.
1896	The International Olympic Committee (IOC) excludes females from participation in the modern Olympic Games.	IOC members state that females are incapable physically and emotionally of competing in elite-level sports. However, the first females compete in the 1900 Paris Olympic Games in tennis and golf. Females also participate with males in sailing, croquet, and equestrian.
1901	A British woman, Constance Applebee, introduces field hockey to females in the United States.	Some women play field hockey in colleges and on club teams, including against teams internationally, while males in the United States choose not to play what they perceive is a feminine sport. Females are not permitted to play field hockey in the Olympic Games until 1980 (males begin to play field hockey in the 1908 London Olympic Games).
1926	The first female, Gertrude Ederle at age nineteen, swims the English Channel in a time that is two hours faster than the men's record.	Ederle, who was a 1924 Olympic champion in swimming, receives a ticket tape parade in New York City. Her remarkable achievement in swimming the English Channel is viewed as the exception to females' interests and abilities in athletics.
1932	Babe Didrikson wins the Amateur Athletic Union (AAU) national team championship by winning the javelin, shot put, baseball throw, eighty-meter hurdles, and broad jump and tying for first in the high jump.	Didrikson captures a silver medal in the high jump and gold medals in the javelin and eighty-meter hurdles in the 1932 Los Angeles Olympic Games. A three-time AAU All-American basketball player who also excels in several other sports, Didrikson wins numerous amateur and professional golf championships.

Year	Event	Description
1954	The Iowa Girls' High School Athletic Union establishes a statewide program for girls' sports equal to that for boys.	This organization focuses on promoting greater sport opportunities for junior and senior high school girls in Iowa and is notably linked with the six-on-six basketball game played in Iowa through 1993.
1943	Chicago Cubs owner Philip Wrigley establishes the All-American Girls Professional Baseball League.	Over 600 female athletes play professional baseball in small Midwestern towns for eleven years. The league folds due to a decentralization of the league and loss of attendance.
1944	Swimmer Ann Curtis becomes the first female to win the Sullivan Award, presented by the Amateur Athletic Union to the outstanding amateur athlete in the United States.	Since its initiation in 1930, seventeen female athletes (including twins Coco and Kelly Miller in 1999) have received this award, which honors their athletic achievements as well as sportsmanship.
1966	The Commission on Intercollegiate Athletics for Women begins to conduct national intercollegiate championships in gymnastics and track and field.	This organization, which becomes the Association for Intercollegiate Athletics for Women in 1971, expands to provide forty-two championships in nineteen sports.
1967	Katherine Switzer registers as K. V. Switzer and becomes the first female to officially enter and run in the Boston Marathon.	When a male race official realizes that a female has entered, he tries to tear her number from her back during the race. Females are allowed to officially run in the Boston Marathon in 1972.
1972	Congress passes the Education Amendments. Title IX of this legislation requires equal opportunity in all educational programs including athletics.	After Congress refuses to exclude athletics from this law and states its application to sport in educational institutions, the participation of females on school teams grows from under 300,000 to over 3 million and on college teams from around 16,000 to over 200,000.
1974	Billie Jean King establishes the Women's Sports Foundation.	Dedicated to advocacy and research on sport issues for women, this organization provides information to encourage sports for females of all ages and skill levels.
1976	NJCAA offers its first national championships for females.	The NJCAA offers twenty-three national championships in thirteen sports for women.
1978	United States Congress passes the Amateur Sports Act.	This act prohibits gender discrimination in amateur sports, thus making training facilities and money more available to women.
1980	NAIA offers its first national championships for females.	The NAIA offers eleven national championships in ten sports for women.
1981	NCAA offers its first national championships for females.	The NCAA offers twenty national championships in each of three divisions for women.

Source: Author.

TABLE 6.6
Basic Requirements of Title IX for Intercollegiate Athletics

Area	Language from Title IX of the 1972 Education Amendments and A Policy Interpretation: Title IX and Intercollegiate Athletics
Financial assistance or athletic grants-in-aid must be available on a substantially proportional basis	"To the extent that a recipient awards athletic scholarships or grants-in-aid, it must provide reasonable opportunities for such awards for members of each sex in proportion to the number of students of each sex participating in interscholastic or intercollegiate athletics." [section 106.37(c)(1) of P. L. 93-568 and Section IV of A Policy Interpretation]
Program areas so males and females receive equivalent treatment, benefits, and opportunities	Equal athletic opportunity to: (section 106.41c P. L. 93-568 and Section IV of A Policy Interpretation) • The provision of equipment and supplies • Scheduling of games and practice time • Travel and per diem allowance • Opportunity to receive coaching and academic tutoring • Assignment and compensation of coaches and tutors • Provision of locker rooms, practice and competitive facilities • Provision of medical and training facilities and services • Provision of housing and dining facilities and services • Publicity • Recruitment of athletes (added in A Policy Interpretation) • Support services for athletes (added in A Policy Interpretation)
Interests and abilities of male and female students are effectively accommodated	Equal athletic opportunity to [section 106.4(c)(1)of P.L. 93-568] "A recipient which operates or sponsors interscholastic, intercollegiate, club or intramural athletics shall provide equal athletic opportunity for members of both sexes. In determining whether equal opportunities are available the Director will consider, among other factors: (1) Whether the selection of sports and levels of competition effectively accommodate the interests and abilities of members of both sexes." Institutions may choose any one of three options for meeting this requirement: (Section VII C.5(a) of A Policy Interpretation) (1) "Whether intercollegiate level participation opportunities for male and female students are provided in numbers substantially proportionate to their respective enrollments; or (2) Where the members of one sex have been and are underrepresented among intercollegiate athletes, whether the institution can show a history and continuing practice of program expansion which is demonstrably responsive to the developing interest and abilities of the members of that sex; or (3) Where the members of one sex are underrepresented among intercollegiate athletes, and the institution cannot show a continuing practice of program expansion such as that cited above, whether it can be demonstrated that the interests and abilities of the members of that sex have been fully and effectively accommodated by the present program."

To fully understand the resistance and challenges to Title IX, Table 6.7 places this legislation in historical context. This table also demonstrates the consistency in application of Title IX to intercollegiate athletics.

Since federal law requires equal opportunity in all educational programs including athletics, it is informative to know the extent to which these institutions have added competitive opportunities for women. While the number of teams tells only part of the story, it does indicate whether or not a good faith effort has been made to provide sport teams for females. Table 6.8 provides historical through current data that show growth in the number of sport teams offered to females attending NCAA (but does not report on NAIA and NJCAA) institutions. This table also documents that over half of the female athletes in NCAA institutions are coached by males. Most of the athletic programs in which female athletes participate are administered by males. This gradually is changing.

In addition to these data for females only, it is important to compare the number of teams for male athletes with the number of teams provided for female athletes. Figure 6.3 graphically shows data from the 2006 institutional reports submitted in compliance with the Equity in Athletics Disclosure Act. Specifically, in the 11 conferences in the NCAA Division I or Football Bowl Subdivision (FBS), the average number of teams for female athletes (10) exceeds the average number of teams for male athletes (8.2).

For ease of reference, the member institutions in each of these conferences are provided in Table 6.9.

An increase in the number of teams offered to females in NCAA institutions is shown in the trend data in Table 6.8. However, the higher average number of teams for females shown in Figure 6.3 fails to fully reveal the number of sport opportunities for male and female athletes. So, it is important to document whether Title IX or other factors have resulted in equitable participation opportunities in sports. Figures 6.4 and 6.5 provide data from the 2006 institutional reports submitted in compliance with the Equity in Athletics Disclosure Act. Figure 6.4 shows a comparison by gender for 430 institutions in the NJCAA, 249 institutions in the NAIA, and 1067 institutions in the NCAA. Disparities by gender are further broken out in Figure 6.5 by division within each governing organization.

TABLE 6.7
Application of Title IX to Intercollegiate Athletics

Date	Legislation, Court Decisions, Letters of Clarification, and other Significant Actions
June 23, 1972	Congress prohibits discrimination on the basis of sex in any federally funded education program or activity.
1974; 1975; 1977	Proposed amendments to Title IX, bills restricting its application to intercollegiate athletics, and resolutions and bills to curtail enforcement of Title IX are repeatedly defeated in Congress.
July 21, 1975	The Department of Health, Education, and Welfare (HEW) issues the final Title IX regulations. It allows an adjustment period of three years for secondary schools and colleges, as long as work toward compliance is expeditious.
December 11, 1979	HEW issues "A Policy Interpretation: Title IX and Intercollegiate Athletics." This policy interpretation includes a three-prong test that details how to provide equal opportunity and specifies how to assess compliance.
May 4, 1980	The Department of Education (DOE) begins operation and includes responsibility for the oversight of Title IX through the Office of Civil Rights (OCR).
February 28, 1984	In the *Grove City vs. Bell* decision, the United States Supreme Court removes the application of Title IX to athletics unless this program receives direct federal financial assistance.
March 22, 1988	The Civil Rights Restoration Act states that educational institutions, if they receive any type of federal financial assistance, must comply with Title IX in their athletics programs.
April 2, 1990	DOE publishes the Title IX Investigative Manual, which replaces the Interim Title IX Intercollegiate Athletics Manual, which had been distributed on July 28, 1980.
February 26, 1992	In the *Franklin vs. Gwinnett County Public Schools* decision, the United States Supreme Court rules that if a defendant intentionally avoids complying with Title IX, a plaintiff filing a lawsuit based on Title IX may receive punitive damages.
July 26, 1993	The NCAA publishes its first Gender Equity Study. It documents that women • Comprise 35% of varsity athletes • Receive 30% of athletic grant-in-aid dollars • Are allocated 17% of recruiting dollars • Receive 23% of operating budget dollars • Have access to 37% of participation opportunities on teams
January 16, 1996	OCR issues a Letter of Clarification that restates, but does not change, the requirements that institutions may choose any of three approaches to demonstrate effective accommodation of the participation needs of the underrepresented sex.
October 1, 1996	The Equity in Athletics Disclosure Act (EADA), which was passed by Congress in 1994, goes into effect. EADA requires each institution receiving federal financial assistance to annually report specific information about all intercollegiate athletics programs.

TABLE 6.7 (*continued*)

Date	Legislation, Court Decisions, Letters of Clarification, and other Significant Actions
July 23, 1998	OCR issues a Letter of Clarification that describes the meaning of "substantially equal" relative to providing financial aid to male and female athletes.
February 26, 2003	The Commission on Opportunities in Athletics, appointed by the Secretary of Education in 2002, recommends weakening the application of Title IX to athletics. Due to a minority report and public criticism of the recommendations, DOE makes no revisions in the regulations of Title IX relative to athletics.
July 11, 2003	OCR issues a Letter of Clarification reaffirming the regulations and policies of Title IX.
March 18, 2005	OCR issues a Letter of Clarification that permits colleges to determine through an e-mail survey whether the interests and needs in participation opportunities for the underrepresented sex are being met.
September 17, 2008	OCR issues a Letter of Clarification to provide guidance to ensure that male and female students are provided equal opportunities to participate in intercollegiate athletics programs.

Sources: Compiled by the author from government documents available at http://www.ed.gov/about/offices/list/ocr/publications.html; http://www.ed.gov/finaid/prof/resources/athletics/eada.html; http://www.ncaa.org/gender_equity/resource_materials/AuditMaterial/Investigator's_Manual.pdf; http://www.law.cornell.edu/supct/html/historics/USSC_CR_0503_0060_ZO.html; http://www.fhwa.dot.gov/environment/ejustice/facts/restoration_act.htm; http://www.oyez.org/cases/1980-1989/1983/1983_82_792/; http://www.ed.gov/about/offices/list/ocr/docs/t9interp.html;

As these two figures illustrate, at every intercollegiate level except NCAA IAAA without football, there are thousands more males than females participating in intercollegiate athletics. Since the institutions in the FBS of the NCAA are most frequently reported in the media, additional data are provided by gender for these institutions in Figure 6.6.

When institutions offer males more than 100 more competitive opportunities than females, it may be due to the large number of athletes playing on football teams. Others argue that there are more male athletes because females are not as interested as males in playing intercollegiate sports; not as many females are skillful enough to play intercollegiate sports; more male athletes are willing to participate on teams even though their playing time is limited, while females are not; and male athletes should be the primary beneficiaries of the revenues earned by males in football and basketball. Another perspective is that athletic directors and other decision makers continue to

TABLE 6.8
Females in Intercollegiate Athletics in NCAA Institutions

Year	Average Number of Sports for Females	Female Head Coaches of Women's Teams	Female Head Administrators of Women's Programs
1972	not available	Over 90%	Over 90%
1978	5.61	58.2%	not available
1982	6.59	52.4%	not available
1986	7.15	50.6%	15.2%
1990	7.24	47.3%	15.9%
1992	7.09	48.3%	16.8%
1996	7.53	47.7%	18.5%
2000	8.14	45.6%	17.8%
2004	8.32	44.1%	18.5%
2006	8.45	42.4%	18.6%
2008	8.65	42.8%	21.3%

Source: Acosta, V. R., and L. J. Carpenter, Women in Intercollegiate Sport. A Longitudinal, National Study Thirty One Year Update, 2008. (Used by permission; full report is available at: www.acostacarpenter.org)

Figure 6.3
Number of Men's and Women's Sports in the Eleven Conferences in the NCAA Football Bowl Subdivision

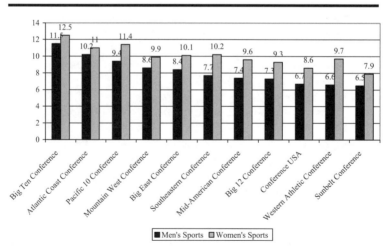

Source: Data compiled from United States Office of Postsecondary Education, Equity in Athletics Data Analysis Cutting Tool, 2006. Available at http://ope.ed.gov/athletics/

TABLE 6.9
Member Institutions in the Conferences in the Football Bowl Subdivision

Atlantic Coast Conference
- Boston College
- Clemson University
- Duke University
- Florida State University
- Georgia Institute of Technology
- North Carolina State University
- University of Maryland
- University of Miami
- University of North Carolina at Chapel Hill
- University of Virginia
- Virginia Polytechnic Institute and State University
- Wake Forest University

Big Ten Conference
- Michigan State University
- Northwestern University
- Ohio State University
- Pennsylvania State University
- Purdue University
- University of Illinois
- University of Indiana
- University of Iowa
- University of Michigan
- University of Minnesota
- University of Wisconsin

Conference USA
- East Carolina University
- Marshall University
- Rice University
- Southern Methodist University
- Tulane University
- University of Alabama at Birmingham
- University of Central Florida
- University of Houston
- University of Memphis
- University of Southern Mississippi
- University of Texas at El Paso
- University of Tulsa

Big East Conference
- DePaul University
- Georgetown University
- Marquette University
- Providence College

- Rutgers University
- Seton Hall University
- St. John's University
- Syracuse University
- University of Cincinnati
- University of Connecticut
- University of Louisville
- University of Notre Dame
- University of Pittsburgh
- University of South Florida
- Villanova University
- West Virginia University

Big 12 Conference
- Baylor University
- Iowa State University
- Kansas State University
- Oklahoma State University
- Texas A & M University
- Texas Tech University
- University of Colorado
- University of Kansas
- University of Missouri
- University of Nebraska
- University of Oklahoma
- University of Texas

Mid-American Conference
- Ball State University
- Bowling Green State University
- Central Michigan University
- Eastern Michigan University
- Kent State University
- Miami University
- Northern Illinois University
- Ohio University
- Temple University
- University of Akron
- University of Buffalo
- University of Toledo
- Western Michigan University

Mountain West Conference
- Air Force Academy
- Brigham Young University
- Colorado State University

(continued)

TABLE 6.9 *(continued)*

Mountain West Conference (Cont.)	
• San Diego State University	• University of South Alabama
• Texas Christian University	• University of Western Kentucky
• University of Nevada at Las Vegas	**Southeastern Conference**
• University of New Mexico	• Auburn University
• University of Utah	• Louisiana State University
• University of Wyoming	• Mississippi State University
	• University of Alabama
Pacific 10 Conference	• University of Arkansas
• Arizona State University	• University of Florida
• Oregon State University	• University of Georgia
• Stanford University	• University of Kentucky
• University of Arizona	• University of Mississippi
• University of California at Berkeley	• University of South Carolina
• University of California at Los Angeles	• University of Tennessee
• University of Oregon	• Vanderbilt University
• University of Southern California	
• University of Washington	**Western Athletic Conference**
• Washington State University	• Boise State University
	• Fresno State University
Sunbelt Conference	• Louisiana Tech University
• Arkansas State University	• New Mexico State University
• Florida Atlantic University	• San Jose State University
• Florida International University	• University of Hawaii
• Middle Tennessee State University	• University of Idaho
• Troy University	• University of Nevada
• University of Arkansas at Little Rock	• Utah State University
• University of Denver	
• University of Louisiana at Lafayette	**Independents in Football**
• University of Louisiana at Monroe	• United States Naval Academy
• University of New Orleans	• United States Military Academy
• University of North Texas	• University of Notre Dame

Source: Author.

resist providing sport opportunities for females despite the federal requirement for equitable educational opportunities.

Another controversial issue facing intercollegiate athletics is the amount of financial support provided to men's and women's athletics. Title IX requires equal opportunity not only in participation opportunities, but also relative to grants-in-aid and program areas such as recruiting, travel, and coaching. To examine this issue, data were compiled and analyzed from institutional reports submitted to comply with the Equity in Athletics Disclosure Act. While over 50 percent of college undergraduate students are females, Figure 6.7 shows that in 2006 females received 44.8 percent of the funding for grants-in-aid,

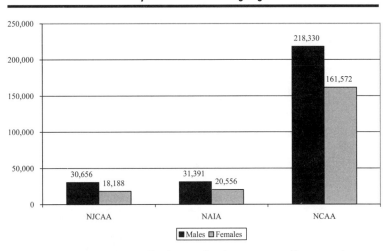

Figure 6.4
Number of Athletes by Gender and Governing Organization in 2006

Source: Data compiled from United States Office of Postsecondary Education, Equity in Athletics Data Analysis Cutting Tool, 2006. Available at http://ope.ed.gov/athletics/

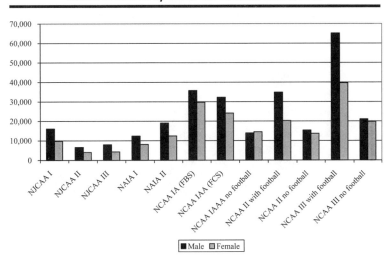

Figure 6.5
Number of Athletes by Gender and Divisional Level in 2006

Source: Data compiled from United States Office of Postsecondary Education, Equity in Athletics Data Analysis Cutting Tool, 2006. Available at http://ope.ed.gov/athletics/

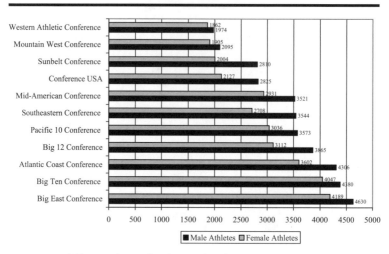

Figure 6.6
Total Number of Male and Female Athletes in Conferences in the NCAA Football Bowl Subdivision

Source: Data compiled from United States Office of Postsecondary Education, Equity in Athletics Data Analysis Cutting Tool, 2006. Available at http://ope.ed.gov/athletics/

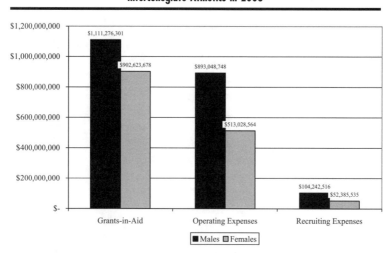

Figure 6.7
Comparison of Financial Support for Males and Females in Intercollegiate Athletics in 2006

Source: Data compiled from United States Office of Postsecondary Education, Equity in Athletics Data Analysis Cutting Tool, 2006. Available at http://ope.ed.gov/athletics/

36.5 percent of the support for operating expenses, and 33.4 percent of the funds for recruiting. One approach to determining if institutions are complying with Title IX is if one gender would accept the financial support and sport opportunities provided to the other gender, then it is likely that equity exists.

Most institutions playing in the NCAA FBS operate their programs as commercial businesses. Some critics allege that this makes these programs ancillary to higher education, even though the NCAA states that maintaining intercollegiate athletics as an integral part of an institution's educational mission is a fundamental purpose. As illustrated comparatively in Figures 6.8 and 6.9, the most media-hyped teams in football and men's basketball in the 11 conferences in the FBS play in stadiums and arenas that were built and expanded to maximize their revenue-producing potential.

These teams are engaged in an athletics "arms race" of trying to keep up with nationally ranked teams, and especially

Figure 6.8
Average Football Stadium Capacities in Conferences in the
NCAA Football Bowl Subdivision

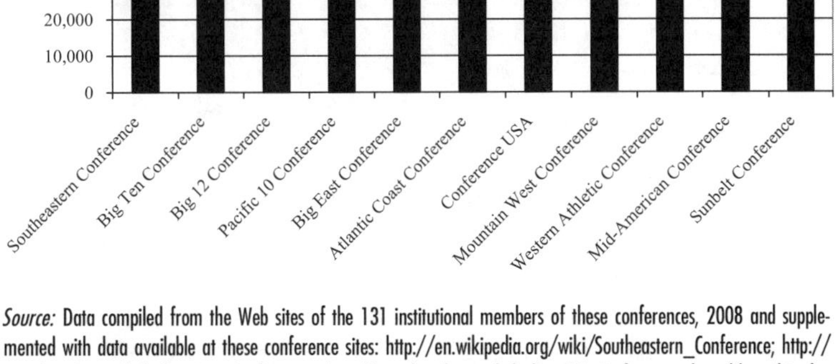

Source: Data compiled from the Web sites of the 131 institutional members of these conferences, 2008 and supplemented with data available at these conference sites: http://en.wikipedia.org/wiki/Southeastern_Conference; http://en.wikipedia.org/wiki/Big_Ten_Conference; http://en.wikipedia.org/wiki/Big_12_Conference; http://en.wikipedia.org/wiki/Pacific-10_Conference; http://en.wikipedia.org/wiki/Big_East_Conference; http://en.wikipedia.org/wiki/Atlantic_Coast_Conference; http://en.wikipedia.org/wiki/Conference_USA; http://en.wikipedia.org/wiki/Mountain_West_Conference; http://en.wikipedia.org/wiki/Western_Athletic_Conference; http://en.wikipedia.org/wiki/Mid-American_Conference; http://en.wikipedia.org/wiki/Sun_Belt_Conference

Figure 6.9
Average Basketball Arena Capacities in Conferences in the
NCAA Football Bowl Subdivision

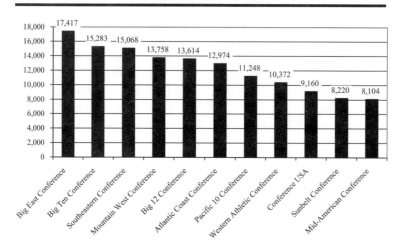

Source: Data compiled from the Web sites of the 131 institutional members of these conferences, 2008 and supplemented with data available at these conference sites: http://en.wikipedia.org/wiki/Big_East_Conference; http://en.wikipedia.org/wiki/Big_Ten_Conference; http://en.wikipedia.org/wiki/Southeastern_Conference; http://en.wikipedia.org/wiki/Mountain_West_Conference; http://en.wikipedia.org/wiki/Big_12_Conference; http://en.wikipedia.org/wiki/Atlantic_Coast_Conference; http://en.wikipedia.org/wiki/Pacific-10_Conference; http://en.wikipedia.org/wiki/Western_Athletic_Conference; http://en.wikipedia.org/wiki/Conference_USA; http://en.wikipedia.org/wiki/Sun_Belt_Conference; http://en.wikipedia.org/wiki/Mid-American_Conference

those in their conferences. Since winning games leads to sold-out stadiums and arenas, coaches must sign the best athletes. Coaches claim that their football and basketball practice facilities, locker rooms, coaches' offices, and training and conditioning facilities must be as good, if not better, than those against whom they compete when recruiting prospective athletes. These same coaches, who are fixated on winning in order to keep their jobs, demand multimillion-dollar salaries, or else they will leave for institutions that will pay them what they believe they deserve for winning games.

In addition to this ever-escalating arms race, many people question whether this money-making push of operating intercollegiate athletic programs in the FBS as commercialized businesses reinforces a belief that colleges have difficulty justifying operating as quasi-farm systems for the National Football League (NFL) and National Basketball Association (NBA).

Further evidence of this business, rather than educational, model is the number of athletes who play these two sports who do not earn college degrees. A lack of seriousness concerning academics characterizes those who view playing football and basketball as a required step in becoming professional athletes.

The overwhelming majority of tickets to intercollegiate football and men's basketball games are sold to nonstudents, further distancing these two sports from the concept that the athletes are students first. In reality, almost every athlete on these teams has been recruited and is receiving financial support dependent on his continued participation on these teams. Since the grants-in-aid received by these athletes are for one year, there is no guarantee of continued receipt of this financial support unless the athlete performs on the field or court, conducts himself in a way consistent with the expectations of the coach, and maintains academic eligibility in conformity with NCAA, conference, and institutional requirements. Some individuals argue that one-year grants overemphasize sport competition over academics and give coaches too much control over the lives of athletes.

These data could indicate that gender equity has not been fully achieved. It also could point to the fact that athletic departments invest more money in football and men's basketball with the idea that it takes money to make money. However, it should be noted, as the NCAA acknowledges, most athletic departments, including their football and men's basketball teams, do not make more money than they spend.

Excerpts from "A Call to Action" from the Knight Commission on Intercollegiate Athletics

Football and men's basketball teams are caught up in an arms race according to the Knight Commission on Intercollegiate Athletics and Myles Brand, president of the NCAA. Thanks to private and institutional support, football stadiums, basketball arenas, and the often palatial training and locker room facilities associated with them are believed to be essential in attracting potential recruits. These recruits are then expected to help win games, which will attract more fans, broadcast rights fees, sponsorship dollars, and private donations. Because of the problems associated with this arms race and the commercialization of intercollegiate athletics, the Knight Commission on Intercollegiate Athletics, as stated in Document 6.4, has concluded that institutions should initiate reforms in their athletic programs in order to reconnect them with the educational mission of higher education.

… The Commission has pursued this work over the years because it believes the nation's best purposes are served when colleges and universities are strong centers of creative, constant renewal, true to their basic academic purposes. In the opening years of the new century, however, those basic purposes are threatened by the imbalance between athletic imperatives and the academy's values. To say it again, the cultural sea change is now complete. Big-time college football and basketball have been thoroughly professionalized and commercialized.

Nevertheless, the Commission believes that the academic enterprise can still redeem itself and its athletic adjunct. It is still possible that all college sports can be reintegrated into the moral and institutional culture of the university. Indeed, in sports other than football and basketball, for the most part that culture still prevails. Athletes can be (and are) honestly recruited. They can be (and are) true "student-athletes," provided with the educational opportunities for which the university exists. The joys of sport can still be honorably celebrated.

But the pressures that have corrupted too many major athletic programs are moving with inexorable force. If current trends continue, more and more campus programs will increasingly mirror the world of professional, market-driven athletics. What that could look like across the board is now present in high-profile form: weakened academic and amateurism standards, millionaire coaches and rampant commercialism, all combined increasingly with deplorable sportsmanship and misconduct.

… It is time to make a larger truth evident to those who want bigger programs, more games, more exposure, and more dollars. It is this: Most Americans believe the nation's colleges and universities are about teaching, learning and research, not about winning and losing. Most pay only passing attention to athletic success or failure. And many big donors pay no attention at all to sports, recognizing in Bart Giamatti's words that it is a "sideshow."

Part of this larger truth requires understanding something that sports-crazed fans are inclined to ignore or denigrate: Loss of academic integrity in the arenas and stadiums of the nation's colleges and universities is far more destructive to their reputations than a dozen losing seasons could ever be.

… In its earlier reports, the Commission defined a "one-plus-three" model, with the "one" - presidential control - directed

toward the "three" - academic integrity, financial integrity, and certification. The Commission here proposes a new "one-plus-three"
model for these new times - with the "one," a Coalition of Presidents, directed toward an agenda of academic reform, de-escalation
of the athletics arms race, and de-emphasis of the commercialization
of intercollegiate athletics. The Coalition of Presidents' goal must be
nothing less than the restoration of athletics as a healthy and integral part of the academic enterprise.

... the Commission makes the following recommendations for
the Coalition's agenda:

Academics. Our key point is that students who participate in athletics deserve the same rights and responsibilities as all other students. Within that broad framework, the Coalition should focus on
the following recommendations:

Athletes should be mainstreamed through the same academic
processes as other students. These specifically include criteria for
admission, academic support services, choice of major, and requirements governing satisfactory progress toward a degree.

Graduation rates must improve. By 2007, teams that do not
graduate at least 50 percent of their players should not be eligible
for conference championships or for postseason play.

Scholarships should be tied to specific athletes until they (or
their entering class) graduate.

The length of playing, practice and postseasons must be reduced
both to afford athletes a realistic opportunity to complete their
degrees and to enhance the quality of their collegiate experiences.

The NBA and the NFL should be encouraged to develop
minor leagues so that athletes not interested in
undergraduate study are provided an alternative route to professional careers.

These recommendations are not new. What is novel is the Commission's insistence that a new and independent structure is needed
to pursue these proposals aggressively.

The Arms Race. The central point with regard to expenditures is the
need to insist that athletic departments' budgets be subject to the
same institutional oversight and direct control as other university
departments. The Coalition should work to:

Reduce expenditures in big-time sports such as football and basketball. This includes a reduction in the total number of scholarships
that may be awarded in Division I-A football.

Ensure that the legitimate and long-overdue need to support
women's athletic programs and comply with Title IX is not used as
an excuse for soaring costs while expenses in big-time sports are
unchecked.

Consider coaches' compensation in the context of the academic institutions that employ them. Coaches' jobs should be primarily to educate young people. Their compensation should be brought into line with prevailing norms across the institution.

Require that agreements for coaches' outside income be negotiated with institutions, not individual coaches. Outside income should be apportioned in the context of an overriding reality: Advertisers are buying the institution's reputation no less than the coaches'.

Revise the plan for distribution of revenue from the NCAA contract with CBS for broadcasting rights to the Division I men's basketball championship. No such revenue should be distributed based on commercial values such as winning and losing. Instead, the revenue distribution plan should reflect values centered on improving academic performance, enhancing athletes' collegiate experiences, and achieving gender equity.

Again, the recommendations put forth here have been heard before. The Coalition offers a chance to make progress on them at long last.

Commercialization. The fundamental issue is easy to state: Colleges and universities must take control of athletics programs back from television and other corporate interests. In this regard, the Coalition should:

Insist that institutions alone should determine when games are played, how they are broadcast, and which companies are permitted to use their athletics contests as advertising vehicles.

Encourage institutions to reconsider all sports-related commercial contracts against the backdrop of traditional academic values.

Work to minimize commercial intrusions in arenas and stadiums so as to maintain institutional control of campus identity.

Prohibit athletes from being exploited as advertising vehicles. Uniforms and other apparel should not bear corporate trademarks or the logos of manufacturers or game sponsors. Other athletic equipment should bear only the manufacturer's normal label or trademark.

Support federal legislation to ban legal gambling on college sports in the state of Nevada and encourage college presidents to address illegal gambling on their campuses.

The Commission is not naïve. It understands that its recommendations governing expenditures and commercialization may well be difficult to accept, even among academics and members of the public deeply disturbed by reports of academic misconduct in athletics programs. The reality is that many severe critics of intercollegiate athletics accept at face value the arguments about the financial exigencies of college sports. In the face of these arguments, they conclude that little can be done to rein in the arms race or to curb the rampant excesses of the market.

Nothing could be further from the truth. The athletics arms race continues only on the strength of the widespread belief that nothing can be done about it. Expenditures roar out of control only because administrators have become more concerned with financing what is in place than rethinking what they are doing. And the market is able to invade the academy both because it is eager to do so and because overloaded administrators rarely take the time to think about the consequences. The Coalition of Presidents can rethink the operational dynamics of intercollegiate athletics, prescribe what needs to be done, and help define the consequences of continuing business as usual....

Source: Knight Commission on Intercollegiate Athletics, *A Call to Action: Reconnecting College Sports and Higher Education*, pp. 22–23; 26–29, 2001. (Used by permission)

Race and Ethnicity

Another ethical issue facing intercollegiate athletics as well as professional sports is whether equity and fairness have been achieved or if discriminatory practices based on race and ethnicity persist. Table 6.10 provides information about past practices in several sports to document the historical exclusion experienced by African Americans in the United States.

While most overt racism has been eliminated from sports by law or societal changes, it is important to determine if progress has been made by African Americans and other minorities in gaining access to competitive opportunities in colleges and on professional teams. The number of athletes is one way to illustrate this, as shown in Table 6.11, which provides data for colleges by gender and ethnicity. According to the 2000 U. S. Census, 12.1 percent of the population is African American, so the number of African American athletes for both genders is higher than would be expected based on the population. The low participation numbers for Hispanics and Latinos does not reflect their 12.5 percent of the population in the 2000 U.S. Census.

With so much emphasis placed on recruiting the best athletes in football and men's basketball to help increase revenues through winning, many coaches, athletic directors, and institutions are accused of placing more emphasis on winning games than on students earning a degree. In the decades since

TABLE 6.10

Examples in Several Sports of Discrimination against and Effects on African Americans

Date	Discriminatory Treatment	Effect or Implication
Baseball		
1884	Moses Walker, who had played baseball at Oberlin College and the University of Michigan, becomes the first African American to play professional baseball with the Toledo Blue Stockings in the American Association. He experiences racist taunts and abuse throughout his one season in the major leagues.	The American Association joins with the National League in a "gentleman's agreement" that bans African Americans from professional baseball. Due to this ban, African Americans form a series of professional baseball Negro Leagues. At times, African Americans athletes in the Negro Leagues compete against and defeat Caucasian professional players in barnstorming games.
1945	Jackie Robinson signs a professional contract with the Brooklyn Dodgers and plays the season with its minor league affiliate in Montreal.	The "gentleman's agreement" ends when Robinson plays for the Brooklyn Dodgers beginning on April 15, 1947. Robinson is subjected to racist taunting and abuse including death threats, but he does not retaliate in order to open the door to MLB to other African Americans. Not until 1967 does the final MLB team, the Boston Red Sox, play African American players.
Basketball		
1923–1949	The New York Renaissance (Rens) dominates basketball among African American teams, but due to segregation, this team is seldom allowed to compete against Caucasian teams.	In 1939, the Rens are permitted to play in the National Basketball League's World Professional Basketball Tournament, which the Rens win. Robert Douglas, who owns and coaches the Rens to over 2500 victories, is the first African American inducted into the Naismith Memorial Basketball Hall of Fame in 1972.
1925	The American Basketball Association, the first true professional basketball league begins, with African Americans banned from playing.	The Harlem Globetrotters, comprised of African Americans since the team's formation in the 1920s, display outstanding basketball skills as a barnstorming team.
Early 1940s	Several African Americans join teams in the National Basketball League.	African Americans are banned from the new Basketball Association of America when it forms in 1946.
1950	Chuck Cooper with the Boston Celtics, Nat Clifton with the New York Knicks, and Earl Lloyd with the Washington Capitols become the first African Americans to play in the NBA.	During the 2007–2008 season, 76% of the players in the NBA are African Americans.
1966	Bill Russell becomes coach of the Boston Celtics, the first African American in the NBA. He is preceded by John McLendon who is hired in 1961 to coach the Cleveland Pipers in American Basketball League.	During the 2007–2008 season, 40% of the head coaches in the NBA are African Americans.

Cycling

1894 — Founded in 1880, the League of American Wheelmen votes to exclude African Americans with a "white only" clause for membership. This prohibition bans African Americans from most races in the United States.

Despite this ban, African American Marshal Taylor wins several cycling races as an amateur and a professional. Excluded from many cycling races in the United States, however, he competes mostly internationally in the early 1900s.

Football

1919 — Fritz Pollard, after starring at Brown University in 1915–1917 and earning All-American acclaim in 1916, becomes one of the two African American players in the new American Professional Football Association (now NFL) in 1920.

The NFL discriminates against African American players by adhering to a "gentleman's agreement" to exclude them between 1934 and 1946.

1923 — Jack Trice, playing his first game for Iowa State, suffers a broken collarbone, but he continues to play until he is trampled by three University of Minnesota players sending him off the field on a stretcher. Trice dies three days later from internal bleeding.

Although a few colleges permit outstanding African Americans to play on their teams, they often are victims of brutality from racist opponents. The football stadium at Iowa State University is named Jack Trice Stadium.

1946 — Kenny Washington and Woody Strode with the Los Angeles Rams and Marion Motley and Bill Willis with the Cleveland Browns re-integrate the NFL.

The Washington Redskins are the last team to sign African American players in 1962. In 2007, 66% of the NFL players are African Americans.

1951 — During a game, Wilbanks Smith playing for Oklahoma A & M repeatedly attacks Drake's Johnny Bright and then deliberately hits him in the face with his fist breaking Bright's jaw.

This vicious, racist attack is captured on film, with the sequence of photos winning a Pulitzer Prize. The football playing field at Drake University is named Johnny Bright Field.

Late 1800s through 1960s — Typically in inter-regional football games, coaches acquiesce to the demands of Southern segregationists and deny African American players the right to compete by leaving them at home or on the bench. Many Southern teams choose to maintain their exclusionary practices by playing against only teams from the South.

Bigotry persists in the former Southwest Conference and especially the Southeastern Conference (SEC). The University of Georgia and University of Mississippi are the last SEC institutions to integrate their football teams in 1972.

1989 — Art Shell becomes the second African American head coach in the NFL. He is preceded by Fritz Pollard, who in 1921 becomes the first African American head coach in the NFL.

In 2007, 19% of the head coaches in the NFL are African Americans.

(continued)

TABLE 6.10 (*continued*)

Date	Discriminatory Treatment	Effect or Implication
Golf		
1960	Charlie Sifford integrates the Professional Golfers' Association of America (PGA), and in 1967 he wins the Hartford Open, a PGA event.	Charlie Sifford is never permitted to enter The Masters at Augusta National because it excludes African Americans.
1964	Althea Gibson integrates the Ladies Professional Golf Association (LPGA).	Only three African American women have ever played in LPGA events, and none has ever won a LPGA tournament.
1975	Lee Elder becomes the first African American allowed to play in The Masters.	Tiger Woods wins The Masters in 1997.
Tennis		
1948	Reginald Weir becomes the first African American to play in a United States Lawn Tennis Association (USLTA) tournament when he is allowed to enter the National Indoor Tennis Championship.	Most tennis tournaments continue to be held at segregated clubs. African Americans compete in tennis events sponsored by the American Tennis Association (ATA), beginning with the first national championships in 1917.
1950	Althea Gibson, who previously had won ten consecutive ATA singles titles beginning in 1947, is invited to play in the USLTA National Championship.	Althea Gibson wins eleven major titles, including the Wimbledon singles crowns and USLTA singles titles in 1957 and 1958.
Track and field		
1866	Track and field is organized in the United States by segregated athletics clubs, such as the New York City Athletic Club.	Some African Americans compete in this sport in clubs, segregated YMCAs, and on teams at northeastern colleges or in historically black colleges and universities.
1936	Jesse Owens becomes the first American to win four gold medals in a single Olympic Games in Berlin in 1936, thereby shattering Adolf Hitler's claim of the superiority of the Aryan race.	Owens is subjected to segregation, racism, and bigotry while a collegiate athlete and later in his life, even after winning the 100 meters, 200 meters, long jump, and as a member of the 4x100 meter relay team in the Olympic Games.
1948	Alice Coachman sets a new world record the high jump in the London Olympic Games, as she becomes the first African American woman to win a gold medal and the first American woman to win a gold medal in track and field.	Despite growing up in the segregated South, Coachman takes advantage of attending Tuskegee Institute, where she wins national championships in the 50-meter dash, 100-meter dash, 400-meter relay, and high jump.

Source: Author.

TABLE 6.11
College Athletes in NCAA Division I Institutions by Gender and Ethnicity

	Caucasian	African American	Latino	American Indian/ Alaskan Native	Asian	Non-Resident Alien	Other
2006–2007							
Male	64.2%	24.7%	3.8%	0.4%	1.6%	N/A	5.3%
Female	72.1%	15.7%	3.7%	0.4%	2.3%	N/A	5.8%
2005–2006							
Male	61.7%	24.6%	3.6%	0.6%	1.7%	4.6%	3.1%
Female	70.1%	15.1%	3.5%	0.4%	2.2%	5.6%	3.1%
2004–2005							
Male	62.2%	24.8%	3.7%	0.4%	1.7%	4.1%	3.1%
Female	70.5%	15.4%	3.3%	0.4%	2.2%	4.9%	3.3%
2003–2004							
Male	62.3%	24.6%	3.6%	0.4%	1.6%	4.4%	3.2%
Female	70.6%	14.9%	3.3%	0.4%	2.1%	5.0%	3.7%
2002–2003							
Male	62.6%	24.6%	3.3%	0.4%	1.6%	4.1%	3.4%
Female	71.9%	14.8%	2.9%	0.3%	2.0%	4.5%	3.7%
2001–2002							
Male	63.1%	24.3%	3.4%	0.4%	1.5%	3.8%	3.7%
Female	72.1%	14.7%	2.8%	0.4%	1.8%	4.2%	3.9%
2000–2001							
Male	61.6%	24.3%	3.3%	0.4%	1.4%	4.7%	4.4%
Female	70.4%	14.8%	2.6%	0.4%	1.7%	5.4%	4.8%

Source: Lapchick, R., The 2008 Racial and Gender Report Card: College Sport, 2009 (The Institute for Diversity and Ethics in Sport, University of Central Florida, Orlando, Florida, 32816), Available at http://web.bus.ucf.edu/documents/sport/2008_college_sport_rgrc.pdf (Used by permission)

institutions could not discriminate against African Americans in their admission policies, many institutions have recruited an increasing number of African Americans to play on these two sport teams. The percentage of African Americans on football and men's basketball teams in NCAA institutions continues to grow.

Like the NFL and NBA, the percentage of African American intercollegiate players continues to exceed the percentage of the population in the United States. Similarly, there are a small number of African American and other minority head coaches in these two sports. The differences between the number of Caucasian players and coaches in comparison with the number of

Figure 6.10
Percentage of Caucasian and African American Football Coaches and Players in NCAA Conferences in the Football Bowl Subdivision

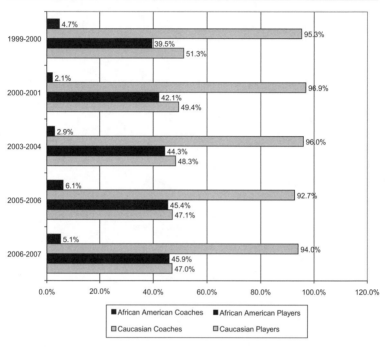

Source: Lapchick, R., The 2008 Racial and Gender Report Card: College Sport, 2009 (The Institute for Diversity and Ethics in Sport, University of Central Florida, Orlando, Florida, 32816), Available at http://web.bus.ucf.edu/documents/sport/2008_college_sport_rgrc.pdf (Used by permission)
*The data for coaches in the last entry are for 2007–2008, rather than 2006–2007.

African American players and coaches are shown in Figure 6.10 for football and Figure 6.11 for basketball. For football, while the number of African American players continues to increase, the number of African American coaches has increased at a slower rate. A wide gap exists between the representation of African Americans as players and coaches. A greater increase is shown for African American coaches in basketball over this time period than for players, although the disparities remain large.

Similar concerns exist relative to the wide disparities between the number of African American players and head coaches in professional football, basketball, and baseball. The continued domination by Caucasian head coaches, owners, presidents, general managers or directors of player personnel,

Figure 6.11
Percentage of Caucasian and African American Basketball Coaches and Players in NCAA Conferences in the Football Bowl Subdivision

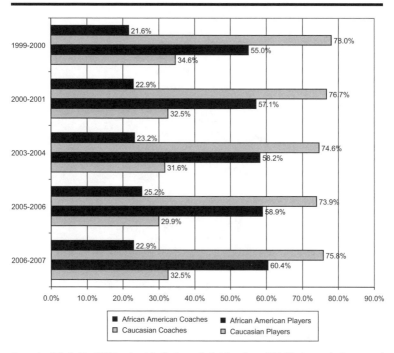

Source: Lapchick, R., The 2008 Racial and Gender Report Card: College Sport, 2009 (The Institute for Diversity and Ethics in Sport, University of Central Florida, Orlando, Florida, 32816), Available at web.bus.ucf.edu/documents/sport/2008_college_sport_rgrc.pdf (Used by permission)

and vice presidents in comparison to African Americans and Latinos in these positions is shown in Figure 6.12.

Olympic Sports

The use of performance-enhancing drugs threatens the integrity of all sports, and especially at the highest competitive levels. While professional sports have dealt with doping in sports in differing ways over the past few years, there has been a more consolidated effort in international sport. As an outgrowth of worldwide conferences that included representatives of governments, the Olympic Movement at all levels, the International Paralympic Committee, athletes, and numerous other stakeholders, the

Figure 6.12
Percentage of Players, Coaches, Owners, and Top Management in Three Professional Leagues

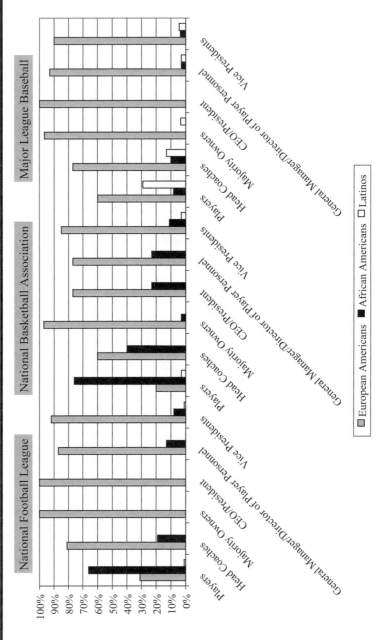

Source: Lapchick, R. E., Racial and Gender Report Card for National Football League, National Basketball Association, Major League Baseball, 2008. (The Institute for Diversity and Ethics in Sport, University of Central Florida, Orlando, Florida, 32816) Available at http://www.bus.ucf.edu/sport/public/downloads/2008_NFL_RGRC_PR.pdf, http://www.bus.ucf.edu/sport/public/downloads/2008_NBA_RGRC_PR.pdf, and http://www.bus.ucf.edu/sport/public/downloads/2008_MLB_RGRC_PR.pdf (Used by permission)

World Anti-Doping Code was developed, adopted, and then implemented on January 1, 2004. One purpose of this code is to protect each athlete's right to participate in doping-free sport while promoting health, fairness, and equality. A second purpose is to coordinate anti-doping programs internationally through detection, deterrence, and prevention of doping. This code harmonizes anti-doping policies, rules, and regulations, and helps implement international standards regarding testing, laboratories, therapeutic use exemptions, and prohibited substances and methods. The code provides universal criteria for determining whether a substance should be banned from use based on whether it enhances performance, poses a threat to athlete health, and violates the spirit of sport. The code also provides standards for sanctions, while permitting flexibility depending on the circumstances.

Not everyone agrees, however, that the use of performance-enhancing drugs should be banned. Table 6.12 lists several positives and negatives about this ethical issue.

The Olympic Games have grown into the most acclaimed international sports festival in the world. The growth in the number of nations sending athletes (from only 14 in the first

TABLE 6.12
Pros and Cons of Using Performance-Enhancing Drugs in Sports

Use of Performance-Enhancing Drugs	Use of Performance-Enhancing Drugs
1. Enhances physical health and well-being	1. Breaks the law when they are obtained illegally
2. Builds strength, muscle mass, and endurance	2. Gives unfair advantages (i.e., which is cheating)
3. Improves athletic performance and recovery	3. Results in harmful physical side effects
4. Has been developed through medical advances and should be treated no differently than technological, training, or other pharmacological enhancements	4. Violates medical opinion that these drugs should be used only by prescription for legitimate medical reasons
5. Excites fans who demand superior performances	5. Causes dependency on the muscular development, increased endurance, or other benefits of using these drugs
6. Levels the playing field when they are made available to all athletes	6. Makes sports impure or artificial, with competitions based on chemicals not on the limits of natural human potential
7. Replaces declining levels of testosterone	7. Costs large sums of money, which could be wasteful or associated with crime
8. Redirects money from wasteful drug testing to more productive sport enhancements to benefit athletes	8. Results in financial and personal losses if an athlete fails a drug test

Source: Author.

Olympic Games to over 200) provides evidence of their popularity and prestige. Throughout the years, though, there have been several ethical controversies. Strong opposition to athletes receiving money based on their athletic ability was a passion of International Olympic Committee (IOC) presidents Pierre de Coubertin and Avery Brundage. Between 1980 and 2001, IOC president Juan Antonio Samaranch led the Olympic Games into an era that welcomed professional athletes and commercialized the Olympic Games as never before. Wars and aftermaths of wars, boycotts, judging scandals, state-subsidized athletes, and recognition or nonrecognition of nations have also plagued the Olympic Games.

Another issue has been should females be allowed to participate in the Olympic Games, and, if so, in what events? Table 6.13 documents the evolution in competitive opportunities for females.

While sports for female athletes were slowly added to the Olympic Games, sports like figure skating, golf, swimming, and tennis open to females were viewed as more appropriate than other sports for females. Track and field, which was the premier sport for males, was not considered acceptable for females. Due to pressures placed on the all-male IOC and the hosting of an international competition for females in track and field, in the 1928 Amsterdam Olympic Games, five track-and-field events (100 meters; 4x100m relay; 800 meters; discus; and high jump) were opened to female athletes. The 800-meter race, because some believed this distance was too demanding for females to run, was eliminated and not resumed until the 1960 Rome Olympic Games. A longer distance race for females, the 1500 meters, began in the 1972 Munich Olympic Games. The marathon for females was added in the 1984 Los Angeles Olympic Games. The winner, Joan Benoit, won in 2 hours, 24 minutes, and 52 seconds, a time that would have won 13 of the 20 previous men's Olympic marathons.

Specific data about the number of nations, events, and athletes by gender illustrate the spreading internationalism of the Olympic Games, as well as the dramatic expansion in opportunities for female athletes. From zero females in 1896, participation of female athletes grew to 40.7 percent in the 2004 Athens Olympic Games. In the 2006 Turin Winter Olympic Games, 38.3 percent of the athletes were females. However, much of this expansion in opportunities has occurred in recent years due to increases in the number of sports for females as listed in Table 6.13 and events within the summer and winter Olympic Games as shown in Tables 6.14 and 6.15.

TABLE 6.13
Sports for Males and Females in the Olympic Games

Summer Sports	Years for Males	Years for Females
Aquatics	1896-present	1912-present
Archery	1900–1908; 1920; 1972-present	1904–1908; 1972-present
Athletics (track and field)	1896-present	1928-present
Badminton	1992-present	1992-present
Baseball	1992–2008	
Basketball	1936-present	1976-present
Boxing	1904-present	
Canoe/kayak	1936-present	1948-present
Cycling	1896-present	1984-present
Equestrian	1900; 1912-present	Mixed teams open to females
Fencing	1896-present	1924-present
Football (soccer)	1900-present	1996-present
Gymnastics	1896-present	1928-present
Handball	1936; 1972-present	1976-present
Hockey (field)	1908; 1920-present	1980-present
Judo	1964; 1972-present	1992-present
Modern pentathlon	1912-present	2000-present
Rowing	1896-present	1976-present
Sailing	1900; 1920-present (mixed team) 1920-present (males only)	1988-present (females only)
Shooting	1972–1992 (mixed team) 1896-present (males only)	1984-present
Softball		1996–2008
Table tennis	1988-present	1988-present
Taekwondo	2000–present	2000-present
Tennis	1896–1924; 1988–present	1900; 1908–1924; 1988-present
Triathlon	2000-present	2000-present
Volleyball	1964-present	1964-present
Weightlifting	1896; 1904; 1920-present	2000-present
Wrestling	1896; 1904-present	2004-present
Winter Sports	**Years for Males**	**Years for Females**
Biathlon	1924; 1960-present	1992-present
Bobsleigh	1924-present	2002-present
Curling	1924; 1998-present	1998-present
Ice hockey	1920-present	1998-present
Luge	1964-present	1964-present
Skating	1908; 1920-present	1908; 1920-present
Skiing	1924-present	1936-present

Source: Compiled from information available on the International Olympic Committee Web site, 2008. Available at http://www.olympic.org/uk/index_uk.asp.

TABLE 6.14

Participation in the Summer Olympic Games

Olympiad	Year	City	Nations	Events	Males	Females	Athletes
I	1896	Athens, Greece	14	43	241	0	241
II	1900	Paris, France	24	95	975	22	997
III	1904	St. Louis, MO	12	91	645	6	651
IV	1908	London, England	22	110	1,971	37	2,008
V	1912	Stockholm, Sweden	28	102	2,359	48	2,407
VI	1916	Berlin, Germany	canceled	due	to	war	
VII	1920	Antwerp, Belgium	29	154	2,561	65	2,626
VIII	1924	Paris, France	44	126	2,954	135	3,089
IX	1928	Amsterdam, Holland	46	109	2,606	277	2,883
X	1932	Los Angeles, CA	37	117	1,206	126	1,332
XI	1936	Berlin, Germany	49	129	3,632	331	3,963
XII	1940	Tokyo, Japan	canceled	due	to	war	
XIII	1944	London, England	canceled	due	to	war	
XIV	1948	London, England	59	136	3,714	390	4,104
XV	1952	Helsinki, Finland	69	149	4,436	519	4,955
XVI	1956	Melbourne, Australia	72	145	2,938	376	3,314
XVII	1960	Rome, Italy	83	150	4,727	611	5,338
XVIII	1964	Tokyo, Japan	93	163	4,473	678	5,151
XIX	1968	Mexico City, Mexico	112	172	4,735	781	5,516
XX	1972	Munich, Germany	121	195	6,075	1,059	7,134
XXI	1976	Montreal, Canada	92	198	4,824	1,260	6,084
XXII	1980	Moscow, USSR	80	203	4,064	1,115	5,179
XXIII	1984	Los Angeles, CA	140	221	5,263	1,566	6,829
XXIV	1988	Seoul, Korea	159	237	6,197	2,194	8,391
XXV	1992	Barcelona, Spain	169	257	6,652	2,704	9,356
XXVI	1996	Atlanta, GA	197	271	6,806	3,512	10,318
XXVII	2000	Sydney, Australia	199	300	6,582	4,069	10,651
XXVIII	2004	Athens, Greece	201	301	6,296	4,329	10,625
XXIX	2008	Beijing, China	204	302			10,500

Source: Information compiled from information available on the International Olympic Committee Web site, 2008. Available at http://www.olympic.org/uk/index_uk.asp.

TABLE 6.15
Participation in the Winter Olympic Games

Olympiad	Year	City	Nations	Events	Males	Females	Athletes
I	1924	Chamonix, France	16	16	247	11	258
II	1928	St. Moritz, Switzerland	25	14	438	26	464
III	1932	Lake Placid, NY	17	14	231	21	252
IV	1936	Garmisch-Parkenkirchen, Germany	28	17	566	80	646
V	1948	St. Moritz, Switzerland	28	22	592	77	669
VI	1952	Oslo, Norway	30	22	585	109	694
VII	1956	Cortina d'Ampezzo, Italy	32	24	687	134	821
VIII	1960	Squaw Valley, CA	30	27	521	144	665
IX	1964	Innsbruck, Austria	36	34	892	199	1,091
X	1968	Grenoble, France	37	35	947	211	1,158
XI	1972	Sapporo, Japan	35	35	801	205	1,006
XII	1976	Innsbruck, Austria	37	37	892	231	1,123
XIII	1980	Lake Placid, NY	37	38	840	232	1,072
XIV	1984	Sarajevo, Yugoslavia	49	39	998	274	1,272
XV	1988	Calgary, Canada	57	46	1,122	301	1,423
XVI	1992	Albertville, France	64	57	1,313	488	1,801
XVII	1994	Lillehammer, Norway	67	61	1,215	522	1,737
XVIII	1998	Nagano, Japan	72	68	1,389	787	2,176
XIX	2002	Salt Lake City, UT	77	78	1,513	886	2,399
XX	2006	Turin, Italy	80	84	1,548	960	2,508

Source: Information compiled from information available on the International Olympic Committee Web site, 2008. Available at http://www.olympic.org/uk/index_uk.asp.

Conclusion

The ethical challenges facing youth sports can be addressed by ensuring that the rights of young athletes are placed foremost. Adults might consider giving the games back to kids so they can have fun, develop sport skills, and learn positive values like respect and honesty along with sportsmanship and teamwork. Instead of national championships for preteen youth, playing multiple sports and positions as they explore their favorites, developing their social and leadership skills, and learning life lessons are more likely to characterize morally sound youth sport programs.

Interscholastic sports are valuable extracurricular experiences that can potentially benefit adolescents. When the emphasis is on further developing sport skills, being a part of a team and striving collectively to reach goals, and learning character lessons about self-discipline, responsibility, and hard work, then interscholastic sports are educational. Playing sports in high school can be a highlight of a young person's life.

Females, by law, can no longer be excluded from sports as they must be provided opportunities to play in sports programs conducted by schools and colleges. Females have demonstrated at the youth through Olympic levels that they are interested in, dedicated to, and capable of achieving at high levels of performance. Many of the discriminatory practices against females have been eliminated, as females have increased their participation levels to 40 percent or higher on most college campuses. Females have made progress toward, but not yet fully achieved, receiving comparable financial support for grants-in-aid and other operational support.

Athletic departments in institutions in the NCAA Football Bowl Subdivision have become commercialized businesses as they seek to maximize their wins and revenues. Attracting and entertaining alumni and other fans require winning, so some coaches and athletes have chosen to behave unethically in order to increase their chances of winning. While many coaches and athletes follow the rules, violations of recruiting and academic rules and regulations occur when there is a one-dimensional pursuit of winning. In order to make intercollegiate athletics more educationally and ethically sound, having athletes earn degrees to prepare for life, rather than a career in professional sports, and keeping winning in perspective in order to rein in the arms race and commercialization in sports seem essential to many.

A regretful time in sports in the United States was characterized by segregation and racism. Thankfully, as integration and civil rights were enforced, most discriminatory practices were eliminated. Some African Americans, however, continue to suffer from fewer opportunities educationally and to serve as coaches and athletics administrators. The moral imperative remains to eliminate prejudice and bias as it negatively affects sports and all those involved.

Performance-enhancing drugs have been used by athletes to gain competitive advantages in the professional sport leagues, Olympic Games, intercollegiate athletics, interscholastic sports, and sometimes even youth sports. Banning performance-enhancing drugs and testing for the use of these drugs are attempts to prevent such cheating. This fight to level the playing field, however, is challenged by the huge rewards associated with being the most successful athletically.

Athletes and all others associated with sport should keep their focus on behaving in morally responsible and ethically appropriate ways. The information and data included in this chapter provide evidence that unethical actions have not yet been fully eliminated, so everyone is asked to be vigilant in helping to make sports ethical.

7

Directory of Organizations

This chapter describes 125 sport and sport-related organizations in the United States and internationally that govern sports for athletes in this country. In the first major group, following the United States Olympic Committee (USOC), the 39 national governing bodies for sports in the summer and winter Olympic Games are described, and the International Sport Federation (ISF) for each is also listed. The names of the sports as identified by the International Olympic Committee (IOC) are used in this alphabetical listing. In addition, six other sport governing bodies recognized by the USOC are included. The second major group is comprised of 24 single-sport organizations, which focus on youth or specific age groups. The third major group contains 15 organizations that offer competitions in several sports, which may or may not be age specific. The fourth major group contains 24 sport-related organizations that contribute to the experiences of athletes. The fifth major group describes 16 professional sport organizations.

As appropriate, these organizations have been placed in historical context. The brief descriptions connect the scope of work of these organizations with sport ethics and ethical behavior in sport. The reader may wish to visit the Web sites or use the contact information to obtain additional information or answers to questions.

United States Olympic Committee and the National Governing Body for Each Sport

United States Olympic Committee (USOC)
http://www.usoc.org
E-mail: http://www.usoc.org/contact_us/ngb
Telephone: 719-632-5551

As authorized by the Amateur Sports Act in 1978, the USOC serves as the national Olympic committee for the United States. In partnership with sport governing bodies, the USOC selects and enters athletes for the summer and winter Olympic Games, Pan American Games, and Paralympic Games. As a nonprofit, nongovernmental organization, it depends on sponsorships and donations to provide training centers, financial support, and coaching to elite athletes. It is responsible for overall rule compliance of teams representing the United States in international competitions.

Summer Sports

Aquatics (includes diving, swimming, synchronized swimming, and water polo)

USA Diving
http://www.usadiving.org/05redesign/main/index.html
E-mail: usadiving@usadiving.org

Diving developed as a sport when German and Swedish gymnasts practiced their movements over water, which helps explain the relationship between these two sports. USA Diving selects and prepares teams to represent the United States in the Olympic Games and other international competitions. It promotes and offers a variety of programs for all ages and skills levels, including junior (under 18 years of age), senior (elite), and masters (over 21 years who no longer compete) divers.

ISF: International Swimming Federation (FINA) www.fina.org

USA Swimming
http://www.usaswimming.org/usasweb/DesktopDefault.aspx
E-mail: comments@usaswimming.org
Telephone: 719-866-4578

USA Swimming is committed to three core objectives: build a base by encouraging young people to discover swimming as an activity they can enjoy for their entire life; promote the sport so more people support and participate in swimming; and achieve and maintain competitive success. USA Swimming offers camps and clinics and selects the open water, short course, and junior and national teams for the Olympic Games and other international competitions.

ISF: International Swimming Federation (FINA) www.fina. org

USA Synchronized Swimming

http://www.usasynchro.org
E-mail: webmaster@usasynchro.org
Telephone: 317-237-5700

Perhaps because of Esther Williams, who was a freestyle swimming champion and popularized water ballet through performances in the San Francisco World's Fair Aquacade in 1940, the following year the Amateur Athletic Union offered the first competitive duet and team events in synchronized swimming. Since 1979, USA Synchronized Swimming has promoted this sport for females beginning in clubs through national teams. Individuals, duets, or teams combine incredible water skills and breath control with strength, endurance, flexibility, grace, and artistry from gymnastics, with elaborate moves precisely timed to music and the other swimmers.

ISF: International Swimming Federation (FINA) www.fina. org

USA Water Polo

http://www.usawaterpolo.org/Home.aspx
E-mail: http://www.usawaterpolo.org/InsideUSAWaterPolo/Staff.aspx
Telephone: 714-500-5445

USA Water Polo seeks to grow this fast-paced team game that emphasizes swimming, passing, and scoring throughout the United States and win gold medals in Olympic, World Championship, and Pan-American Games. U.S. leagues provide a low-cost, entry-level membership for water polo clubs, while Masters Water Polo encourages and promotes participation in lifelong fitness and competitive water polo.

ISF: International Swimming Federation (FINA) www.fina. org

Archery
USA Archery
http://www.usarchery.org
E-mail: info@usarchery.org

USA Archery seeks to develop the interest and abilities of individuals of all ages in archery with the goal of producing Olympic, Pan-American, and world champions. USA Archery's junior program for individuals from ages 8 to 18 includes club activities and tournaments for beginners through world competitions. Its junior programs emphasize character development as well as skill development.

ISF: International Archery Federation (FITA) http://www.archery.org

Athletics
USA Track and Field (USATF)
http://www.usatf.org
E-mail: membership@usatf.org
Telephone: 317-261-0500

USATF traces its organizational history to the late nineteenth century athletic clubs that offered track and field competitions. Today, USATF fosters sustained competitive excellence, interest, and participation in track and field, long-distance running, and race walking. USATF begins with running programs at the grassroots level, sanctions over 4,000 events annually, and selects the national teams that compete in the Olympic Games and other international competitions. The USATF has around 100,000 members and 2,500 affiliated local clubs.

ISF: International Association of Athletics Federations (IAAF) www.iaaf.org

Badminton
USA Badminton
http://www.usabadminton.org
E-mail: usab@usabadminton.org

Since it began as the American Badminton Association in 1936, USA Badminton has promoted the game and prepared players for national competitions. Badminton became an Olympic sport in 1992. USA Badminton encourages recreational players to compete through clubs and a grassroots national championship for nonelite players. In addition to players developing their talents and performing to their highest levels, the stated goal is for players at all levels to enhance the quality of their lives.

ISF: Badminton World Federation (BWF) http://www.internationalbadminton.org

Baseball
USA Baseball
http://web.usabaseball.com/index.jsp
E-mail: info@usabaseball.com

USA Baseball governs more than 12,000,000 amateur players and between 1992 and 2008 chose and prepared the Olympic team. Among the baseball teams it selects for international competitions are 14 and under, 16 and under, 18 and under, collegiate or national, and the women's national team. In 2006, for the first time USA Baseball included the first professional players in the World Baseball Classic.

ISF: International Baseball Federation (ISAF) http://www.ibaf.org

Basketball
USA Basketball
http://www.usabasketball.com
E-mail: fanmail@usabasketball.com

USA Basketball, which has 15 member organizations, selects and prepares teams for international competitions sponsored by the International Basketball Federation (IBF). It began in 1974 as the Amateur Basketball Association of the United States of America, but changed to USA Basketball after the IBF opened international competitions to professional players. USA Basketball sponsors Hoop Summit, a game featuring top senior high school boys competing against a team of the world's top 19 years or younger players; a Youth Development Festival for selected high school sophomore and junior boys and girls; and USA Basketball Select Teams, which participate in international tournaments while helping players gain valuable foreign experience and cultural exposure.

ISF: International Basketball Federation (FIBA) http://www.fiba.com

Boxing
USA Boxing
http://usaboxing.org
E-mail: http://usaboxing.org/contact_us/ngb
Telephone: 719-866-2300

USA Boxing promotes amateur, Olympic-style boxing, which is limited to four two-minute rounds. While there are 11 weight classes in the Olympic Games, the Junior Olympic program is based on age and weight categories. Since 1993, USA Boxing has allowed females to box against females in sanctioned competition. USA Boxing sponsors national and international competitions and clinics and training camps for athletes and coaches.

ISF: International Boxing Association (AIBA) http://www.aiba.org

Canoe/kayak
USA Canoe/Kayak (USACK)
http://canoekayak.teamusa.org
E-mail: http://canoekayak.teamusa.org/contact_us/ngb
Telephone: 719-632-5551

USACK promotes flatwater sprint and whitewater slalom and selects elite athletes for Olympic and international competitions. In addition to promoting canoe and kayak racing, it sanctions recreational paddling sports including marathon, freestyle (rodeo), wildwater, polo, canoe sailing, outrigger, and dragon boat events.

ISF: International Canoe Federation (ICF) http://www.canoeicf.com

Cycling
USA Cycling
http://www.usacycling.org
E-mail: http://cycling.teamusa.org/contact_us/ngb
Telephone: 719-866-4581

Track cycling traces its history in the United States back to the late 1800s. USA Cycling promotes several types of cycling and selects teams for the Olympic Games and other international competitions. USA Cycling sanctions over 2,500 local, regional, and national events including road, track (on a velodrome, which is a steeply banked oval track), mountain (such as cross country, slalom, and downhill), cyclo-cross, and BMX (bicycle motocross for racing and freestyle with 20-inch wheel cycles).

ISF: International Cycling Union (UCI) http://www.uci.ch/Templates/UCI/UCI5/layout.asp?MenuID=MTYxNw

Equestrian
US Equestrian Federation (USEF)
http://www.usef.org
E-mail: webmaster@usef.org

The Association of American Horse Shows, which was organized in 1917, unified men and women from all regions of the country with the purpose of clean competition and fair play in the show ring. Its successor, USEF, advances the level of horsemanship beginning at the junior level, ensures the well-being of horses, and pursues excellence in the Olympic Games and other international competitions. In its mission statement, the USEF emphasizes the encouragement of sportsmanship and protection of horses from abuse.

ISF: International Equestrian Federation (FEI) http://www.fei.org/Pages/Default.aspx

Fencing
USA Fencing (USFA)
http://www.usfencing.org/usfa
E-mail: info@USFencing.org

In 1891, the Amateur Fencers League of America was established to promote this sport. Its successor, USFA, works with local clubs and colleges to offer amateur competitions for juniors, collegians, and veterans. The sport of fencing includes three weapons: foil, a light-weight sword often used to train for duels; épée, a freestyle dueling sword; and saber, a slashing cavalry sword. USFA selects and prepares elite fencers for international competitions including the Olympic Games.

ISF: International Fencing Federation (FIE) http://www.fie.ch

Football
USA Soccer
http://ussoccer.com
E-mail: http://soccer.teamusa.org/contact_us/ngb
Telephone: 312-808-1300

USA Soccer, which was originally founded in 1913 as the United States Football Association, seeks to make soccer a preeminent sport in the United States by developing it at recreational through the Olympics and World Cup levels. It works with and through USA Youth Soccer, the American Youth Soccer Association, SAY Soccer, U.S. Club Soccer, United States Adult Soccer Association, its development academy, and the professional soccer leagues in integrating player participation and development. USA Soccer selects the men's and women's national teams, and the youth national teams in the under 17 and under 20 categories for both genders for the Olympic Games and World Cup.

ISF: Federation of Association Football (FIFA) http://www.fifa.com

Gymnastics

USA Gymnastics

http://www.usa-gymnastics.org

E-mail: http://gymnastics.teamusa.org/contact_us/ngb

Telephone: 317-237-5050

USA Gymnastics selects and prepares teams to represent the United States in the Olympic Games and World Championships. It also develops men's and women's artistic gymnastics, rhythmic gymnastics, trampoline and tumbling, and acrobatic gymnastics at the grassroots through national levels. Over 90,000 athletes engage in competitive programs, while 20,000 others are professional, instructor, and club members. Through local clubs, YMCA or YWCAs, or parks and recreation programs, USA Gymnastics teaches gymnasts flexibility, strength, grace, discipline, control, coordination, goal orientation, confidence, creativity, leadership, the importance of maintaining a healthy body, and positive self-esteem.

ISF: International Gymnastics Federation (FIG) http://fig.sportcentric.org

Handball

USA Team Handball

http://www.usateamhandball.org

E-mail: info@USAteamhandball.org

This team sport, which is most popular in European nations, has seven players (one of which is a goalkeeper) who pass or bounce a ball into the opponent's goal, which is similar to, but smaller than, a soccer goal. Because this game is infrequently played in this country, USA Team Handball recruits intercollegiate athletes in baseball, football, soccer, softball, triathlon, volleyball, and water polo. USA Team Handball selects the teams to represent the United States in international competitions including the Olympic Games.

ISF: International Handball Federation (IHF) http://www.ihf.info/front_content.php?idcat=57

Hockey

USA Field Hockey

http://www.usfieldhockey.com

E-mail: information@usafieldhockey.com

Possibly because field hockey was introduced into the United States by a woman, played in many women's colleges, and the United States Field Hockey Association in 1922 was organized by women, this sport has been played almost exclusively by females in this country. USA Field Hockey has 17,000 members and supports programs including high school camps, the National Hockey Festival, partner camps, championships for club hockey, grassroots development programs, futures program, and high-performance training centers. USA Field Hockey selects the national teams for international competition including the Olympic Games.

ISF: International Hockey Federation (FIH) http://www.worldhockey.org

Judo
USA Judo
http://www.usjudo.org
E-mail: http://judo.teamusa.org/contact_us/ngb
Telephone: 719-866-4730

The martial art of judo involves throwing and grappling on the ground, including pins, arm locks, and control holds. Strict rules govern competition and ensure safety, making it open to individuals of all ages and skill levels, with separate weight divisions for men, women, boys, and girls. In addition to developing body control, balance, and reflexive action, judo teaches self-discipline, self-confidence, concentration, and respect for others and self. USA Judo oversees instructional programs and competitive opportunities for juniors, seniors, Team USA, and Paralympic athletes.

ISF: International Judo Federation (IJF) http://www.ijf.org

Modern pentathlon
USA Pentathlon
http://pentathlon.teamusa.org
E-mail: http://pentathlon.teamusa.org/contact_us/ngb

The founder of the modern Olympic Games, Baron Pierre de Coubertin, initiated this event in 1912 because he believed that it would test a man's (and since 2000 a woman's) moral qualities as well as physical resources and skills. The pentathlon consists of five events: pistol shooting by firing a 10-meter air pistol 20 times at 20 stationary targets; fencing through one-touch bouts against every other competitor using épée swords;

swimming in a free-style race over 200 meters; riding or equestrian show jumping, while riding a randomly assigned horse, jump over 12 hurdles (15 jumps) over a course length of 350 to 450 meters; cross-country running through a 3,000 meter race on uneven terrain, all completed on one grueling day. USA Pentathlon selects the men's and women's teams that represent the United States in the Olympic Games.

ISF: International Modern Pentathlon Union (UIPM) http://www.pentathlon.org

Rowing
US Rowing
http://www.usrowing.org/index.aspx
E-mail: http://www.usrowing.org/contactus/index.aspx
Telephone: 1-800-314-4ROW

Organized rowing traces its history to the National Association for Amateur Oarsmen founded in 1872 for men. US Rowing promotes lifelong participation in rowing by offering youth, junior, scholastic, collegiate, adaptive, and masters educational programs and competitions. US Rowing selects the men's and women's (since 1976) national teams that compete in the Olympic Games and other international competitions. Rowers use either two oars (sculls) or one oar (sweeps). The events include single sculls, double sculls, and quadruple sculls, coxless pair, coxless four, and eight with coxswain, who faces the direction the boat is traveling, steers it, and coordinates the power and rhythm of the rowers.

ISF: International Federation of Rowing Associations (FISA) http://www.worldrowing.com

Sailing
US Sailing
http://www.ussailing.org
E-mail: info@ussailing.org
Telephone: 401-683-0800

Sailing traces its origin to 1897 when the North American Yacht Racing Union was organized to promote yacht racing and to unify the rules. US Sailing promotes getting started in sailing through learning symposiums and sailing festivals. It offers 18 national championships in fleet, match, and team racing in skiff, dinghy, windsurfer, keelboat, and multihull boats, and selects sailors for the Olympic and Paralympic Games. It also provides educational programs for powerboat and power cruising. US

Sailing annually presents a National Sportsmanship Award for exemplifying the spirit of sportsmanship in sailing.

ISF: International Sailing Federation (ISAF) http://www.sailing.org

Shooting
USA Shooting
http://www.usashooting.com
E-mail: http://shooting.teamusa.org/contact_us/ngb
Telephone: 719-866-4670

USA Shooting manages shooting development programs, sanctions events at local, state, regional, and national levels, and prepares shooters to win medals at the Olympic Games. The shooting disciplines include pistol, rifle, and shotgun (skeet, trap, and double trap).

ISF: International Shooting Sport Federation (ISSF) http://www.issf-sports.org

Softball
Amateur Softball Association (ASA)
http://www.asasoftball.com
E-mail: webmaster@softball.org
Telephone: 405-424-5266

Begun in 1933, ASA oversees softball from grassroots programs through national teams that compete internationally. The ASA youth program includes over 80,000 teams with 1,300,000 players and 300,000 coaches. ASA conducts over 90 championships in slow pitch, modified pitch, and fast pitch for over 30,000 players of all ages. One of its objectives is to promote the spirit of sportsmanship and principles of ethical behavior in softball.
ISF: International Softball Federation (ISF) http://www.internationalsoftball.com

Table tennis
USA Table Tennis (USATT)
http://www.usatt.org/index.shtml
E-mail: usatt@usatt.org

USATT is comprised of over 8,000 members who play table tennis in over 240 clubs and offers 300 annual tournaments. USATT oversees the Olympic and cadet, junior, and national teams that compete internationally.

ISF: International Table Tennis Federation (ITTF) http://www.ittf.com

Taekwondo
USA Taekwondo
http://www.usa-taekwondo.us
E-mail: http://usa-taekwondo.us/contact_us/ngb
Telephone: 719-632-5551

Taekwondo, a Korean martial art that emphasizes fighting with the fists and feet, seeks to enhance life through the development of mind and body. USA Taekwondo seeks to develop world-class athletes for the achievement of sustained competitive excellence. It also works through an athlete development process beginning with junior programs leading to national teams in four categories: base programming, developmental, high-performance, and world-class. Taekwondo competitions typically consist of 16 weight classes, 8 for men and 8 for women, except in the Olympics where these classes are limited to half this number.
ISF: World Taekwondo Federation (WTF) http://www.wtf.org/#

Tennis
United States Tennis Association (USTA)
http://www.usta.com
E-mail: memberservices@usta.com
Telephone: 914-696-7000

The USTA, since its establishment initially for men in 1881, has been dedicated to the growth of tennis, which today ranges from Quick Start Tennis for youth, to championships for players of all ages, to the U.S. Open for professionals. USTA player development programs for juniors emphasize learning a sport that can be enjoyed throughout life, achieving fitness, and enhancing social and emotional skills. The USTA has over 700,000 members and 7,000 organizational members. The USTA oversees professional tour events and selects teams for the Davis Cup (for men), Fed Cup (for women), Olympic Games, and Paralympic Games.
ISF: International Tennis Federation (ITF) http://www.itftennis.com

Triathlon
USA Triathlon (USAT)
http://www.usatriathlon.org
E-mail: http://usatriathlon.org/contact_us/ngb
Telephone: 719-597-9090

USA Triathlon sanctions over 2,000 local to high-profile events for its 110,000 members and seeks to create interest and participation through camps, clinics, races, and educational opportunities. USA Triathlon selects and prepares teams to represent the United States in the Olympic Games and other international competitions. Triathletes compete in this endurance event over varying distances in swimming, cycling, and running.

ISF: International Triathlon Union (ITU) http://www.triathlon.org/?call=TVRFMg==&fed=MTEz&keep=sh

Volleyball
USA Volleyball (USAV)
http://www.usavolleyball.org
E-mail: postmaster@usav.org

After being developed at a YMCA in 1895 and spread internationally through the YMCA, in 1928 the United States Volleyball Association was formed and sponsored its first tournament. USAV continues this work as it seeks competitive success and sport growth and enhancement for players of all ages through a game that offers team cooperation and spirit. Volleyball clubs provide learning and competitive opportunities, and the USAV sponsors championships for youth and juniors, indoor and beach programs for adults, and indoor and beach national teams, and three disabled national teams.

ISF: International Volleyball Federation (FIVB) http://www.fivb.org

Weightlifting
USA Weightlifting (USAW)
http://weightlifting.teamusa.org
E-mail: usaw@usaweightlifting.org

USAW conducts Olympic weightlifting programs and selects male and female competitors for the Olympic Games and other international events. In addition to local weightlifting competitions sponsored by affiliates at the school age, junior, senior, and master levels, USAW sanctions five national championships in all age groups.

ISF: International Weightlifting Federation (IWF) http://www.iwf.net

Wrestling
USA Wrestling
http://www.themat.com
E-mail: webmaster@usawrestling.org
Telephone: 719-598-8181

In 1968, the United States Wrestling Federation was established, with leadership provided by college coaches. The successor, USA Wrestling, promotes wrestling through developmental programs and camps, educational programs for coaches, and competitive opportunities up through the Olympic Games. USA Wrestling selects members of the national teams in bantam, midget, novice, schoolboy/girl, cadet, junior, and women's divisions, senior national teams in men's and women's freestyle and men's Greco-Roman, and Olympic teams in men's and women's freestyle and men's Greco-Roman.

ISF: International Federation of Associated Wrestling Styles (FILA) http://www.fila-wrestling.com

Winter Sports

Biathlon
USA Biathlon (USBA)
http://www.usbiathlon.org
E-mail: USBiathlon@aol.com

USBA works with local clubs to develop interest, promote participation, and prepare elite performers. Biathlon, which combines the physical demands of cross-country skiing with the precision of rifle marksmanship, while relatively unknown in the United States, is the top-rated winter sport on European television. Since 1980, USBA has promoted this sport, which has grown to 18 clubs nationally and over 1,000 members, who compete in the winter and summer (with running rather than skiing) versions of the sport.

ISF: International Biathlon Union (IBF) http://www.biathlonworld.com/eng/news/default.htm

Bobsleigh
USA Bobsled and Skeleton Federation (USBSF)
http://www.usbsf.com
E-mail: info@usbsf.com

USBSF promotes and develops athletes for the Olympic Games in bobsledding and skeleton. Bobsled competitions consist of four-man (a pilot, a brakeman, and two pushers), two-man (without the two pushers), and two-woman teams making timed runs down a narrow, twisting, banked, and iced track on gravity-powered sleds. Skeleton (sometimes called tobogganing) is an individual sport in which the athlete lies in a prone, head-first position and drives the sled as fast as possible down an iced track. Given the virtual obscurity of these winter sports in the United States, many of the athletes on the national teams are recruited from other sports. Athletes from sports requiring strength and speed can become pushers in bobsled. Since every athlete must be a pusher and driver in skeleton, athletes with great foot speed with a natural talent for driving are recruited.

ISF: International Bobsleigh and Tobogganing Federation (FIBT) http://www.fibt.com

Curling
USA Curling (USAC)
http://dev.topfloormedia.com/usca
E-mail: info@usacurl.org

Teams of four players compete in curling by taking turns sliding a heavy, polished granite stone down the ice, while two of the players using brooms seek to help position the stone closest to the target. Women in 1948 and men in 1958 organized national associations for curling. USAC has over 13,000 curlers and 135 clubs and seeks to grow the sport of curling and win medals in world championships, the Olympic Games, and the Paralympic Games.

ISF: World Curling Federation (WCF) http://www.world curling.org

Ice hockey
USA Hockey
http://www.usahockey.com
E-mail: usah@usahockey.org

USA Hockey has over 585,000 ice and inline hockey players, coaches, officials, and volunteers and supports programs at the grassroots through elite levels. It offers programs for youth, junior, disabled, college, and adult players. USA Hockey selects and manages national team development, national sled (disabled), and men's and women's national teams.

ISF: International Ice Hockey Federation (IIHF) http://www.iihf.com

Luge
USA Luge
http://www.usaluge.org/index.php
E-mail: http://luge.teamusa.org/contact_us/ngb
Telephone: 800-USA-LUGE

In luge, one or two athletes lay supine and feet first on a sled while speeding along an iced track with banked curves and walled-in straights. USA Luge recruits, prepares, and equips the national luge team for international and Olympic competition and promotes the growth of this sport. USA Luge is committed to athletic excellence with the highest degree of sportsmanship, honor, and dedication.

ISF: International Luge Federation (FIL) http://www.fil-luge.org

Skating
USA Figure Skating
http://www.usfsa.org
E-mail: info@usfigureskating.org

Local ice skating clubs sponsored competitions beginning in the mid-nineteenth century, long before the United States Figure Skating Association was established in 1921. USA Figure Skating begins with instructional programs in basic skills and offers competitive levels for figure skaters as they increase their proficiency. Elite skaters compete in regional, sectional, and national championships, and international events like the Olympic Games and World Championships.

ISF: International Skating Union (ISU) http://www.isu.org

USA Speed Skating
http://www.usspeedskating.org
E-mail: http://speedskating.teamusa.org/contact_us/ngb
Telephone: 719-632-5551

USA Speed Skating is responsible for providing grassroots programs, such as development camps, as well as the selection and preparation of Olympic speed skaters in short-track and long-track events. It works with local clubs in sponsoring competitions.

ISF: International Skating Union (ISU) http://www.isu.org

Skiing
United States Ski and Snowboard Association (USSA)
http://www.ussa.org
E-mail: http://www.ussa.org/magnoliaPublic/ussa/en/contact.html
Telephone: 435-649-9090

USSA supports athletic excellence in Olympic skiing and snow-boarding and national development systems emphasizing its core values of loyalty, integrity, respect, perseverance, and accountability. The USSA provides education, development, and competitive opportunities in over 4,000 sanctioned events for young athletes through a network of 400 clubs.

ISF: International Ski Federation (FIS) http://www.fis-ski.com

Non-Olympic Sports with National Governing Bodies

Bowling
United States Bowling Congress (USBC)
http://www.bowl.com
E-mail: Associationservices@bowl.com
Telephone: 1-800-514-BOWL

The USBC was formed in 2005 from a merger of the American Bowling Congress, Women's International Bowling Congress, Young American Bowling Alliance, and USA Bowling to serve over 2,600,000 amateur adult and youth bowlers. The USBC states as its values: credibility, dedication, excellence, heritage, inclusiveness, integrity, philanthropy, and sportsmanship. While USBC selects Team USA for international events, bowling is not an Olympic sport.

ISF: International Bowling Federation (FIQ) http://www.fiq.org

Karate
USA Karate
http://www.usa-karate.net
E-mail: http://karate.teamusa.org/contact_us/ngb
Telephone: 719-632-5551

Karate is an attacking martial art that uses kicks, punches, and strikes, as well as blocking movements. Classes begin for students as early as four years old and continue throughout life. This martial art can help improve concentration, coordination, self-esteem, self-discipline, self-confidence, and leadership skills while reducing stress, improving grades, and controlling weight. Through its educational programs and competitions, USA Karate emphasizes helping participants develop healthier minds and bodies as they work to improve personal defense skills. Karate is not an Olympic sport, nor does USA Karate select national teams.

ISF: World Karate Federation (WKF) http://www.karate-world.org

Racquetball

USA Racquetball

http://www.usra.org

E-mail: http://racquetball.teamusa.org/contact_us/ngb

Telephone: 719-635-5396

This organization traces its founding to 1969, which was the year after this sport was developed. While not recognized as an Olympic sport, racquetball is played by all ages and skill levels at local tournaments through international competitions for the top players. Intercollegiate programs operate in over 60 institutions at club and varsity levels.

ISF: International Racquetball Federation (IRF) http://www.internationalracquetball.com

Roller Sports

USA Roller Sports (USARS)

http://www.usarollersports.org

E-mail: http://rollersports.teamusa.org/contact_us/ngb

Telephone: 402-483-7551

USARS creates, enhances, and conducts programs and competitions in roller sports, including inline speed skating, roller figure skating, inline hockey, hardball hockey, and fitness and recreational activities for beginners through elite athletes. Although USARS has not yet been successful in its bid to become an Olympic sport, several athletes who have won medals in the Olympic Games began their athletic careers in one of the USARS sports.

ISF: International Roller Sports Federation (FIRS) http://www.rollersports.org/default.asp?load=726041252A001

Squash

US Squash

http://www.us-squash.org

E-mail: http://squash.teamusa.org/contact_us/ngb

Telephone: 212-268-4090

US Squash traces its roots to 1904 when the United States Squash Racquets Association was founded and became a pioneer in promoting competition for females as well as males. While squash is not an Olympic sport, this organization conducts tournaments and governs the over 11,000 members who play this racket and ball game in over 1,000 facilities nationwide. US Squash stresses enriching the experiences, health, and well-being of players.

ISF: World Squash Federation (WSF) http://www.worldsquash.org.uk

Water Skiing
USA Water Ski
http://www.usawaterski.org
E-mail: usawaterski@usawaterski.org

USA Water Ski promotes the growth and development of recreational water skiing, as well as organizes and governs competitive water skiing, working with over 600 local water ski clubs for individuals of all ages. Nearly 80 percent of its members compete in annual tournaments featuring slalom and trick events, although this sport is not in the Olympic Games. The first championships were held in 1939 when USA Water Ski was founded.

ISF: International Water Ski Federation (IWSF) http://www.iwsf.com

Single-Sport Organizations

American Canoeing Association (ACA)
http://www.americancanoe.org
E-mail: aca@americancanoe.org

Founded in 1880, the ACA promotes canoeing, kayaking, and rafting as wholesome lifetime recreational activities through event sponsorship, safety education, instructor certification, waterway stewardship, water trails, paddler's rights and protection, and public information campaigns. Approximately 50,000 members participate in nearly 1,400 ACA-sanctioned paddle sport events annually. ACA emphasizes education, recreation, and stewardship.

American Youth Football (AYF)
http://www.americanyouthfootball.com
E-mail: Jlaufer@americanyouthfootball.com

AYF, established in 1996, promotes the development of youth through football and cheerleading with over 450,000 members internationally. It promotes good sportsmanship, teamwork, high moral and physical standards, and the importance of scholarship and academic achievement among players and cheerleaders. A hallmark of AYF is its commitment to giving back to the community, such as providing financial grants to leagues, working with corporate sponsors to provide shoes for players and fields for teams, and sending inner-city kids to football camp.

American Youth Soccer Organization (AYSO)
http://soccer.org/home.aspx
E-mail: http://soccer.org/About/Contact/Default.htm
Telephone: 800-872-2976

Begun in 1964 for boys, with girls included since 1971, the AYSO has grown to involve over 650,000 players. AYSO is committed to ensuring that every child plays at least half of every game and the teams are balanced to help create evenly matched games. Over 250,000 volunteers benefit from educational programs provided by AYSO based on following written soccer rules and also the spirit of the game.

Babe Ruth League
http://www.baberuthleague.org
E-mail: info@baberuthleague.org
Telephone: 800-880-3142

The Babe Ruth League was founded in 1951 to provide wholesome baseball for boys 13 to 15. Its leagues for players from the ages of 5 to 12, added in 1982, in 2000 became Cal Ripken Baseball. In 1984, Babe Ruth Softball for girls ages 5 to 18 was added. Over 1,000,000 players compete annually in all of these programs. The goal of the Babe Ruth League is to use baseball and softball to teach mental and physical development, respect for the rules of the game, and the basic ideals of sportsmanship and fair play.

Biddy Basketball International
http://www.biddybb.com
E-mail: biddybb@cox.net

Serving over 20,000 boys and girls in 300 leagues, this developmental program adapts the size of the ball, height of the goal, and distance for shooting free throws, so players can learn basketball skills as they grow and mature. Athletes can compete in district, regional, and international championships.

Boston Athletic Association (BAA)
http://www.bostonmarathon.org
E-mail: info@baa.org

The BAA was established in 1887 to manage athletic events, especially running events, and promote a healthy lifestyle through sports. BAA conducted its first road race, which became known as the Boston Marathon, in 1897. This marathon, the world's oldest annual marathon, is regarded by most as the most prestigious in the world. The BAA remains as an active running club for recreational through elite runners and sponsors races for all ages.

Golden Gloves
http://www.goldengloves.com/welcome
E-mail: executivedirector@goldengloves.com

Since its first boxing tournament in 1923, Golden Gloves has sponsored local and regional tournaments to promote amateur boxing. Golden Gloves, working through its 30 franchises, has helped develop the majority of this nation's competitors in the Olympic Games and Pan-American Games. Golden Gloves is dedicated to enhancing the physical and emotional well-being and social development of young athletes and developing individual athletic skills, a work ethic, discipline, sportsmanship, self-respect, pride, and personal character.

Little League Baseball
http://www.littleleague.org/Little_League_Online.htm
E-mail: http://www.littleleague.org/Learn_More/About_Our_
Organization/contacts.htm
Telephone: 570-326-1921

Little League Baseball began in 1939 to provide organized baseball competitions for 9- to 12-year-old boys and has expanded nationally and internationally. In 1974, Little League Baseball began to allow girls to play on baseball teams. Today, there are baseball leagues for boys and girls ages 5 to 18 and for girls in softball. The goals of Little League Baseball are to develop citizenship, discipline, teamwork, fair play, sportsmanship, physical well-being, character, courage, and loyalty.

Mid-America Youth Basketball (MAYB)
http://www.mayb.com/index1.shtml
E-mail: mayb@mayb.com

Since 1993, MAYB has organized youth basketball tournaments, growing to over 170 summer, spring, and winter tournaments in 22 states involving 3,700 teams. Boys and teams in grades 3 through 12 are encouraged to join teams so they can practice their skills and enjoy participating in basketball.

National Softball Association (NSA)
http://www.playnsa.com
E-mail: nsahdqtrs@aol.com

The NSA focuses on meeting the needs of parks and recreation departments and softball complex owners to serve youth through adult players. It provides state, regional, and world tournaments to NSA-sanctioned leagues through qualifying tournaments.

NFL Youth Football
http://www.nflyouthfootball.com/site12.aspx
E-mail: NFL@active.com

In addition to its sponsorship of the Punt, Pass, and Kick program for boys and girls and NFL Flag that emphasizes teamwork and sportsmanship, NFL Youth Football sponsored a Junior Development Program for 12- to 14-year-old boys and a High School Development Program. These instructional programs teach offensive and defensive skills with an emphasis on the development of life skills and character. It also offers a Girls Flag Football Leadership Program with funding for equipment for every high school that initiates a girls' flag football program.

PONY Baseball/Softball
http://www.pony.org/home/default.asp
E-mail: info@pony.org

PONY, an acronym for Protect Our Nation's Youth, began in 1951 to sponsor baseball for boys to help them grow into healthier and happier adults. PONY Baseball, with over 450,000 players in 4,000 leagues, is organized into teams in two-year age increments: Shetland League (ages 5 and 6), Pinto League (ages 7 and 8), Mustang League (ages 9 and 10), Bronco League (ages 11 and 12), PONY League (ages 13 and 14), Colt League (ages 15 and 16), and Palomino League (ages 17 through 19). Even though girls may play in the baseball leagues, PONY began offering fast-pitch and slow-pitch softball in 1976. The age divisions for the softball leagues, which have more that 4,000 teams, are similar to those for baseball.

Pop Warner Little Scholars (PWLS)
http://www.popwarner.com
E-mail: webupdate@popwarner.com

This program, named for the legendary Hall of Fame coach Glenn "Pop" Warner, began in 1929 to provide youth football programs, which have expanded to 41 states and internationally. The program was renamed Pop Warner Little Scholars in 1959 in recognition of its emphasis on academic achievement in an atmosphere conducive to developing sound character while having fun. In the 1970s, cheerleading was officially recognized as a competitive program and majorettes, pom squads, dancing boots, and pep squads also have been added. Pop Warner programs serve over 400,000 boys and girls ages 5 to 16.

Soccer Association for Youth (SAY)
http://www.saysoccer.org/pages
E-mail: sayusa@saysoccer.org
Telephone: 800-233-7291

SAY provides recreational grassroots soccer programs for children, emphasizing low fees, balanced teams, and equal participation. SAY, through its 20,000 coaches and 1,900 volunteer administrators, serves over 100,000 players. It provides low-cost and free materials to coaches.

T-Ball USA Association
http://www.teeballusa.org
E-mail: info@retailport.com

The T-Ball USA Association seeks to develop the game of T-ball by offering a variety of programs and services as it serves over 2,200,000 participants. It works with local, regional, and national youth baseball leagues like Little League Baseball, and community groups such as parks and recreation departments and Boys and Girls Clubs.

United States Adult Soccer Association (USASA)
http://www.usasa.com
E-mail: communications@usasa.com
Telephone: 317-541-8564

USASA, along with 54 national state organizations, offers a player development program and stages national competitions for club teams, veterans' teams, and coed teams. It emphasizes fun, fair play, and friendship.

United States Golf Association (USGA)
http://www.usga.org/home/index.html
E-mail: membership@usga.org
Telephone: 908-234-2300

USGA sponsors programs for players of all ages and annually conducts 13 national championships, including the U.S. Open, U.S. Women's Open, U.S. Senior Open, and national amateur championships and state team championships. Since its founding in 1894, USGA has worked with the Royal and Ancient Golf Club in St. Andrews, Scotland, to write and interpret the rules of golf, which include playing by the letter, spirit, and etiquette of the game.

United States Masters Swimming (USMS)
http://www.usms.org
E-mail: http://www.usms.org/admin/email.php?To=Tracy+Grilli&a=info
Telephone: 800-550-SWIM

USMS is dedicated to its over 40,000 swimmers, ages 18 to over 100. It provides organized workouts, competitions, clinics, and workshops for noncompetitive and competitive swimmers who seek to improve their fitness through swimming.

USA Football
http://www.usafootball.com
E-mail: http://www.usafootball.com/contact_us
Telephone: 877-5-FOOTBALL

This organization, which does not sponsor leagues or teams, hosts educational programs for coaches, officials, and administrators and skill development programs for young players. It annually awards over $500,000 in equipment grants to youth leagues and high schools, and another $500,000 to subsidize background checks for volunteer youth coaches. Funding comes from an endowment established by the NFL and NFL Players Association in 2002.

US Club Soccer
http://www.usclubsoccer.org
E-mail: leaguesupport@usclubsoccer.org

Since its establishment in 2000, US Club Soccer has grown to over 2,300 members in 48 states. It supports competitive soccer clubs and the development of elite players through planning, marketing, managing, and financing programs. US Club Soccer sponsors events from the Youth World Series at the introductory level through the National Cup.

US Lacrosse
http://www.uslacrosse.org/index.phtml
E-mail: info@uslacrosse.org

In 1998, US Lacrosse unified youth, men's, and women's lacrosse. Youth participation is around 250,000, while there are about 200,000 interscholastic players and 500 college club teams.

US Youth Soccer
http://www.usyouthsoccer.org
E-mail: http://www.usyouthsoccer.org/contactus.asp
Telephone: 800-4SOCCER

Over 600,000 volunteers and administrators and 300,000 coaches enable US Youth Soccer to serve over 3,000,000 youth players ages 5 to 19. Its programs include underserved areas, athletes with physical disabilities, recreational players, competitive athletes, and elite athletes. Every child is guaranteed playing time, with an emphasis on physical, mental, and emotional growth and development, and fun.

Youth Basketball of America (YBOA)
http://www.yboa.org/About.aspx
E-mail: yboahq@yboa.org

YBOA promotes youth basketball worldwide through leagues and hosts three tournaments, an international tournament, and national championships for boys and girls. This organization emphasizes the personal growth and development of youth athletes and encourages teamwork, sportsmanship, and fun through the spirit of basketball.

Youth Football USA (YFUSA)
http://www.yfusa.org
Email: joeb@yfusa.org

YFUSA is comprised of about 300,000 coaches, administrators, and players committed to sportsmanship, safety, and scholarship. This organization works to create safe and healthy participation, assists leaders as they develop the skills of youth, and promotes high moral standards.

Multi-Sport Organizations

Amateur Athletic Union (AAU)
http://aausports.org/default.asp
E-mail: membership@aausports.org
Telephone: 1-8-AAU-4USA

After its establishment in 1888, the AAU led this nation's participation in the Olympic Games by serving as the national sport
federation for several sports. Beginning with swimming and
track and field in 1967, the AAU has conducted the Junior Olympics. Over 16,000 boys and girls representing all 50 states and
several U.S. territories participate at the grassroots level and
advance to this annual multisport national competition. Today,
the AAU through over 60,000 volunteers serves over 500,000 participants through its "Sports for All, Forever" philosophy.

Disabled Sports USA (DS/USA)

http://www.dsusa.org/about-overview.html
E-mail: information@dsusa.org

DS/USA offers nationwide sport rehabilitation programs in
winter skiing, water sports, summer and winter competitions,
fitness, and special sporting events. These are open to individuals with a permanent disability including visual impairments,
amputations, spinal cord injury, dwarfism, multiple sclerosis,
head injury, cerebral palsy, and other neuromuscular and orthopedic conditions. A goal of DS/USA is to provide individuals
of all ability levels with opportunities to gain confidence and
dignity through participation in sports.

International Olympic Committee (IOC)

http://www.olympic.org/uk/index_uk.asp
E-mail: pressoffice@olympic.org
Telephone: 41-21-621-61-11 (Lausanne, Switzerland)

The IOC has 205 affiliated national Olympic committees and 35
international sport federations. In addition to hosting the largest
multisport international sport festivals in the summer and winter
Olympic Games, the IOC emphasizes fair competition by seeking
to eliminate performance-enhancing drugs.

International Paralympic Committee (IPC)

http://www.paralympic.org/release/Main_Sections_Menu/
index.html
E-mail: info@paralympic.org
Telephone: 49-228-2097-200 (Bonn, Germany)

Olympic-style games for individuals with disabilities began in
1960 and have grown to include over 4,500 athletes from over 140
nations. This global governing body organizes the summer Paralympic Games in 20 sports and winter Paralympic Games in

5 sports, and coordinates world championships and other competitions. By IOC policy, all future host cities for the summer and winter Olympic Games will also host the Paralympic Games.

National Association of Intercollegiate Athletics (NAIA)
http://naia.cstv.com
E-mail: http://naia.cstv.com/member-services/about/staff.htm
Telephone: 816-595-8000

Formed in 1952 by smaller institutions that had previously instituted a basketball tournament, the NAIA (now with nearly 300 members) has grown to include championships in 11 sports for males. In 1980, the NAIA began national championships for females and now offers them in 10 sports. Launched in 2000, the Champions of Character program emphasizes how student-athletes and coaches should model core values of respect, responsibility, integrity, servant leadership, and sportsmanship.

National Collegiate Athletic Association (NCAA)
http://www.ncaa.org/wps/portal
E-mail: pmr@ncaa.org
Telephone: 317-917-6222

The NCAA, which began in 1906, is comprised of three divisions based on enrollment, number of sports, and the awarding of grants-in-aid. (Division I has 331 members; Division II has 291 members; Division III has 445 members.) The NCAA offers national championships in each of these divisions in 19 sports each for males and females. The NCAA recognizes one male and one female athlete who have shown sportsmanship, fairness, civility, honesty, unselfishness, respect, and responsibility as competitors through an annual Sportsmanship Award.

National Federation of State High School Associations (NFHS)
http://www.nfhs.org
E-mail: http://www.nfhs.org/custom/ContactUs
Telephone: 317-972-6900

Since 1920, the NFHS has provided leadership to and supported educationally based interscholastic sports. Over 7,000,000 students (over 54 percent of the students enrolled in high schools) participate in interscholastic sports. The most popular sports for girls are basketball, outdoor track and field, and volleyball, while more boys participate in football, basketball, and outdoor track and field. The other sports are baseball, cross country, gymnastics, field hockey, ice hockey, lacrosse, soccer, softball, swimming and diving, and wrestling. The NFHS encourages communities to invest in youth through supporting interscholastic sports and helping develop their character.

National Intramural-Recreational Sports Association (NIRSA)
http://www.nirsa.org//AM/Template.cfm?Section=
Welcome
E-mail: nirsa@nirsa.org
Telephone: 541-766-8211

NIRSA was established in 1950 and now provides professional development to about 4,000 members, who serve an estimated 5,500,000 students. Through its members, NIRSA fosters quality recreational programs, facilities, and services for diverse populations within colleges and universities.

National Junior College Athletic Association (NJCAA)
http://www.njcaa.org
E-mail: wbaker@njcaa.org
Telephone: 719-590-9788

The NJCAA, which began in 1938, offers national championships in 15 sports for males and in 13 sports for females in its over 430 member institutions. NJCAA promotes intersectional and national competitions for athletes in two-year institutions in ways consistent with the educational missions of member institutions.

National Association of Police Athletic/Activities League (National PAL)
http://www.nationalpal.org
E-mail: copnkid@nationalpal.org
Telephone: 561-745-5535

National PAL provides local chapters with resources and opportunities to organize young athletes for competing in a championship environment in sports like boxing and basketball.

National Senior Games Association (NSGA)
http://www.nsga.com/DesktopDefault.aspx
E-mail: http://www.nsga.com/DesktopDefault.aspx?Params=454b0
4071756536c150001527f00000002aeTelephone: 415-269-3658

NSGA is dedicated to motivating men and women over 50 to lead healthy lives through participating in state through national senior athletic events. The biennial Summer National Senior Games, which began in 1987, include competitions in archery, badminton, basketball, bowling, cycling, golf, horseshoes, race walk, racquetball, road race, shuffleboard, softball, swimming, table tennis, tennis, track and field, triathlon, and volleyball.

Special Olympics
http://www.specialolympics.org/Special+Olympics+Public+Website/default.htm
E-mail: info@specialolympics.org
Telephone: 202-628-3630

Begun as a day camp in 1962 and expanded into the first International Special Olympics Games in 1968, the Special Olympics annually provide educational and competitive experiences for over 2,500,000 individuals with intellectual disabilities in over 180 countries. In local through international competitions in 30 summer and winter sports, the Special Olympics empower individuals to become physically fit, productive, and respected members of society.

United States Association of Blind Athletes (USABA)
http://www.usaba.org/Pages/usabainformation/aboutus.html
E-mail: mlucas@usaba.org
Telephone: 719-630-0422

Since its establishment in 1976, USABA has been committed to enhancing the lives of blind and visually impaired individuals through participation and achievement in sports. USABA conducts sports and recreation programs to help people learn the skills needed to participate in sports and life alongside their sighted peers. USABA enables over 3,000 athletes to compete in cycling, judo, powerlifting, skiing, swimming, track and field, wrestling, five-a-side football, and goalball (a team sport with the objective to throw a ball with embedded bells into the opponent's goal).

USA Deaf Sports Federation (USADSF)
http://www.usdeafsports.org
E-mail: HomeOffice@usdeafsports.org
Telephone: 605-367-5760

Since 1945, when the American Athletic Union of the Deaf was established, sport competitions have been offered to individuals without hearing. USADSF selects athletes for teams in the Deaflympics and other international competitions in badminton, baseball, basketball, bowling, curling, cycling, golf, ice hockey, martial arts, orienteering, shooting, ski and snowboard, soccer, swimming, table tennis, team handball, tennis, track and field, triathlon, volleyball, water polo, and wrestling.

Wheelchair Sports, USA (WSUSA)
http://www.wsusa.org/index.php?option=com_frontpage& Itemid=1
E-mail: http://www.wsusa.org/index.php?option=com_contact& task=view&contact_id=1&Itemid=3
Telephone: 636-614-6784

Since its establishment in 1956 as the National Wheelchair Athletic Association, Wheelchair Sports, USA has focused on providing participation and competitive sport opportunities for athletes with disabilities. It provides programs for juniors, women, and quadriplegics (those with paralysis in upper as well as lower extremities). Wheelchair Sports, USA works with the USOC to ensure that the athletic experiences for athletes with disabilities parallel those of the able-bodied, from novice through elite levels.

Sport-Affiliated Organizations

American College of Sports Medicine (ACSM)
http://www.acsm.org/AM/Template.cfm?Section=Home
E-mail: http://www.acsm.org/_frm/departments/indexnew.asp? area=general
Telephone: 317-637-9200

Founded in 1954, ACSM is dedicated to the integration of research, education, and practical application of sports medicine and exercise science to maintain and enhance physical performance, fitness, health, and quality of life. The over 20,000 regional, national, and international members of ACSM apply knowledge about medicine and exercise science to promote healthier lifestyles for people and excellence in sports, including the diagnosis, treatment, and prevention of sports-related injuries.

Association for Applied Sport Psychology (AASP)
http://appliedsportpsych.org
E-mail: http://appliedsportpsych.org/About/Contact-AASP.html
Telephone: 608-443-2475

Since its founding in 1986, AASP has grown to 1,200 members in 28 countries who provide leadership for the development of theory, research, and applied practice in sport, exercise, and health psychology. AASP members provide professional services to athletes, coaches, teams, parents, and other groups involved in exercise, sport participation, and rehabilitation.

Boys and Girls Clubs
http://www.bgca.org
E-mail: info@bgca.org

Sports often attract youth to local Boys and Girls Clubs, where they can develop their skills, make friends, and have fun. Boys and Girls Clubs are positive places for kids and help instill in them a sense of competence, usefulness, belonging and influence.

Citizenship Through Sports Alliance (CTSA)
http://www.sportsmanship.org
E-mail: tbreidenthal@sportsmanship.org
Telephone: 816-474-7264

A coalition of 12 school, college, Olympic, and professional sport organizations begun in 1997, CTSA promotes values realized through sportsmanship and ethical play in sports. It is dedicated to helping sport participants become better citizens and learn the values necessary to teach and learn respect for self and others.

Institute for International Sport (IIS)
http://www.internationalsport.com/nsd/index.cfm
E-mail: iis102@etal.uri.edu
Telephone: 800-447-9889

Since 1991, IIS has sponsored National Sportsmanship Day (held annually on the first Tuesday in March) to promote thoughtful discussions and activities by athletes, parents, coaches, and administrators about how sports can serve as a positive force in society. As part of National Sportsmanship Day, IIS sponsors All-American Sportsmanship School Awards to honor the elementary, middle, and high school schools and colleges that demonstrate exceptional sportsmanship programs. IIS annually names Sport Ethics Fellows, who develop honorable competition on a local scale and serve as role models for fair play and sportsmanship.

Josephson Institute
http://josephsoninstitute.org/sports
E-mail: http://charactercounts.org/contact.html
Telephone: 310-846-4800

Since 1987, the Josephson Institute has developed and delivered services and materials to increase ethical commitment, competence, and practice in all segments of society. The Josephson Institute's character education program for youth, Character Counts, emphasizes trustworthiness, respect, responsibility, fairness, caring, and citizenship. The Pursuing Victory with Honor program applies these six pillars of character to sport.

National Alliance for Youth Sports (NAYS)
http://www.nays.org
E-mail: nays@nays.org
Telephone: 800-688-KIDS

This organization partners with over 3,000 community-based organizations, including parks and recreation departments, Boys and Girls Clubs, YMCAs, and YWCAs. The NAYS certifies volunteer coaches and administrators of youth sport programs to help them meet its national standards for quality programs for children.

National Association for Athletics Compliance (NAAC)
http://nacda.cstv.com/naacc/nacda-naacc.html
E-mail: jgalaska@nacda.com
Telephone: 440-892-4000

NAAC seeks to foster the highest possible professional and ethical standards in athletics compliance and uphold the ideals of higher education.

National Association for Sport and Physical Education (NASPE)
http://www.aahperd.org/naspe
E-mail: http://www.aahperd.org/aahperd/template.cfm?template=contactus.cfm
Telephone: 800-213-7193

NASPE advocates for teaching values through youth and school sports. In addition to its educational materials and advocacy efforts, NASPE provides the *National Standards for Sport Coaches*, which provide direction for administrators, coaches, athletes, and the public about the skills and knowledge that coaches should possess to ensure optimal sport experiences for youth and adolescents.

National Association of Collegiate Directors of Athletics (NACDA)

http://nacda.cstv.com
E-mail: http://nacda.cstv.com/feedback/nacda-feedback.html
Telephone: 440-892-4000

NACDA provides professional development opportunities and serves as an advocate in addressing the nature, scope, issues, and challenges facing intercollegiate athletics. It seeks to develop a collegial and mutually beneficial relationship among athletic administrators, faculty, and students.

National Athletic Trainers' Association (NATA)

http://www.nata.org
E-mail: membership@nata.org
Telephone: 214-637-6282

The NATA, established in 1950, is comprised of about 30,000 certified athletic trainers who seek to enhance the quality of health care they provide. NATA sets standards for professionalism, education, certification, research, and practice. Its code of ethics is an example of the high standard of professionalism expected of certified athletic trainers who assist athletes of all ages through the prevention, assessment, treatment, and rehabilitation of sports injuries.

National Consortium for Academics and Sports (NCAS)

http://www.ncasports.org/home.htm
E-mail: info@ncasports.org
Telephone: 407-823-4770

NCAS focuses on the educational attainment of students who are also athletes and uses the power and appeal of sport to positively affect social change. Established in 1985, college and university members agree to provide free tuition to former athletes who did not complete their degree requirements if these individuals participate in school outreach and community service programs addressing social issues of America's youth.

National Council of Youth Sports (NCYS)

http://www.ncys.org
E-mail: youthsports@ncys.org
Telephone: 772-781-1452

NCYS works to enhance the experiences of youth in sports through member organizations that serve 44,000,000 children. Local communities emphasize children in youth sports having fun through healthy physical activities and developing self-esteem, fair play, and good citizenship. NCYS sponsors the STRIVE Awards to recognize coaches, administrators, and volunteers at the local level who demonstrate a heartfelt passion, an enthusiastic commitment, and a contagious spirit to help kids succeed in youth sports and show young people that sports potentially can teach respect, initiative, values, and excellence.

National High School Coaches Association (NHSCA)
http://www.nhsca.com
E-mail: nhsca@nhsca.com
Telephone: 610-923-0900

NHSCA is committed to meeting the needs of administrators, coaches, athletes, and parents who make up the athletic community in schools. In addition to offering a coach certification program, it provides information to help coaches attain and maintain the professional expertise to fulfill their responsibility to develop the sports skills and character of young people.

National Recreation and Park Association (NRPA)
http://www.nrpa.org
E-mail: info@nrpa.org
Telephone: 703-858-0784

NRPA advocates for making parks, open spaces, and recreational opportunities available to all to increase their quality of life. Through coalitions and partnerships with allied organizations, NRPA facilitates community initiatives to use parks and recreational activities to enhance people's emotional, social, and physical needs.

National Sports Center for the Disabled
http://www.nscd.org
E-mail: http://www.nscd.org/about/contact.htm
Telephone: 303-293-5711

Courage, strength, and determination are the qualities that describe the individuals served since 1970 by the National Sports Center for the Disabled. Through adaptive and therapeutic recreational activities and over 20 sports, the lives of children and adults with physical or mental challenges are positively impacted on ski slopes, in canoes, on mountain trails, and on golf courses as they learn more about sports and themselves.

National Strength and Conditioning Association (NSCA)
http://www.nsca-lift.org
E-mail: nsca@nsca-lift.org
Telephone: 719-632-6722

Since its establishment in 1978, the NSCA has grown to around 30,000 members in 52 countries. NSCA members disseminate and apply research-based knowledge on strength training and conditioning practices to improve athletic performance and fitness.

North American Society for the Psychology of Sport and Physical Activity (NASPSPA)
http://www.naspspa.org
E-mail: naspspa@hotmail.com

NASPSPA members engage in the scientific study of individuals engaged in sport and physical activity and improve the quality of research and teaching in the psychology of sport, motor development, and motor learning and control.

National Youth Sports Safety Foundation (NYSSF)
http://www.nyssf.org
E-mail: NYSSF@aol.com
Telephone: 617-277-1171

NYSSF promotes the healthy development, safety, and well-being of youth by keeping them physically active and participating in sports for life. Given that over 5,000,000 youth athletes require treatment in hospital emergency rooms because of sports injuries, NYSSF is dedicated to reducing the number and severity of injuries youth sustain in sports and fitness activities by educating health professionals, program administrators, coaches, parents, and athletes.

Positive Coaching Alliance (PCA)
http://www.positivecoach.org/default.aspx
E-mail: pca@positivecoach.org
Telephone: 866-725-0024

PCA seeks to transform youth sports so sports can transform youth. It works with 1,100 youth sport partner organizations, leagues, schools, and cities and has conducted over 6,000 workshops for youth sport coaches, parents, organizational leaders, and athletes. The PCA stresses that youth athletes honor the game by striving to win through a positive, character-building environment while learning life lessons.

United States Anti-Doping Agency (USADA)
http://www.usantidoping.org
E-mail: webmaster@usantidoping.org
Telephone: 719-785-2000

USADA is committed to ensuring clean sport by eliminating doping in sport and preserving the well-being of Olympic and Paralympic sport, the integrity of competition, and ensuring the health of athletes.

World Anti-Doping Agency (WADA)
http://www.wada-ama.org/en
E-mail: info@wada-ama.org
Telephone: 514-904-9232

WADA is committed to fostering doping-free sport throughout the world. In its fight against the use of performance-enhancing drugs, WADA takes a seven-prong approach: worldwide acceptance of the World Anti-Doping Code; identification and detection of doping substances and methods; a coordinated Web-based management system of anti-doping activities and compliance; shared resources to implement doping control and anti-doping education; effective doping prevention strategies and education; informational outreach to athletes; and no-notice out-of-competition testing.

Young Men's Christian Association (YMCA)
http://www.ymca.net
E-mail: fulfillment@ymca.net
Telephone: 800-872-9622

Through over 2,600 local entities, the YMCA seeks to meet the critical social needs of over 21,000,000 children and adults of all ages, races, faiths, backgrounds, abilities, and income levels. Since 1851, the mission of the YMCA has grown to include deepening the values of youth, strengthening family and community bonds, and enhancing the spiritual, mental, and physical well-being of each individual, often through participation in sporting activities.

Young Women's Christian Association (YWCA)
http://www.ywca.org/site/pp.asp?c=djISI6PIKpG&b=284783
E-mail: info@ywca.org
Telephone: 202-467-0801

Established in the United States in 1858, the YWCA advocates for women's rights and civil rights, provides safe places for girls and women, and helps develop strong women leaders. It achieves its mission of eliminating racism and empowering women through job training, career counseling, providing child care, and developing the health and fitness of 2,600,000 members in 300 local associations.

Professional Sport Organizations

Arena Football League (AFL)
http://www.arenafootball.com/HomePage.dbml?DB_OEM_ID=3500
E-mail: http://www.arenafootball.com/CreateTicket.dbml?ATCLID=919439&SPSID=73546&SPID=1563&DB_OEM_ID=3500
Telephone: 212-252-8100

AFL offers indoor, high-scoring football as a cost-effective, total entertainment experience to fans of all ages. Established in 1987, the AFL opened a minor league (afl2) in 2000, averaged over 12,000 fans per game in 2007, and grew to 17 teams in 2008. The top two teams at the end of each season compete in the ArenaBowl.

Association of Tennis Professionals (ATP)
http://www.atptennis.com/1/en/home
E-mail: http://www.atptennis.com/en/aboutatp/contact.asp
Telephone: 904-285-8000

Established in 1972, ATP works to promote the interests of male tennis professionals. Beginning in 1990, it began to organize what is today known as the worldwide ATP Tour.

Association of Volleyball Professionals (AVP)
http://web.avp.com/index.jsp
E-mail: contact@avp.com
Telephone: 310-426-8000

Through AVP, established in 1983, male and female professionals compete on the nation's only pro beach volleyball tour.

Ladies Professional Golf Association (LPGA)
http://www.lpga.com/default_new.aspx
E-mail: feedback@lpga.com
Telephone: 386-274-6200

The LPGA, founded in 1950, includes the LPGA Tour and LPGA Teaching and Club Professionals. A unique feature of the

LPGA is its focus on charity through its tournaments, grassroots junior and women's programs, and affiliation with Susan G. Komen for the Cure (of breast cancer).

Major League Baseball (MLB)
http://mlb.mlb.com/index.jsp
E-mail: http://mlb.mlb.com/mlb/help/contact_us.jsp
Telephone: 212-931-7800

While professional baseball began in 1869, the coming together of the National League and American League in 1903 formed MLB, the highest level of professional play.

Major League Soccer (MLS)
http://web.mlsnet.com/index.jsp
E-mail: feedback@mlsnet.com
Telephone: 212-450-1227

MLS, founded in 1996, is the top-level professional soccer league in the United States, with 14 teams in 2008.

Minor League Baseball (MiLB)
http://web.minorleaguebaseball.com/index.jsp
E-mail: webmaster@minorleaguebaseball.com
Telephone: 866-644-2687

In 1901, the National Association of Professional Baseball Leagues was established for players needing to develop their skills in hopes of advancing into MLB. Minor League Baseball today, with its 19 leagues, operates as an umbrella organization for leagues that have agreements to operate as affiliates of MLB.

National Association for Stock Car Auto Racing (NASCAR)
http://www.nascar.com
E-mail: fanfeedback@nascar.com
Telephone: 866-722-5299

Begun in 1948, NASCAR has grown to sanction over 1,200 races at 100 tracks in more than 30 states, Canada, and Mexico. NASCAR boasts the most brand-loyal fans and status as the number-one spectator sport and the second-rated regular-season televised sport. NASCAR includes the Sprint Cup Series, Nationwide Series, and Craftsman Truck Series.

National Basketball Association (NBA)
http://www.nba.com
E-mail: http://www.nba.com/email_us/contact_us.html
Telephone: 212-407-8000

The NBA was formed in 1946 as the Basketball Association of America and adopted its current name after merging with the National Basketball League in 1949. The top professional league is comprised of 30 teams, including numerous international players.

National Football League (NFL)
http://www.nfl.com
E-mail: http://www.nfl.com/contact-us

The NFL, which began in 1920 as the American Professional Football Association, is comprised of 32 teams at the highest level of competition. The most popular sport in the United States, the NFL's Super Bowl is consistently one of the most watched television events each year.

National Hockey League (NHL)
http://www.nhl.com
E-mail: http://www.nhl.com/ice/feedback.htm

The NHL, formed in 1917 in Montreal, Canada, is the highest level of professional ice hockey with 30 teams in North America. The top two teams compete each year for the Stanley Cup, the oldest professional sports trophy awarded in North America.

National Lacrosse League (NLL)
http://www.nll.com
E-mail: comments@nll.com
Telephone: 212-764-1390

The NLL began play in 1987 and has grown to include 12 teams in North America in 2008. The summer professional indoor league, which is played on turf inside the confines of an ice hockey rink with the glass and rink boards intact, combines the physical play of hockey and the high scoring, fast pace, and playmaking of basketball.

Professional Bowlers Association (PBA)
http://www.pba.com
E-mail: info@pba.com
Telephone: 206-332-9688

The PBA is comprised of over 4,200 male and female professional bowlers throughout the world who compete in 21 official events. Established in 1958, the PBA is the major league of worldwide bowling.

TABLE. 7.1

Examples of and Access Information for Codes of Ethics for Athletes, Fans, Coaches, and Others Involved with Sports

Sport Organization	Type of Code	URL
International Olympic Committee	Code of Ethics	http://multimedia.olympic.org/pdf/en_report_1295.pdf
National Basketball Association	NBA Fan Code of Conduct	http://www.nba.com/news/code_of_conduct_050217.html
National Football League	Fan Code of Conduct	http://www.nfl.com/news/story?id=09000d5d809c28f9&template=without-video&confirm=true
National Youth Sports Coaches Association	Code of Ethics	http://www.nays.org/IntMain.cfm?Cat=3&Page=5
National Association for Sport and Physical	Coaches Code of Conduct	http://www.aahperd.org/naspe/pdf_files/pos_papers/coaches.pdf
National Athletic Trainers' Association	Code of Ethics	http://www.nata.org/codeofethics/code_of_ethics.pdf
National Federation of State High School Associations	Coaches Code of Ethics	http://www.nfhs.org/web/2004/01/the_coaches_code_of_ethics.aspx
United States Tennis Association	The Code	http://dps.usta.com/usta_master/sitecore_usta/USTA/Document%20Assets/2008/05/29/doc_13_22409.pdf
USA Gymnastics	Code of Ethics	http://gymnastics.teamusa.org/content/index/483

TABLE. 7.2
Code of Ethics for Athletes, Coaches, Parents, and Fans in Sports

As an athlete. . .
1. I will show respect to opponents, officials, coaches, and teammates.
2. I will try my hardest to improve my skills and fitness so that I can be a contributing member of my team.
3. I will praise and positively reinforce the play of my teammates and enjoy having them as teammates.
4. I will play by the rules of the game as well as the spirit of the game.
5. I will take responsibility for my behavior at all times, play fair, and show sportsmanship.
6. I will put forth my best effort, realizing that this determines whether I win or lose.

As a coach, parent, and fan. . .
1. I will be supportive of and positive toward all players and their efforts to do their best.
2. I will model respectful behavior toward officials, coaches, and all athletes and act responsibly at all times.
3. I will keep winning in perspective and always demonstrate sportsmanship.

Source: Author.

Professional Golfers' Association of America (PGA)

http://www.pga.com/home
E-mail: http://www.pga.com/about/feedback
Telephone: 561-624-7672

Established in 1916, the PGA is comprised of 28,000 male and female golf professionals who promote, teach, and manage the game. In 1968, male professional players broke away from the PGA to form their own organization, which is called the PGA Tour.

Women's National Basketball Association (WNBA)

http://www.wnba.com
E-mail: http://www.wnba.com/contact_us/contact_wnba.html

The WNBA, which is financially supported by the NBA, began play in 1997. This 13-team league plays between May and August and mostly in the same arenas as the NBA teams that helped establish the teams.

Women's Tennis Association (WTA)

http://www.sonyericssonwtatour.com
E-mail: http://www.sonyericssonwtatour.com/3/thewtatour/contact
Telephone: 727-895-5000

The WTA traces its heritage to the first women-only professional tennis event in 1970, even though it was not formally established until 1973. It organizes the worldwide WTA Tour for over 2,000 players representing 90 nations.

Many of these organizations have established a code of ethics or conduct for players, coaches, and fans. These codes help set a standard that expects everyone to behave in morally responsible and sportsmanlike ways. Table 7.1 provides several examples. These codes reinforce that one important goal of sport at all levels is that everyone involved will help make sporting experiences as positive and rewarding as possible. Guidance given in Table 7.2 can serve as a model for how to behave ethically in sports.

8

Print and Nonprint Resources

This chapter includes selected and annotated bibliographies of print resources including reference works, books, magazine and journal articles, and nonprint resources of databases, DVDs, videotapes, and Internet sites. For ease in locating information of specific interest, these resources are organized by five topics: sport for all, youth sport, interscholastic sport, intercollegiate sport, and international sport.

Print Resources

Ethical Issues in Sport for All

Reference Works

Ashe, A. R., Jr. 1988. *A Hard Road to Glory: A History of the African-American Athlete* (194 pp.); *A Hard Road to Glory: A History of the African-American Athlete, 1919–1945* (497 pp.); *A Hard Road to Glory: A History of the African-American Athlete since 1946* (571 pp.). New York: Warner Books.

These books tell the historical story of discriminatory treatment of African American athletes as they sought equal opportunities to demonstrate their talents in sports. Written by a former African American tennis champion, these volumes graphically recount the barriers experienced by athletes seeking a level playing field regardless of their race.

Bartlett, R., C. Gratton, and C. Rolf, eds. 2006. *Encyclopedia of International Sports Studies.* London: Routledge, 3 vols., 1520 pp.

This reference work includes entries in sports medicine, sport science, social science of sport, sport engineering, and technology in sport. It includes discussions of psychological and sociological aspects of sports.

Berlow, L. H. 1994. *Sport Ethics: A Reference Handbook.* **Santa Barbara, CA: ABC-CLIO, 204 pp.**

This book examines ethical issues associated with youth sport, intercollegiate athletics, the Olympic Games, and professional sports. Biographical sketches, documents, and organizations are discussed, as well as specific topics like racism, women in sports, and drug abuse.

Cashmore, E. 2000. *Sports Culture: An A–Z Guide.* **New York: Routledge, 482 pp.**

The author presents information about issues, events, organizations, and people and places, each in a social and cultural context.

Christensen, K. A., A. Guttmann, and G. Pfister, eds. 2001. *International Encyclopedia of Women and Sports.* **New York: Macmillan, 3 vols.**

These volumes include detailed information about the history of and current situation in women's sports. They include more than 230 biographies, 170 sports entries, and 75 country profiles; plus, this work examines cultural, social, and ethical issues of women's sports.

Deardorff, D. L., and R. J. Higgs. 2000. *Sports: A Reference Guide and Critical Commentary, 1980–1999.* **Westport, CT: Greenwood Press, 361 pp.**

The authors examine sport as it relates to history, business, law, education, race and ethnicity, gender, literature, philosophy and religion, popular culture, psychology, science and technology, and sociology.

Frank, A. M. 2003. *Sports and Education: A Reference Handbook.* **Santa Barbara, CA: ABC-CLIO, 226 pp.**

This chronology helps the reader learn about sport and significant issues, individuals, and organizations in sport.

Jones, D. G., and E. L. Daley. 1992. *Sports Ethics in America: A Bibliography, 1970–1990.* New York: Greenwood Press, 320 pp.

This comprehensive bibliography provides nearly 2,900 entries listing books, journal articles, magazines, and newspapers published in the United States since 1970. Although the citations are not annotated, they are topically arranged into five categories: general works; teams, players, and coaches; the game, competition, and contestants; sports and society; and reference works.

Levinson, D., and K. Christensen. 1998. *Encyclopedia of World Sport: From Ancient Times to the Present.* New York: Oxford University Press, 488 pp.

This comprehensive volume is filled with detailed information about hundreds of sports and how they are played. It also explores issues in sport as a part of the human experience.

Wiggins, D. K., ed. 2004. *African Americans in Sports.* Armonk, NY: Sharpe Reference, 2 vols.

Numerous authors provide information about African American players, sports, teams, institutions, organizations, and other key personnel. Within the listings are descriptions of cultural themes and social issues that place each entry in historical context.

Books

Coakley, J. 2009. *Sports in Society. Issues and Controversies,* 10th ed. Boston: McGraw-Hill, 704 pp.

This book examines the major issues in the interface between sports and society, including racial and gender equity, violence, deviance, economic issues, social class, the media, politics, and socialization. In this comprehensive book, the author examines many of these issues from an ethical perspective.

Eitzen, D. S. 2006. *Fair and Foul: Beyond the Myths and Paradoxes of Sport.* Lanham, MD: Rowman and Littlefield Publishers, 185 pp.

The author, a sport sociologist, uses a point-counterpoint approach in discussing the role of sport in society. He examines ethical issues such as whether sport unites or divides, is fair or foul, is healthy or destructive, is expressive or controlled, and whether it is myth or reality that sport serves as a pathway to success.

Engh, F. 1999. *Why Johnny Hates Sports: Why Organized Youth Sports Are Failing Our Children and What We Can Do about It.* **Garden City Park, NY: Avery Publishing Group, 208 pp.**

The founder of the National Alliance for Youth Sport writes about the moral and ethical misbehaviors that have led to the dropout of youth from sports. Instead of harming children, youth sports should teach sportsmanship and ensure that youth have fun playing sports.

Feezell, R. M. 2004. *Sport, Play, and Ethical Reflection.* **Urbana: University of Illinois Press, 173 pp.**

After discussing sport's playful nature, the author presents contrasts between sportsmanship and cheating in sports. The case is made that character can be enhanced through sport, but only through respecting the game.

Finley, P. S., and L. L. Finley. 2006. *The Sports Industry's War on Athletes.* **Westport, CT: Praeger, 198 pp.**

The authors expose the big, bad world of sports and the lack of ethical behavior therein. They discuss doping, eating disorders, playing while hurt, cheating, dirty play, violence, recruiting scandals, academic fraud, hazing, racism, and sexism.

Lumpkin, A., S. K. Stoll, and J. M. Beller. 2003. *Sport Ethics: Applications for Fair Play,* **3rd ed. Boston: McGraw-Hill, 274 pp.**

This book focuses on applying basic ethical principles to many of the problems facing all levels of sport. The authors discuss intimidation, gamesmanship, violence, eligibility, elimination, commercialism, gender equity, racial equity, performance-enhancing drugs, and technology and provide numerous ethical dilemmas to encourage the use of moral reasoning to address real sport issues.

McCloskey J., and J. E. Bailes. 2005. *When Winning Costs Too Much: Steroids, Supplements, and Scandal in Today's Sports.* **Lanham, MD: Taylor Trade Publishing, 344 pp.**

Doping in sports is examined, from kids using steroids through the BALCO scandal with elite athletes using designer drugs.

The physical, social, and ethical issues associated with seeking to gain advantages by using drugs in sports are discussed.

Rhoden, W. C. 2006. *$40 Million Slaves: The Rise, Fall, and Redemption of the Black Athlete.* **New York: Crown Publishers, 286 pp.**

This historical examination of African Americans in sport describes how they have been discriminated against, excluded, and exploited in sport. The author argues that African American athletes remain largely on the periphery of power in the multibillion-dollar sport industry that their talents helped build.

Simon, R. L. 2004. *Fair Play: The Ethics of Sport.* **Boulder, CO: Westview Press, 244 pp.**

The author examines issues in the ethics of sport including competition, sportsmanship, drugs, violence, gender, educational sport, commercialization, and values.

Wooden, J. R., and S. Jamison. 1997. *Wooden: A Lifetime of Observations and Reflections on and off the Court.* **Lincolnwood, IL: Contemporary Books, 201 pp.**

Former UCLA basketball coach John Wooden shares the importance of developing character and living a life based on values. He describes the characteristics for a values-based life in his pyramid of success.

Magazine or Journal Articles

Eitzen, S. 1996. "Ethical Dilemmas in American Sport." *Vital Speeches of the Day* **62 (6): 182–185.**

Given the adoration given athletes for their achievements, coaches and players at times resort to unethical actions to gain competitive advantages as a winning-at-all-costs approach has become the prevailing code of conduct. The author states that participation in sport, rather than building character, stifles moral reasoning and moral development.

Howe, L. A. 2004. "Gamesmanship." *Journal of the Philosophy of Sport* **31 (2): 212–225.**

The author discusses competition, excellence, fairness, sportsmanship, winning and losing, and competition and suggests how these concepts interact in the world of sports.

Kretchmar, R. S. 2005. "Why Do We Care So Much about Mere Games? (And Is This Ethically Defensible?)" *Quest* 57 (2): 181–191.

People of all ages and for many eras of time seem to care a great deal about the outcome of games, even though more pressing issues like world poverty, war, and political injustice exist. The author suggests that it is easy to understand why humans gravitate to less serious games with their artificial problems for recreational respite and to escape from the demands of life.

Lomax, S. 2008. "Whatever Happened to America's Ethical Values?" *Business and Economic Review* 55 (1): 15–18.

Cheating and other unethical activities are prevalent among corporate executives, government officials, and athletes as widespread cheating characterizes the educational system and workplace. The author stresses the importance of parents serving as role models for positive values and a child's ethical development.

Mathias, M. B. 2004. "The Competing Demands of Sport and Health: An Essay on the History of Ethics in Sports Medicine." *Clinics in Sports Medicine* 23 (2): 195–214.

Historically, tension has existed between the emphasis on winning in sport and the health of athletes. At times, athletes, athletic trainers, and physicians have pursued victory at the cost of the health of athletes.

Nucci, C., and K. Young-Shim. 2005. "Improving Socialization through Sport: An Analytic Review of Literature on Aggression and Sportsmanship." *Physical Educator* 62 (3): 123–129.

The authors discuss aggression and sportsmanship in sports. They also describe how socialization and the development of social skills can potentially occur in and through sports.

Rudd, A. 2005. "Which 'Character' Should Sport Develop?" *Physical Educator* 62 (4): 205–211.

The author examines two types of character that can potentially be developed through sports: social values and moral values. The recommendation is that sport should emphasize the development of moral character.

Rudd, A., and S. K. Stoll. 1998. "Understanding Sportsmanship." *Journal of Physical Education, Recreation, and Dance* **69 (9): 38–42.**

The authors state that it is important for athletes to understand the true meaning of sportsmanship. When athletes know and appreciate the concept, they are more likely to make morally reasoned decisions in sports.

Stovitz, S. D., and D. J. Satin. 2004. "Ethics and the Athlete: Why Sports are More than a Game but Less than a War." *Clinics in Sports Medicine* **23 (2): 215–225.**

The authors review key ethical concepts and provide a practical framework for interpreting and assessing the moral status of an athlete's behavior. They suggest a close relationship exists between ethics and athletes.

Tatum, L. 2002. "Girls in Sports: Love of the Game Must Begin at an Early Age to Achieve Equality." *Seton Hall Journal of Sport Law* **12 (2): 281–310.**

The author provides a strong rationale, based on a review of equal protection clauses and litigation at the college, school, and community levels, that only through a broad and an early expansion of opportunities in sports can females finally achieve equality.

Other Types of Print Works

Cox, R. S. 2001. "Sportsmanship: Is Bad Behavior Ruining American Sports?" *Congressional Quarterly Researcher* **11 (11): 225–248.** Available at: http://library.cqpress.com/cqresearcher/document.php?id=cqresrre2001032300.

With sports reflective of societal values, this electronic resource examines how unsportsmanlike behaviors have become acceptable in sport at all competitive levels. Trash talking and violence are illustrative of these unethical behaviors.

Tanner, J. 2001. "Women in Sports: Can They Reach Parity with Men?" *Congressional Quarterly Researcher* **11 (18): 401–424.**

Available at: http://library.cqpress.com/cqresearcher/document.php?id=cqresrre2001051100.>

The author examines women in sports from a historical and current context. Specific questions discussed include whether colleges are playing number games rather than fully complying with Title IX, women's professional leagues can survive, and if female athletes posing for sexy photographs diminish women's accomplishments in sports.

Women's Sports Foundation. 2008. *Go Out and Play: Youth Sports in America.* Available at: http://www.womenssportsfoundation.org/~/media/Files/Research%20Reports/Go%20Out%20and%20Play%20report%209%2018%2008.pdf, 192 pp.

Reporting on a nationwide survey of youth in grades 3 through 12 and parents, sports are found to have a positive impact on family satisfaction and linked with improved physical and emotional health, academic achievement, and quality of life. This report concludes that a gender gap exists, with males benefiting from greater opportunities in sports in rural and urban areas. Ethnic minority females are discriminated against by race and gender, while youth with disabilities are disadvantaged because of fewer participation opportunities in sports.

Ethical Issues in Youth Sport
Books
Bigelow, B., T. Moroney, and L. Hall. 2001. *Just Let the Kids Play: How to Stop Other Adults from Ruining Your Children's Joy and Success in Youth Sports.* Deerfield Beach, FL: Health Communications Incorporated, 336 pp.

The authors describe several problems in youth sports, such as elite teams that exclude players, out-of-control adults, and physical and psychological injuries to young athletes. To address unethical conduct associated with youth sports, the authors suggest playing by the rules and adapting the games to children; plus, they provide success stories that yield ideas for change.

Farrey, T. 2008. *Game On: The All-American Race to Make Champions of Our Children.* New York: ESPN Books, 383 pp.

This investigative work examines in detail the major societal and ethical concerns associated with children's involvement in sports. Using the framework of ages 3 through 14, the author explores the various choices parents face in deciding how much emphasis to place on sports for their children.

Gatz, M., M. A. Messner, and S. J. Ball-Rokeach. 2002. *Paradoxes of Youth and Sport.* **Albany: State University of New York Press, 277 pp.**

This book examines ethical issues including violence, racial and gender inequity, the media, the obsession to win, and commercialization and, given this problems, whether youth sport can build character. Special emphasis is placed on the role of sport in the lives of youth in urban settings.

Murphy, S. 1999. *The Cheers and the Tears: A Healthy Alternative to the Dark Side of Youth Sports Today.* **San Francisco: Jossey-Bass, 230 pp.**

Alleging a crisis in youth sport, the author provides guidance to parents for avoiding the pitfalls of an overemphasis on sports for their children. This sport psychologist advocates ensuring that young athletes enjoy positive sport experiences.

National Association for Sport and Physical Education. 2008. *National Standards for Sport Coaches,* **2nd ed. Reston, VA: National Association for Sport and Physical Education, 42 pp.**

This book describes the eight domains of coaching competencies to guide coaches in providing quality learning and playing experiences for youth and adolescents. The first domain, philosophy and ethics, prioritizes the importance of using an athlete-centered coaching philosophy and ensuring professional accountability for fair play.

Ryan, J. 1995. *Little Girls in Pretty Boxes: The Making and Breaking of Elite Gymnasts and Figure Skaters.* **New York: Doubleday, 243 pp.**

Through the lens of the two sports most abusive of girls, the author challenges the morality of a too-early, too-specialized, and too-competitive involvement in gymnastics and figure skating. The ethical issues discussed lead to questions about how to break this exploitive cycle.

Selleck, G. A. 2003. *Raising a Good Sport in an In-Your-Face World: Seven Steps to Building Character on the Field—and Off.* Chicago: Contemporary Books, 194 pp.

The author discusses moral and ethical aspects of sport with an emphasis on sportsmanship and how a person lives.

Sheehy, H., and D. Peary. 2002. *Raising a Team Player: Teaching Kids Lasting Values on the Field, on the Court, and on the Bench.* North Adams, MA: Storey Books, 152 pp.

A small-town coach shares his life-tested wisdom on work ethic, goal setting, winning and losing, competition, enthusiasm, sportsmanship, and character.

Thompson, J. 1995. *Positive Coaching: Building Character and Self-Esteem through Sports.* Portola, CA: Warde Publishers, 400 pp.

This book focuses on helping coaches, parents, and teachers build the character and self-esteem of youth playing sports. The author suggests specific strategies that address the psychological health of young athletes.

Thompson, J. 2003. *The Double-Goal Coach—Positive Coaching Tools for Honoring the Game and Developing Winners in Sports and Life.* New York: HarperCollins, 346 pp.

Written by the founder of the Positive Coaching Alliance, this book provides best-practices coaching tools. The author offers a framework for how coaches and parents can help youth enjoy sports while they learn valuable life lessons.

Magazine or Journal Articles

Bach, G. 2002. "Youth Sports Organizers Call Time Out: An Estimated 70% of All Youth Sports Programs Are Operated by Parent-Interest Groups; and Each Parent's Motives and Morals Influence How the Program Is Run." *Parks and Recreation* 37 (6): 60–63.

This article discusses the Recommendations for Communities, a joint initiative of the National Recreation and Park Association and National Alliance for Youth Sports.

Dougherty, N. 2007. "Rules for Rowdiness." *Athletic Management* **19 (4): 59–63.**

Examples of negative behaviors in high school and college sports are described. The author then discusses efforts made by school administrators to curtail these ethical problems.

Goldstein, J. D., and S. E. Iso-Ahola. 2006. "Promoting Sportsmanship in Youth Sports: Perspectives from Sport Psychology." *Journal of Physical Education, Recreation, and Dance* **77 (7): 18–24.**

After examining theoretical and practice information about sportsmanship in youth sport, the authors offer suggestions for providing a better sporting environment for youth.

Kavanagh, B., and M. Fall. 1995. "Coaches Can Encourage Morality and Fairplay." *Strategies* **8 (1): 25–29.**

The authors recommend a six-step approach to guide youth sport coaches in teaching and serving as a model for morality and good sportsmanship. These steps include reflecting on their personal values, investigating the perceptions, values, and attitudes of athletes, establishing plans for teaching morality and sportsmanship, holding team meetings to share expectations, informing parents of goals and expectations, and allocating time to discuss and reinforce ethical conduct and moral issues.

Lee, M., J. Whitehead, and N. Ntoumanis. 2007. "Development of the Attitudes to Moral Decision-making in Youth Sport Questionnaire (AMDYSQ)." *Psychology of Sport and Exercise* **8 (3): 369–392.**

The authors developed a questionnaire to assess the attitudes of young competitors toward moral decision-making in sport. They report that males, older athletes, team sport athletes, and athletes competing at higher levels score higher than females, younger athletes, and individual sport athletes on acceptance of cheating and gamesmanship. Female athletes were more likely to keep winning in perspective.

McCallister, S. G., E. M. Blinde, and W. M. Weiss. 2000. "Teaching Values and Implementing Philosophies: Dilemmas of the Youth Sport Coach." *Physical Educator* **57 (1): 35–45.**

Through interviews of coaches, this study examines the values and life skills that they view as important and the extent to which they seek to teach these to young athletes. Even though coaches recognize the importance of teaching a wide range of positive values and life skills, those interviewed struggle to instill these values and life skills in young athletes.

Ryska, T. A. 2003. "Sportsmanship in Young Athletes: The Role of Competitiveness, Motivational Orientation, and Perceived Purposes of Sport." *Journal of Psychology* **137 (3): 273–293.**

This study found that intrinsic reasons for sports participation by young athletes predicted higher levels of sportsmanship, while extrinsic purposes for participation in sports, such as to obtain social status and a high-status career, contributed to lower levels of sportsmanship. The author recommends developing a competitive sport setting to promote ethical standards of behavior by young sport participants.

Sage, G. H. 1998. "Does Sport Affect Character Development in Athletes?" *Journal of Physical Education, Recreation, and Dance* **69 (1): 15–18.**

The author states that despite claims to the contrary, there is no evidence that sports build character. Rather, organized sport for youth may adversely affect moral development as an "anything goes" pursuit of winning shapes athletes' values in negative ways.

Wells, M. S., G. D. Ellis, K. P. Paisley, B. Arthur, and D. Skye. 2005. "Development and Evaluation of a Program to Promote Sportsmanship in Youth Sports." *Journal of Park and Recreation Administration* **23 (1): 1–17.**

The authors discuss the serious and growing problem of poor sportsmanship in youth sports. They describe the "Play Hard, Play Fair, Play Fun" youth basketball program as an example of how to shift the focus from winning to an atmosphere characterized by sportsmanship, cooperation, and positive relationships among participants on competing teams. Effective strategies used to enhance sportsmanship include introducing the players and referees, posting signs supporting sportsmanship, rewarding players for good sportsmanship, resetting the score to zero when the score discrepancy between the two teams became too large, hosting a postgame social event for players and coaches, and providing a league Web site with photographs of each team's weekly sportsmanship award winner.

Wiersma, L. D., and C. P. Sherman. 2005. "Volunteer Youth Sport Coaches' Perspectives of Coaching Education/Certification and Parental Codes of Conduct." *Research Quarterly for Exercise and Sport* 76 (3): 324–338.

Based on focus group interviews with 25 volunteer youth sport coaches, the authors identify areas of need for educating coaches, barriers and problems faced in and recommendations for offering coaching education, and the importance of codes of conduct for parents.

Other Types of Print Works

National Alliance for Youth Sports. 2007. *National Standards for Youth Sports.* Available at: http://www.nays.org/TimeOut/National%20Standards08FINAL.pdf, 16 pp.

Nine standards should guide operations and outcomes of youth sport programs according to individuals involved with organizing and administering these programs. The sixth standard calls on everyone involved to display sportsmanship.

Ethical Issues in Interscholastic Sport

Books

Alberts, C. L. 2003. *Coaching Issues and Dilemmas: Character Building through Sport Participation.* Reston, VA: National Association for Sport and Physical Education, 187 pp.

This book describes the importance of coaches modeling positive values and developing character. Practical scenarios are provided to help guide coaches in dealing with ethical issues.

Bissinger, H. G. 1990. *Friday Night Lights: A Town, a Team, and a Dream.* Reading, MA: Addison-Wesley Publishing Company, 357 pp.

This eyewitness account of a football season at Permian High School in Odessa, Texas, reveals one community's obsession with the team's success. The author describes many of the social, racial, and gender problems associated with football shaping a town's identity.

Brown, B. E. 2003. *Teaching Character through Sport: Developing a Positive Coaching Legacy.* **Monterey, CA: Coaches Choice, 140 pp.**

The author provides coaches with specific strategies for teaching values and developing character through sport.

Carocci, V. P. 2008. *Building Character—Harry's Way: The Story of Harry DeFrank and the Value of Sport in the Lives of Our Youngsters When Done the Right Way by the Right People.* **Carlisle, PA, 196 pp.**

This book tells the story of Harry DeFrank, a high school girls' basketball team coach. He teaches players values and how to play the game of basketball and live their lives the right way.

Gough, R. W. 1997. *Character is Everything: Promoting Ethical Excellence in Sports.* **Fort Worth, TX: Harcourt Brace College Publishers, 100 pp.**

This book discusses sportsmanship, ethics, and the development of character through sport. The author emphasizes the importance of role models who exemplify ethical excellence.

Griffin, R. S. 1998. *Sports in the Lives of Children and Adolescents: Success on the Field and in Life.* **Westport, CT: Praeger, 158 pp.**

The author examines the interface between sports and academics, the importance of sports in schools, girls in sports, class and race in sports, parenting a child in sports, and defining success in sports.

May, R. A. B. 2008. *Living through the Hoop: High School Basketball, Race, and the American Dream.* **New York: New York University Press, 243 pp.**

The author explores high school basketball through the lens of race with specific reference to the impact of drugs, drinking, and delinquency of athletes. It is challenging for sportsmanship and the need to win to coexist.

Miracle, A. W., and C. R. Rees. 1994. *Lessons of the Locker Room: The Myth of School Sports.* Amherst, NY: Prometheus Books, 243 pp.

The authors question whether the claim that sports build character is true or a myth perpetuated through an obsession about the importance of sports in schools. Achieving educational goals to prepare for life should be complemented by interscholastic sports rather than overshadowed by a winning-at-all-costs locker room mentality.

Ripken, C., and R. Wolff. 2006. *Parenting Young Athletes the Ripken Way: Ensuring the Best Experience for Your Kids in Any Sport.* New York: Gotham Books, 240 pp.

After his Hall of Fame career when he played baseball with sportsmanship and class, Cal Ripken Jr. has focused on youth. He offers advice as a father and coach about how to reduce the overemphasis on winning and emphasize the fun of playing sports.

Shea, E. J. 1996. *Ethical Decisions in Sport: Interscholastic, Intercollegiate, Olympic, and Professional.* Springfield, IL: C. C. Thomas, 223 pp.

The author emphasizes the moral and ethical aspects of sports and making morally reasoned decisions in competitive sports at the school, college, Olympic, and professional levels.

Magazine or Journal Articles

Beller, J. M., and S. K. Stoll. 1995. "Moral Reasoning of High School Student Athletes and General Students: An Empirical Study versus Personal Testimony." *Pediatric Exercise Science* 7 (4): 352–363.

This study analyzes the cognitive moral reasoning of high school athletes and nonathletes. The authors report that interscholastic athletes reason from a less consistent, impartial, and reflective perspective than do nonathletes.

Fierberg, D. E. 2000. "High School, Where Hazing is Amazing." *Education Digest* 66 (4): 48–51.

Hazing is behavior that threatens or causes physical or psychological harm to an athlete as a condition of participating on a team. School administrators and coaches have not been diligent enough to prevent the continuation of hazing, which is illegal.

Green, T., and C. Gabbard. 1999. "Do We Need Sportsmanship Education in Secondary School Athletics?" *Physical Educator* **56 (2): 98–104.**

The authors advocate that sportsmanship education is needed in secondary schools as a way to help instill social values. Through specifically designed learning experiences, athletes can develop sportsmanship.

Lumpkin, A. 2008. "Teaching Values through Youth and Interscholastic Sports." *Strategies: A Journal for Physical and Sport Educators* **21 (4): 19–23.**

After discussing the goals for youth and adolescents in sports and some issues of concern, the author suggests numerous strategies for teaching character and moral values through sports. By explaining, demonstrating, modeling, and reinforcing respect and responsibility and related values, keeping winning in perspective, and making sports fun, youth and adolescent athletes are more likely to develop character through their participation in sports.

Marsh, H. W., and S. Kleitman. 2003. "School Athletic Participation: Mostly Gain with Little Pain." *Journal of Sport and Exercise Psychology* **25 (2): 205–228.**

The authors state that playing interscholastic sports leads to positive effects on academic performance, self-esteem, subsequent college enrollment, and eventual educational attainment. These positive outcomes hold true across the range of participation levels and demographic subgroups of socioeconomic status, gender, and ethnicity.

Said, E., and S. N. Blair: 2005. "Sports Gone beyond Wild ... But Not Completely without Hope." *Physician and Sportsmedicine* **33 (7): 6–7.**

An orthopedic surgeon and exercise physiologist address problems in school sports. Specifically, they discuss the use of anabolic steroids, aggressive parents and fans, unethical behaviors of coaches, and a "winning-at-all-costs" approach.

Shields, D. L., B. Bredemeier, D. Gardner, and A. Bostrom. 1995. "Leadership, Cohesion, and Team Norms Regarding Cheating and Aggression." *Sociology of Sport Journal* 12 (3): 324–336.

The authors examine whether a sport team's collective norms influence behavior, and specifically cheating and aggression as correlated with age, year in school, and years playing baseball or softball. They report higher expectations of peer cheating and aggression among males than females, community college than high school athletes, winning team members, and nonstarters.

Sloan, T. 2003. "It's Not Cheating Unless You Get Caught." *Referee* 28 (2): 24–28.

The author discusses the fine line between gamesmanship and cheating in sports. Using examples from baseball, football, and soccer, the author explains how officials sometimes contribute to the confusion leading to more unethical behavior in sports.

Vandenabeele, R. 2004. "S.O.S.: Save Our Sportsmanship." *Coach and Athletic Director* 74 (1): 72.

The author discusses strategies for teaching sportsmanship and ethical behaviors through interscholastic sports. Specifically, the call is for defining sportsmanship, emphasizing participation rather than winning, teaching positive values, and educating and involving parents to reinforce these desired outcomes.

Zimmer, D. 2004. "Values and Priorities and Where They Begin." *Coach and Athletic Director* 74 (5): 30–32.

At times, coaches fail to take advantage of the opportunities they have to influence the development of moral values in athletes. The author encourages coaches to use teachable moments in sport to develop sportsmanship and model character.

Other Types of Print Works

Hansen, B. 2004. "Hazing: Should More Be Done To Stop It?" *Congressional Quarterly Researcher* 14 (1): 1–24. Available at: http://library.cqpress.com/cqresearcher/document.php?id=cqresrre2004010900&type=hitlist&num=8

Those who haze others claim it is fun, is exciting, and builds camaraderie when they initiate newcomers into the culture of a team, fraternity, or another group, although there is no evidence that hazing builds cohesiveness. The victims of physical and verbal hazing may participate because they want to prove themselves, they feel peer pressure to get along, or are afraid not to participate. Rather than build character, hazing can lead to physical and psychological injuries, alcohol poisoning, and death.

National Association for Sport and Physical Education. 2008. *National Coaching Report,* **160 pp.**

This report summarizes available information on the status of coaching education and the coaching profession in interscholastic and youth sports. It provides data on participation rates, governance, and credentialing of coaches in interscholastic and youth sports.

Ethical Issues in Intercollegiate Sport
Books
Bowen, W. G., and S. A. Levin. 2003. *Reclaiming the Game: College Sports and Educational Values.* **Princeton, NJ: Princeton University Press, 490 pp.**

Using data from elite institutions, this investigative report examines the admissions advantages, academic performances, and campus cultures associated with intercollegiate athletics. Debunking myths, the authors call for national reform based on their findings of preferential treatment of athletes and their underperformance in the classroom.

Byers, W., with C. Hammer. 1995. *Unsportsmanlike Conduct: Exploiting College Athletes.* **Ann Arbor: University of Michigan Press, 413 pp.**

The former head of the National Collegiate Athletic Association exposes some of the exploitive rules and actions used to further the goals of college athletic programs at the expense of athletes. The author expresses concern about several questionable aspects of college sports, especially as played at the highest competitive level.

Carpenter, L. J., and R. V. Acosta. 2005. *Title IX.* **Champaign, IL: Human Kinetics, 270 pp.**

The authors provide a comprehensive examination of the content and application of Title IX of the 1972 Education Amendments to sports.

French, P. A. 2004. *Ethics and College Sports: Ethics, Sports, and the University.* **Lanham, MD: Rowman and Littlefield Publishers, 193 pp.**

The stated role of intercollegiate athletics stands in contrast to the myths of amateurism, character development, gender equity, and financial equity. In reality, intercollegiate athletics at the highest level is in the entertainment business.

Gerdy, J. R. 2006. *Air Ball: American Education's Failed Experiment with Elite Athletics.* **Jackson: University Press of Mississippi, 270 pp.**

The author argues that the current system of intercollegiate athletics has failed. He suggests reform measures for rebuilding this system, but realizes it will take courage to enact changes.

King, C. R., and C. F. Springwood. 2001. *Beyond the Cheers: Race as Spectacle in College Sport.* **Albany: State University of New York Press, 214 pp.**

This book exposes the racism associated with team logos and mascots, as well as the predominance of whiteness in college sports.

Sack, A. L., and E. J. Staurowsky. 1998. *College Athletes for Hire: The Evolution and Legacy of the NCAA's Amateur Myth.* **Westport, CT: Praeger, 184 pp.**

A decline in the amateur spirit accompanied the giving of grants-in-aid to athletes and the emerging commercialization of college sports. While initially excluded from the changing culture in intercollegiate athletics, females are now part of the business of college sports.

Shulman, J. L., and W. G. Bowen. 2001. *The Game of Life: College Sports and Educational Values.* **Princeton, NJ: Princeton University Press, 447 pp.**

Using data from elite colleges, the authors investigate admissions, academic performance, postcollegiate lives, and whether athletes donate to the institutions they attended. The authors share empirical data to support their conclusions and the ethical implications of their findings.

Sperber, M. A. 2000. *Beer and Circus: How Big-Time College Sports Is Crippling Undergraduate Education.* New York: Henry Holt and Company, 322 pp.

Comparing intercollegiate athletics to Animal House, the author discusses admission scams, cheating, the collegiate party culture associated with intercollegiate athletics, faculty apathy toward athletics, and an overall undermining of undergraduate education. The picture painted about how important intercollegiate athletics has become on some campuses is not a pretty one.

Thelin, J. R. 1996. *Games Colleges Play: Scandal and Reform in Intercollegiate Athletics.* Baltimore: Johns Hopkins University Press, 252 pp.

Intercollegiate athletics, higher education's peculiar institution, is examined from the perspective of scandals, academic controversies, and lack of faculty control. The author calls for reform to more closely align college sports with academic expectations.

Zimbalist, A. S. 1999. *Unpaid Professionals: Commercialism and Conflict in Big-Time College Sports.* Princeton, NJ: Princeton University Press, 252 pp.

This work explores the economic issues associated with gender equity for athletes and coaches, commercialism, media, and the NCAA and its member institutions. Recommendations for reform are offered.

Magazine or Journal Articles

Brand, M. 2006. "The Role and Value of Intercollegiate Athletics in Universities." *Journal of the Philosophy of Sport* 33 (1): 9–20.

The author, as president of the National Collegiate Athletic Association, suggests that the role of intercollegiate athletics has been undervalued. He claims that intercollegiate athletics make an important contribution to the undergraduate education of athletes and positively contribute to campus culture.

Calvert, C., and R. D. Richards. 2004. "Fans and the First Amendment: Cheering and Jeering in College Sports." *Virginia Sports and Entertainment Law Journal* 4 (1): 1–53.

Using a First Amendment framework and a model of balancing rights and freedoms with good sportsmanship and the rights of other fans, the authors review policies of athletic conferences.

Diacin, M. J., J. B. Parks, and P. C. Allison. 2003. "Voices of Male Athletes on Drug Use, Drug Testing, and the Existing Order in Intercollegiate Athletics." *Journal of Sport Behavior* 26 (1): 1–16.

Eight intercollegiate athletes were asked about their perceptions of drug use and drug testing. These athletes support drug testing despite privacy and fairness issues. These athletes also discuss the ambiguities and contradictions between athletics and academics.

Jordan, J. S., T. C. Greenwell, A. L. Geist, D. L. Pastore, and D. F. Mahony. 2004. "Coaches' Perceptions of Conference Code of Ethics." *Physical Educator* 61 (3): 131–145.

Head coaches of college sports teams are asked to identify what should be included in a code of ethics in order to encourage positive ethical behavior. They rate the ideals of sportsmanship, promotion of values like honesty, integrity, and fair play, a healthy environment, and professional conduct as most important.

Kavussanu, M., and G. C. Roberts. 2001. "Moral Functioning in Sport: An Achievement Goal Perspective." *Journal of Sport and Exercise Psychology* 23 (1): 37–54.

The authors examine the achievement goals, unsportsmanlike attitudes, and judgments about the legitimacy of intentionally injurious acts in male and female college basketball players. Male athletes show lower levels of moral functioning and greater approval of unsportsmanlike behaviors and are more likely than females to judge injurious acts as legitimate.

Lawry, E. G. 2005. "Academic Integrity and College Athletics." *Phi Kappa Phi Forum* 85 (3): 20–23.

Too often money and incentives for winning obscure academic integrity in intercollegiate athletics as academically unmotivated athletes cheat and academic regulations are circumvented to keep star athletes eligible to play. As possible solutions, the author suggests reducing the size and influence of athletic departments, preventing athletic departments from being responsible for athletes' academic performance, enforcing academic rules, and requiring more disclosure of athletes' academic records.

Lumpkin, A. 2008. "A Call to Action for Faculty Regarding Intercollegiate Athletics." *Phi Kappa Phi Forum* 88 (1): 21; 24.

The author identifies ethical issues in intercollegiate athletics, such as escalating coaches' salaries, overcommitment of hours by athletes to their sports, preferred admissions for underqualified students, and failure to graduate by many athletes. These are associated with an overemphasis on winning, growing commercialization of sports, and reallocation of resources to cover budgetary shortfalls in athletics. Recommendations to more closely align intercollegiate athletics with educational and ethical outcomes are provided.

Priest, R. F., J. V. Krause, and J. Beach. 1999. "Four-year Changes in College Athletes' Ethical Value Choices in Sports Situations." *Research Quarterly for Exercise and Sport* 70 (2): 170–178.

This longitudinal study reports on the moral development of intercollegiate and intramural sport athletes at the United States Military Academy. The data show a decrease in ethical value choice in sport situations, reveal that males and females change ethical choices to the same extent, and indicate that athletes think coaches are more likely to make unethical choices than athletes are.

Thelin, J. R. 2008. "Academics and Athletics: A Part and Apart in the American Campus." *Journal of Intercollegiate Sports* 1 (1): 72–81.

The author discusses the special privileges granted to athletic departments, misbehaviors of coaches, financial issues associated with academics and athletics, and the inclination of some coaches and athletic directors to violate rules. Specific examples are provided in this examination of policy and ethical issues.

Tricker, R. 2000. "Painkilling Drugs in Collegiate Athletics: Knowledge, Attitudes, and Use of Student Athletes." *Journal of Drug Education* 30 (3): 313–324.

In a study of more than 500 college athletes, the author reports that 29% believe there is nothing unethical about using painkilling drugs to mask injuries so they can compete. Perceptions of societal norms and expectations may contribute to the extent of use of these drugs. The author makes recommendations for coaches, athletic trainers, and administrators who are concerned about controlling the use and abuse of painkilling drugs by athletes.

Other Types of Print Works

Acosta, V. R., and L. J. Carpenter. 2008. *Women in Intercollegiate Sport: A Longitudinal, National Study Thirty-One Year Update, 1977–2008*, 41 pp.

The authors report on a longitudinal basis the status of females in intercollegiate athletics. The data include number of teams for female athletes, head and assistant coaches of teams for females, athletic directors, head athletic trainers, head sports information directors, and females employed in intercollegiate athletics.

Knight Commission on Intercollegiate Athletics. 1991. *Keeping Faith with the Student Athlete: A New Model for Intercollegiate Athletics*. Available at: http://www.knightcommission.org/images/uploads/1991-93_KCIA_report.pdf, 70 pp.

The Commission's original report calls for a one-plus-three model. The *one* is presidential control of intercollegiate athletics directed toward the *three* of academic integrity, financial integrity, and accountability through certification.

Knight Commission on Intercollegiate Athletics. 2001. *A Call to Action: Reconnecting College Sports and Higher Education*. Available at: http://www.knightcommission.org/images/uploads/KCfinal-06-2001.pdf, 27 pp.

Given the lack of sufficient progress made in achieving the recommended one-plus-three model, the Commission a decade later calls for a stronger commitment to academic standards in intercollegiate athletics.

Knight Commission on Intercollegiate Athletics. 2004. *Challenging the Myth*. Available at: http://www.knightcommission.org/images/uploads/KCfinal-06-2001.pdf, 36 pp.

Cornell University economist Robert Frank reviews the economic literature on intercollegiate athletics. Specifically, he investigates whether successful athletic programs stimulate increased applications and great contributions by alumni and other donors. Since the findings are mixed, any indirect benefits in admissions and donations are small.

Knight Commission on Intercollegiate Athletics. 2006. *Athletics Recruiting and Academic Values: Enhancing Transparency, Spreading Risk and Improving Practice.* **Available at: http://www.knightcommission.org/images/uploads/Recruiting EssayKnight.pdf, 11 pp.**

This roundtable discussion sought to enhance communication among athletics and academic leaders and promote transparency in recruiting and admissions in intercollegiate athletics. A clarification and application of values are required to ensure integrity in the recruiting process.

Knight Commission on Intercollegiate Athletics. 2007. *Faculty Perceptions of Intercollegiate Athletics.* **Available at: http:// www.knightcommission2.org/faculty_perceptions_final.doc, 172 pp.**

This survey examines faculty members' beliefs about and satisfaction with intercollegiate athletics. The data collected indicates whether professors would join in the work for meaningful change to address identified concerns.

National Collegiate Athletic Association. 2008. *1981–1982 to 2006–2007 NCAA Sports Sponsorship and Participation Rates Report.* **Available at: http://www.ncaapublications.com/ ProductsDetailView.aspx?sku=PR2008, 207 pp.**

This report provides longitudinal and comparative data on the teams and athletes for member institutions in the NCAA. The number of teams and athletes continues to grow as does the number of women's teams competing in NCAA championships. The average number of male athletes (216) per NCAA member institution is higher than for female athletes (162).

National Collegiate Athletic Association. 2008. *The 2005–2006 NCAA Gender Equity Study,* **97 pp.**

This report provides data on participation of athletes, number and salaries of head and assistant coaches, recruiting expenses, athletically related financial aid, and overall revenues and expenses for intercollegiate athletic programs. Some of the data are categorized for football and men's and women's basketball.

National Women's Law Center. 2007. *Breaking Down Barriers: A Legal Guide to Title IX and Athletic Opportunities.* Available at: http://www.nwlc.org/pdf/Breaking%20Down%20 Barriers%202007.pdf, 126 pp.

This guide provides information about discrimination in athletics and describes how to make a claim based on a violation of Title IX. This resource for plaintiffs and their attorneys describes how private parties can help enforce Title IX on behalf of the rights of athletes in educational institutions.

Women's Sports Foundation. 2008. *Who's Playing College Sports? Money, Race and Gender.* Available at: http://www.womenssports foundation.org/~/media/Files/Research%20Reports/Money% 20Race%20%20%20Gender.pdf, 48 pp.

While Title IX has expanded opportunities in sports for females, this report concludes that increases in expenditures in football and men's basketball are constraining participation opportunities. This study specifically examines high school participation trends as they influence intercollegiate sports, the impact of rising health care costs on sports with high injury rates, increased number of international athletes, and enrollment management strategies that favor sports played by athletes who are well-prepared academically, able to pay high tuition costs, and less diverse in race and ethnicity.

Ethical Issues in International Sport
Books
Bahrke, M. S., and C. E. Yesalis, eds. 2002. *Performance-Enhancing Substances in Sport and Exercise.* Boston: McGraw-Hill, 373 pp.

This edited book provides an extensive description of the physiological effects of the use of performance-enhancing drugs. It also includes information on drug testing and the ethical issues associated with the use of these drugs.

Barney, R. K., S. R. Wenn, and S. G. Martyn. 2002. *Selling the Five Rings: The International Olympic Committee and the Rise of Olympic Commercialism*. Salt Lake City: University of Utah Press, 384 pp.

This historical examination of the Olympic Games emphasizes commercialization, especially from the selling of television rights and obtaining corporate sponsorships. This well-researched book provides in-depth information about the key leaders, processes, and rationales associated with the evolution of the International Olympic Committee as a corporate entity, along with the associated ethical issues that characterized its evolution.

Beamish, R., and Ritchie, I. 2006. *Fastest, Highest, Strongest: A Critique of High-Performance Sport*. New York: Routledge, 194 pp.

The authors discuss doping in sports and specifically the Olympic Games. They also examine associated ethical issues.

Girginov, V., and S. J. Parry. 2005. *The Olympic Games Explained: A Student Guide to the Evolution of the Modern Olympic Games*. New York: Routledge, 272 pp.

After discussing the history of the Olympic Games, the authors examine topics such as politics, the media, marketing, economics, use of drugs, and the ethics of Olympic sports.

Maraniss, D. 2008. *Rome 1960: The Olympics That Changed the World*. New York: Simon and Schuster, 478 pp.

The author artfully weaves politics, history, and sport in this comprehensive examination of the 1960 Rome Olympic Games. Using unforgettable characters and dramatic contests as context, the author describes how the Olympic Games began to be forever changed, such as through the crumbling of amateurism, doping, and commercialization.

Pound, R. W. 2004. *Inside the Olympics: A Behind-the-Scenes Look at the Politics, the Scandals, and the Glory of the Games*. Etobicoke, Canada: J. Wiley and Sons, 288 pp.

An International Olympic Committee member provides an insider's perspective about judging scandals, negotiating television rights, doping, securing corporate sponsorships, and bidding scandals. Integrally involved as a leader in growing the Olympic Movement, the author is committed to guarding its integrity.

Simson, V., and A. Jennings. 1992. *The Lords of the Rings: Power, Money and Drugs in the Modern Olympics.* **London: Simon and Schuster, 289 pp.**

The authors examine the interplay between how the International Olympic Committee has expanded its worldwide reach while confronting the major problem of drug abuse in sports. Particular emphasis is placed on the politics behind this story.

Voet, W. 2001. *Breaking the Chain. Drugs and Cycling: The True Story.* **London: Yellow Jersey, 128 pp.**

A former rider in the Tour de France discusses the interwoven nature of drugs and international cycling. The author claims that in pursuit of competitive advantages, most riders have chosen to use performance-enhancing drugs.

Wilson, W., and E. Derse. 2001. *Doping in Elite Sport: The Politics of Drugs in the Olympic Movement.* **Champaign, IL: Human Kinetics, 295 pp.**

This edited book examines the use of performance-enhancing drugs in the Olympic Games from multiple perspectives from testing to scandals. The chapter authors place the issue of doping in historical, sociological, global, and ethical context.

Woodland, L. 2003. *The Crooked Path to Victory: Drugs and Cheating in Professional Bicycle Racing.* **San Francisco: Cycle Publishing, 192 pp.**

Professional racing has for decades attracted cheaters who have sought unfair advantages through drugs. Even though many cyclists lie about and deny the use of performance-enhancing drugs, this book describes many forms of their cheating and recounts how some cyclists have paid the ultimate price with their lives.

Magazine or Journal Articles

Carr, C. L. 2008. "Fairness and Performance Enhancement in Sports." *Journal of the Philosophy of Sport* **35 (2): 193–207.**

The author questions from a philosophical perspective whether the use of performance-enhancing drugs represents unfair behavior by athletes. Since all athletes have the freedom to break the rules that ban these drugs, it is argued that using performance-enhancing drugs is merely a technological innovation in training.

Catlin, D. H., and T. H. Murray. 1996. "Performance-Enhancing Drugs, Fair Competition, and Olympic Sport." *Journal of the American Medical Association* 276 (3): 231–237.

The authors provide an overview of the drug testing process for the 1996 Atlanta Olympic Games, which included testing prior to athletes' arrival in Atlanta, immediately after events, and on short notice or no notice. Although some athletes claim that drug testing violates their personal liberties, most athletes support drug testing for banned substances including stimulants, anabolic steroids, diuretics, hormones, and marijuana.

DeFrantz, A. L. 2001. "The Future of the Olympic Movement." *Journal of the International Council for Health, Physical Education, Recreation, Sport, and Dance* 37 (2): 37–41.

The author states that the Olympic Games enjoy global appeal because they affirm universal values like the pursuit of excellence, sportsmanship, international cooperation, peace, and respect for all. The International Olympic Committee (of which the author is a member), in the role of guardian, must preserve and nurture Olympic values and not permit commercialism to interfere with achieving these values.

Kalinski, M. I. 2003. "State-Sponsored Research on Creatine Supplements and Blood Doping in Elite Soviet Sport." *Perspectives in Biology and Medicine* 46 (3): 445–451.

Using previously restricted information, the author reveals that athletes in the former Soviet Union used creatine supplements and blood doping in the 1970s and 1980s. This evidence shows that charges at that time against some successful Soviet athletes for using performance-enhancing drugs and practices could not be substantiated because of the secrecy surrounding Soviet research in exercise biochemistry.

Milton-Smith, J. 2002. "Ethics, the Olympics and the Search for Global Values." *Journal of Business Ethics* 35 (2): 131–142.

The author states that the economic globalization of the Olympic Games has been plagued by commercial exploitation, intense national rivalries, cronyism, cheating, corruption, and a winning-at-any-cost approach. To revitalize the Olympic spirit, suggestions are offered for building a framework of global values to counterbalance naked economic priorities.

Panagiotopoulos, D. 1998. "The Legal Aspects of Sports Ethics and the Protection of Fair Play." *International Journal of Physical Education* 35 (3): 99–105.

In order to safeguard the spirit of fair play, the author states that deviant behavior should be punished. Eligibility rules, promotion of integrity, propriety, purity, and fair judgment, and moral principles should be legislated, enforced, and respected in international sports.

Parry, J. 2006. "Sport and Olympism: Universals and Multiculturalism." *Journal of the Philosophy of Sport* 33 (2): 188–204.

The author suggests that the Olympics play a significant role in globalization, multiculturalism, and the struggle for universal principles. With the growing interdependency among societies and people, the Olympic Games can help bring about liberal ideals and universal values, such as living together in mutual respect.

Ritchie, I. 2003. "Sex Tested, Gender Verified: Controlling Female Sexuality in the Age of Containment." *Sport History Review* 34 (1): 80–98.

The author explores the sociohistorical construction of the sex test, which was a policy known as gender verification. Female athletes in major international competition from the 1960s until the 2000 Sydney Olympic Games were subjected to invasive verification procedures to prove their gender and eligibility to compete.

Rogge, J. 2003. "Olympian Efforts." *Harvard International Review* 25 (1): 16–20.

Writing prior to the 2004 Athens Olympic Games, the author, as the president of the International Olympic Committee, reflects on the values associated with the ideals of the Olympic Movement. Founder Baron Pierre de Coubertin in espousing this utopian ideal believed that sport could teach the world's youth basic human values leading to friendship and peace among all communities.

Schneider, A. J., and R. B. Butcher. 1993. "For the Love of the Game: A Philosophical Defense of Amateurism." *Quest* 45 (4): 460–469.

The authors describe the end of amateurism in the Olympic Games and along with it an end to the hypocrisy of illicit payments. Rather than monetary payments, though, competing for the love of the game should define the motivation behind amateurism, while cheating harms the game.

Other Types of Print Works

Jost, K. 2004. "Sports and Drugs: Are Stronger Anti-Doping Policies Needed?" *Congressional Quarterly Researcher* 14 (26): 613–636. Available at: http://library.cqpress.com/cqresearcher/document.php?id=cqresrre2004072300.

Using examples of athletes like Tim Montgomery, Marion Jones, and Barry Bonds and the BALCO scandal, the author examines the extent of drug use in elite sports. Drug policies, testing, and penalties have affected, but not eliminated, the use of performance-enhancing drugs in sports as cheaters continue to seek competitive advantages.

World Anti-Doping Agency. 2004. *World Anti-Doping Code.* Available at: http://www.wada-ama.org/rtecontent/document/code_v3.pdf, 44 pp.

Adopted by over 1,000 representatives of governments, the International Olympic Committee, International Paralympic Committee, Olympic and Paralympic sports and national committees, and athletes, this code leads the fight against doping in sport. Through a uniform set of rules, this code harmonizes anti-doping policies, rules, regulations, and enforcements within sport organizations and among public authorities.

Nonprint Resources

Ethical Issues in Sport for All

American filmmakers use sports to tell compelling stories of conflict, triumph, and individual achievement. The following book examines the evolution of how athletes and sports have been represented and evolved over time: Baker, A. 2003.

Contesting Identities: Sports in American Film. Urbana: University of Illinois Press, 162 pp.

DVDs/Videotapes

The Athlete in Society: What Price Glory? VHS. Alexandria, VA: PBS Adult Learning Satellite Service, 1993.

A panel including former tennis champion Arthur Ashe explores moral and ethical questions in sports.

Media and Sports: Watchdog or Lapdog? VHS. New York: Insight Media, 1999.

Frank Deford, Jennings Bryant, Val Pinchbeck Jr., and Michael Oriard at the First International Conference on Ethics and Sport discuss the relationship between the media and sports and related ethical issues.

Playing Hurt: Ethics and Sports Medicine. DVD. Princeton, NJ: Films for the Humanities and Sciences, 2005.

A panel of experts representing the Orthopaedic Society for Sports Medicine discusses ethical and medical issues associated with injured athletes.

The Sociology of Sports in the United States. DVD. New York: Insight Media, 2005.

This program describes sports as a social phenomenon. In exploring the interface between sports and society, it examines the relationship of sports to religion, social roles, citizenship, morality, class, race, gender, and the institutionalization of sports.

Sports and Life: Students, Athletes and Life Skills. VHS. Dubuque, IA: Kendall/Hunt, 2000.

Bill Curry, Bonnie Blair, and Kareem Abdul-Jabbar discuss how important sports are in life and what sports can do for and to athletes.

Sportsmanship, Gamesmanship and Character. Do Good Sports Make Good People? VHS. New York: Insight Media, 1999.

Daniel Doyle, Jan Boxill, Scott Kretchmar, Bill Shelton, and Brenda Jo Bredemeier discuss how gamesmanship and sportsmanship affect the character of athletes.

Violence, Aggression, and Sport. VHS. Tampa, FL: Philosophy Lab, 1999.

At the First International Conference on Ethics and Sports, panelists explore the ethical implications of violence in sports. They discuss the impact of violence in sports on the off-the-field behavior of athletes, how violent and illegal acts of athletes influence the behavior of young fans, and what teams should do when athletes are accused of violence.

Databases

ABI/INFORM is a business information database. It includes citations dealing with the financial and business aspects of sports and associated ethical issues.

Education Abstracts, a bibliographic database, cites articles from more than 400 periodicals, yearbooks, and books (after 1995). This database offers 50- to 150-word abstracts describing the content of about two-thirds of the citations, some of which deal with issues in sport sponsored by educational institutions.

Periodicals Index Online is an electronic index of millions of articles published in the arts, humanities, and social sciences. Some articles deal with college sports, athletics, and the Olympic Games.

Pubmed is the Web access name of Medline, which is the biomedical database of articles indexed from more than 3,700 international journals. Doping in sports and sports medicine are among the topics included.

Readers Guide Abstracts provide citations from the 240 popular general-interest magazines indexed in *Readers Guide to Periodical Literature*. Abstracts are provided for the feature articles and news stories, some of which deal with ethical issues in sports.

Sociological Abstracts provide citations of journal articles from more than 1,800 publications, book reviews, and links to dissertations and conference papers. It includes citations on sport violence, teams, athletes, spectators, sports participation, and related topics.

SPORTDiscus is a comprehensive database of more than 350 journals in the field of sports and contains more than 700,000 references from thousands of periodicals, books, e-journals, conference proceedings, theses, dissertations, and Web sites.

The Philosopher's Index links to articles by subject and author in more than 600 journals. Sport ethics, athletes, athletics, coaching, competition, and related topics are included from articles and books.

PsycINFO includes citations from more than 2,000 scholarly journals, books, and dissertations. Within this index are citations about athletic performance, attitudes toward sports, sport spectators, and related topics.

Internet Sites
http://www.educ.uidaho.edu/center_for_ethics

This site of the Center for ETHICS at the University of Idaho describes some of the research being conducted in the area of sport ethics. Sharon Stoll and her colleagues are leaders in applying moral reasoning to the development of character in and through sport.

www.sportsmanship.org

The Citizenship through Sports Alliance is a coalition of amateur and professional sport organizations that promote the development of character at all levels of sport. This alliance provides online resources to support its promotion of fair play and the importance of building a sport culture that encourages respect for self, others, and the game.

http://www.internationalsport.com/iishome.cfm

The Institute for International Sport (IIS) seeks to foster friendship, goodwill, peace, humanitarianism, and global awareness among nations through sports. IIS promotes ethical behavior, good sportsmanship, and sound guidance by sport educators and parents and sponsors National Sportsmanship Day.

Ethical Issues in Youth Sport
DVDs/Videotapes
Enjoy the Game. VHS. Blue Springs, MO: Enjoy the Game, Inc., 2003.

This short video emphasizes the development of sportsmanship and values in elementary and middle school students. It is designed to support character-based educational programs.

Give It Your All: Defining Yourself through Sports Participation. Ames, IA: Championship Productions, 2003.

Former intercollegiate athlete and current athletic director at Ohio State University, Gene Smith delivers a passionate and motivational message directed to athletes and parents. He discusses sportsmanship as the way to handle challenges in sports and life, the importance of achieving academically, the roles of coaches and parents, and how to resist temptation by making values-based decisions.

Just a Game. VHS. New York: ABC News, 2002.

Violence too often characterizes youth sports as well as the behaviors of adults who coach and watch youth sports. This special report warns of the consequences of out-of-control parents who disrupt their children's sports and model inappropriate behavior.

Sports and Children: Training or Child Abuse? VHS. New York: Insight Media, 1999.

Panelists discuss the ethical aspects of emphasizing the development of young children for highly competitive sports. They explore whether youth sport is characterized by overzealous parents or coaches seeking to develop elite competitors.

Sports and Primary and Secondary Education: Student or Player Development? VHS. Dubuque, IA: Kendall Hunt, 2000.

Bill Curry, Rick Wolff, and Scott Kretchmar at the First International Conference on Ethics and Sports discuss sports and values for school students.

Winning Respect. VHS. Champaign, IL: American Sport Education Program, 1998.

Guidance is provided to youth sport coaches as they help their athletes develop character, respect, and responsibility. The importance of winning respect both inside and outside sport is stressed.

Internet Sites
http://www.asep.com

American Sport Education Program offers instructional sessions leading to certifications to coaches, officials, sport administrators, and parents. A range of courses helps volunteer, club, and high school coaches provide athletes with developmentally appropriate skill instruction and values-based learning experiences.

http://www.internationalsport.com/csp

The Center for Sports Parenting offers parents and coaches information to help them guide young athletes in dealing with the psychological and physical challenges in sports. Through its sports parenting social network, parents have opportunities to interact with one another online and to learn from sports parenting experts.

http://courseware.vt.edu/users/rstratto/CYSLinks.html

This Coaching Youth Sports Web site provides links to numerous sport-related sites, including some for coaches, parents, and officials, and some with information about specific sports.

http://ed-web3.educ.msu.edu/ysi

The Institute for the Study of Youth Sports at Michigan State University was established in 1978 to address negative practices in youth sports. This institute conducts research on ways to maximize the physical, psychological, and social benefits of participating in youth sports while minimizing detrimental effects.

http://josephsoninstitute.org/sports

The Josephson Institute Center for Sport Ethics uses six pillars of character—trustworthiness, respect, responsibility, fairness, caring and citizenship—to help coaches, parents, and athletes build character. Its "pursuing victory with honor" program emphasizes that character counts as the basis for becoming a true champion.

www.positivecoach.org

The Positive Coaching Alliance is dedicated to helping youth sport leaders, coaches, and parents ensure a positive playing environment for young athletes. Its goal of "transforming youth sports so sports can transform youth" is achieved through advocacy efforts, publications, and educational seminars that emphasize helping young athletes learn life skills that will serve them well beyond the playing field.

http://www.cbsnews.com/stories/2005/09/29/earlyshow/series/main890850.shtml

"The rules of good sportsmanship: What parents should know to have a good game."

This segment from the CBS *Early Show* on September 30, 2005, features Terry Hanratty, former college and professional quarterback, Jill Friedland, and her 13-year-old daughter and soccer player, Kasey, discussing the importance of good sportsmanship. Tips for good sportsmanship can guide parents and coaches as they help young athletes become good sports.

http://www.ethics.org/resources/articles-general-ethics.asp?aid=833

Larson, L. 2003. "Reflecting on How Sports Influences Character." Ethics Resource Center.

If sports are to build character, then positive outcomes and values like discussions about teamwork, leadership, honesty, responsibility, accepting mistakes, appreciating different levels of achievement, self-confidence, tranquility, and respect for teammates, other players, and referees should be occurring. Rather than the unsportsmanlike, unethical, and illegal conduct of some athletes at all levels of competition, people involved in sports are encouraged to show sportsmanship, because sports are only games played for fun.

Ethical Issues in Interscholastic Sport

DVDs/Videotapes

Citizenship through Sports and Fine Arts Curriculum for High School Activities. **VHS. Kansas City, MO: National Federation of State High School Associations, 1998.**

This program promotes the values of citizenship to high school students through their participation in sports. It includes a video about how coaches can help athletes develop character, respect, and responsibility.

Coach Carter. DVD. Hollywood, CA: Paramount Pictures, 2004.

Based on a true story, this movie recounts how a high school basketball coach, despite intense criticism, benches his undefeated team due to how poorly some of the athletes are performing in their academic work.

Crossing the Line. DVD. Los Angeles: Starlight Home Entertainment, 2003.

Problems confront a high school basketball team and its coach when a parent violently erupts at a game. This story examines the issue of parents losing control at sports events.

Friday Night Lights. Universal City, CA: Universal, 2004.

Based on H. G. Bissinger's book by the same name, this video chronicles the 1988 high school football season in socially and racially divided Odessa, Texas. Overwhelming pressures are felt by Coach Gary Gaines and the Permian High School Panthers as they try to win the state championship while struggling with real-life issues.

Hoop Dreams. VHS. Atlanta, GA: Turner Home Entertainment, 1994.

This video follows the high school careers of two adolescents from inner-city Chicago as they pursue their dream of playing professional basketball. They face ethical choices relative to family, academics, confidence, and their future.

Know the Score: The Dangers of Performance-Enhancing Drugs. VHS. Mount Kisco, NY: Human Relations Media, 2002.

This program exposes the physical ailments like headaches, muscular weakness, and irregular heartbeats associated with the use of performance-enhancing drugs. These abused drugs include steroids, creatine, human growth hormones, diuretics, blood-doping hormones, ephedrine, and amphetamines.

Power, Passion, and Glory: The Real Story of Texas Football Madness. DVD. Ken Heckmann Productions Inc. and Game Partners, Ltd., 2005.

This depicts the real story of the Celina Bobcats, a team that has won more games than any other team in Texas history.

Remember the Titans. **DVD. Burbank, CA: Walt Disney Home Video, 2001.**

In the context of forced school integration in Alexandria, Virginia, in 1971, the successful white coach, Bill Yoast, is replaced by an African American coach, Herman Boone. These two coaches model how to overcome their personal and philosophical differences in developing a championship high school football team comprised of boys of both races.

Science and Sports: Performance Enhancing Drugs. **VHS. Dubuque, IA: Kendall-Hunt, 2000.**

Panelists at the First International Conference on Ethics and Sports discuss the use of performance-enhancing drugs in sports.

Steroids: The Hard Truth. **VHS. New York: Castleworks, 2002.**

This program examines the use of steroids by adolescent boys and girls who seek to enhance their athletic performance and self-image. Former drug users and experts reveal several dangers and misconceptions about steroids.

Internet Sites
http://www.heartofachampion.org

The Heart of a Champion program focuses on nine core character traits: commitment, leadership, perseverance, teamwork, respect, integrity, responsibility, self-control, and compassion. This research-based program offers curricular materials and activities that teach and reinforce positive character traits.

http://www.nfhs.org/web/2008/02/nfhs_steroids_awareness_video.aspx

This steroid-awareness video provided by the National Federation of State High School Associations discusses the permanent physical damage caused by the use of anabolic steroids. Several speakers and real-life examples help adolescents learn about the harmful effects of steroid use as the video encourages them to choose not to use drugs.

Ethical Issues in Intercollegiate Sport
DVDs/Videotapes

Blue Chips. DVD. Hollywood, CA: Paramount Pictures, 2005.

Caught up in ethical struggles in trying to win, a college basketball coach allows alumni to provide under-the-table payments leading to the successful recruiting of highly talented players. Ethical issues such as keeping sport in perspective versus winning are played out.

Ethically Speaking: Diplomas or Trophies? DVD. Charlottesville, VA: Commonwealth Public Broadcasting, 2002.

University of Virginia sociology professor Paul Kingston and director of athletics Craig Littlepage debate how intercollegiate athletics relate to the function, value, and academic mission of universities and whether college athletes are being monetarily exploited. This program explores the intersection of ethics, public policy, and personal life.

Game Plan. VHS. New York: ABC News, 2003.

ABC News in this *Nightline* story analyzes then Vanderbilt University Chancellor Gordon Gee's call for reforms in college athletics. This new approach requires athletes to meet the requirements of a core curriculum and ties the number of scholarships to the graduation rate.

Glory Road. DVD. Burbank, CA: Walt Disney Home Entertainment, 2006.

Coach Don Haskins of Texas Western College recruits African American players to this small, remote institution and develops a winning team. In the 1966 NCAA Men's Division I Basketball Championship, Haskins's all-African American starting lineup defeats the all-Caucasian team from the University of Kentucky.

Johnny Be Good. DVD. Santa Monica, CA: MGM Home Entertainment, 1988.

The recruitment of quarterback Johnny Walker is filled with drinking, women, and monetary kickbacks as two "football factories" attempt to get a prize athlete to attend their institutions.

One on One. VHS. Burbank, CA: Warner Home Video, 1992.

A high school basketball star from a small town is recruited to play for a big-time college. He finds himself ill-prepared for the brutal realities of his new team and the "winning is everything" situation.

Race, Stereotyping, and Sports: Do Blacks Lose by Winning at Sports? VHS. New York: Insight Media, 1999.

A panel discusses the interconnections among race, stereotypes, opportunity, and equality in sports.

Sports for Sale. VHS. Alexandria, VA: PBS Video, 1991.

Bill Moyers hosts a panel discussion exploring the commercialized business of intercollegiate football and basketball and how this business emphasis threatens the academic integrity of athletes.

Sports and Higher Education: Academics, Athletics and Financial Opportunity. VHS. St. Petersburg, FL: Philosophy Lab Corporation, 2000.

At the First International Conference on Ethics and Sports, Bill Curry, Murray Sperber, and Dick DeVenzio discuss the interface between sports and colleges.

Sports and Justice: Title IX and Gender Equity. VHS. St. Petersburg, FL: Philosophy Lab, 1999.

Through interviews and panel discussions, the participants examine gender equity in sports, including the impact of Title IX of the 1972 Education Amendments.

Databases
http://ope.ed.gov/athletics

The Equity in Athletics Disclosure Act requires institutions to annually report data on their intercollegiate athletic programs. The analytical (cutting) tool on this site permits access to institutional and aggregated data for number of athletes by team, number of coaches and their salaries, and revenues and expenses by team and category.

Internet Sites
http://chronicle.com

The *Chronicle of Higher Education*, a weekly newspaper that covers higher education issues in the United States, frequently includes articles on ethical issues of intercollegiate athletics. Click on *athletes* to search for topical articles of interest.

http://naia.collegesports.com/champions-character

The Champions of Character program, launched by the National Association of Intercollegiate Athletics in 2000, seeks to help develop character through sport in athletes, coaches, and parents by providing practical tools for modeling the values of respect, responsibility, integrity, servant leadership, and sportsmanship. This educational outreach initiative reaches hundreds of thousands of college students to influence them to live their lives based on the tenets of character and integrity.

http://www.tidesport.org

The Institute for Diversity and Ethics in Sport (TIDES) conducts research on issues related to gender, race, gambling, violence, and the use of performance-enhancing drugs in amateur, intercollegiate, and professional sports. TIDES publishes numerous studies, including the *Racial and Gender Report Card* that provides an assessment of hiring practices in coaching and sport management in professional and college sport. For example, *The 2008 Racial and Gender Report Card: College Sport* (58 pp.) provides data that are used as the basis for assigning a grade on gender hiring practices in intercollegiate athletics for race (C+) and gender (B). These data include racial and gender demographics for athletes in NCAA-member institutions, head and assistant coaches, athletic directors, associate and assistant athletic directors, senior women administrators, and other athletic department staff members.

Ethical Issues in International Sport

DVDs/Videotapes
Dope: The Battle for the Soul of Sport. VHS. Woolloomooloo, New South Wales: Hilton Cordell and Associates, Film Finance Corporation Australia, 2004.

This video describes efforts by scientists like United States specialist Don Catlin and Australian geneticist Dr. John Rasko to make the 2004 Athens Olympic Games drug free. In looking at the detection of athletes using performance-enhancing drugs, they discuss scandals involving track-and-field athletes from the United States and Australian cyclists.

The Great Olympic Makeover. **VHS. Sydney: Australian Broadcasting Corporation, 2000.**

Andrew Jennings reveals how Olympic representatives attempted to deflect criticism about claims of corruption within the Olympic Movement.

International Aspects of Sports: Managing a World of Sports. **VHS. Dubuque, IA: Kendall/Hunt, 2000.**

Todd Boyd, Robert Huizenga, Armen Keteyian, Richard Lapchick, Bill Morgan, and Angela Schneider discuss ethical and management issues in international sports.

Running Brave. **VHS. Burbank, CA: Englander Productions, 1983.**

Sioux Indian Billy Mills wins the gold medal in the 1964 Tokyo Olympic Games in the 10,000-meter race. Mills, who grew up on an impoverished South Dakota Indian reservation, achieves his phenomenal upset victory despite challenging cultural barriers and deeply rooted insecurities.

Tarnished Gold. **VHS. New York: A and E Home Video, 2000.**

This investigative report describes the corruption and bribery associated with the 2002 Winter Olympic Games in Salt Lake City, Utah.

Internet Sites

http://portal.unesco.org/education/en/ev.php-URL_ID=2223& URL_DO=DO_TOPIC&URL_SECTION=201.html

The Code of Ethics of the United Nations Educational, Scientific and Cultural Organization states that fair play is integral to all sporting activity as well as the management of sport programs. This code defines fair play, explains the responsibility for fair play, and describes the duties and behaviors of governments, sport organizations, and individuals who should ensure that fair play becomes the winning way.

http://www.gmathletes.net

This Web site provides resources and news items from various sources in support of Andy Miah's book *Genetically Modified Athletes: Biomedical Ethics, Gene Doping and Sport.*

These resources provide a wealth of information to anyone interested in learning more about the ethical issues and problems that confront sports at all levels. These resources also provide suggestions and strategies for how to achieve the goal of developing character through sport.

Glossary

amateurism   Love of, such as a love for playing sports.

arms race   Term used to describe building bigger and more luxurious athletic facilities and paying higher and higher salaries to football and men's basketball coaches, especially by institutions playing in the NCAA Football Bowl Subdivision.

barnstorming   Term used to describe teams that travel from location to location competing in entertaining exhibitions and sporting events, including with local teams.

beneficence   Playing fairly or doing good.

bidding scandal   During the process of selecting the host city for future summer and winter Olympic Games, representatives of prospective organizing committees provide lucrative benefits to members of the International Olympic Committee to influence votes in their favor.

blood doping   Occurs when athletes have a portion of their blood removed, which causes the body to replenish the extracted red blood cells; just prior to competition, their blood is reinfused, thus increasing the volume of red blood cells and oxygen-carrying capacity of the blood, which results in increased endurance; is a banned performance-enhancing practice.

bookmaking   Accepting bets and paying winnings depending on the outcome of a sporting event.

boycott   Voluntarily refusing to compete in the Olympic Games in order to protest some action, situation, or set of circumstances; often associated with political or ethnic issues.

bracketed morality   When individuals engaging in immoral actions in sports justify their actions within sport competitions.

British Amateur Sports Ideal   Belief that social and moral values are learned, practiced, and reinforced through sport.

burnout Occurs when an athlete becomes physically or psychologically exhausted or lacks the motivation or interest to continue participating in a sport.

character Mental, social, and ethical traits that make each person unique.

character education Instructing people to know, value, and do what is morally right.

cheating Actions that violate the written rules and unwritten rules and expectations of the game.

code of ethics Values, principles, and standards that guide conduct.

cognitive dissonance Questioning approach through which people examine what is the right thing to do.

commercialism Operating as a business, which characterizes some intercollegiate athletic programs, especially in institutions playing in the Football Bowl Subdivision.

death penalty Punishment assessed by the NCAA against an institution for major, repeated rule violations that disallows a team from competition.

discrimination Prejudicial mistreatment of an individual or group based on a characteristic such as race, ethnicity, or gender.

doping Use of performance-enhancing drugs and methods by athletes.

dropout Occurs when an athlete stops participating in a sport, often due to lack of fun, skill, and other interests.

drug testing Process of determining whether the person has used a prohibited drug or method.

eligibility Requirements regarding academic performance, age, weight, and other stipulations used to determine whether an athlete is permitted to play.

ethical relativism Each individual determines what is true, with all points of view equally valid.

ethics Study of morals, moral values, and character.

gamesmanship Actions not prohibited by the rules, but done to gain advantages by whatever means possible to increase the chance of winning.

gentleman's agreement Unwritten rule in Major League Baseball, National Football League, Basketball Association of America, and other sport organizations to exclude African Americans, thus discriminating against them based solely on race.

grant-in-aid Financial award given by an athletic department to an athlete for playing a sport in college.

groupthink   Occurs when pressure for conformity from group members results in individuals not making a morally right decision.

honesty   Keeping promises, telling the truth, and being trustworthy.

integrity   Living consistent with a person's moral values.

intercollegiate athletics   Competitions between students in colleges.

interscholastic sports   Competitions between students in schools.

intimidation   Actions intended to keep opponents from performing as skillfully as they potentially could.

justice   Treating others with fairness.

justice as fairness ethical theory   Advocates guaranteeing equal rights and equality of opportunity while providing the greatest benefit to those least advantaged.

moral callousness   Hardened feelings that lead to rationalizing acting in morally wrong ways.

moral development   Examines how and through what processes people learn and develop morally, even when confronted with psychological and social detractors.

moral reasoning   Process of evaluating personal values and developing a consistent, impartial set of moral principles by which to live.

moral values   Relative worth an individual places on virtuous behaviors.

morals   Right and good motives, intentions, and actions.

nationalism   Loyalty to one's national identity.

no pass, no play   Policy in many schools that requires a specified level of academic achievement in order to be eligible to play sports.

nonconsequential (Kantian) ethical theory   Advocates an absolute moral code of behavior.

Olympic Movement   Collaborative activities of the International Olympic Committee, national Olympic committees, international and national sport federations, host city organizing committees, and athletes that bring Olympic values and programs to life.

performance-enhancing drugs   Substances or processes used to gain physiological advantages.

point spread   The publicized difference in the projected scores of two teams before the game is played.

preferred admissions   When an educational institution admits a prospective student who does not meet the academic requirements for admission.

proscriptive rules   Rules forbidding or prohibiting certain actions to reduce and prevent violent actions that cause serious injuries and harm athletes.

punitive damages Financial awards made by the court for violations of the law as a deterrent to future misdeeds intolerable to society.

racism Belief that specific human traits produce superiority of a particular race resulting in discrimination against individuals of another race.

recruiting Process of a coach trying to convince an athlete to attend a specific educational institution in order to play on an athletic team; typically a recruited athlete receives some type of financial award.

redshirting Keeping a student out of competition for an academic year; in intercollegiate athletics, this approach is used to allow athletes to develop physically, is due to an injury, or occurs because other athletes preclude the likelihood of playing; in interscholastic sports, this approach is used prior to the high school years so a child can gain a physical development advantage.

responsibility Fulfilling one's duty and being a person who can be counted on to carry out what is expected.

select teams Comprised of highly skilled players who focus on winning and advancing to higher levels of competition; often includes playing year-round and competing at regional and national levels; sometimes called travel, elite, or club teams.

sexism Discriminatory treatment against one gender based on prejudicial attitudes or beliefs that results in the denial of benefits or opportunities.

sex testing Process formerly required of female athletes in the Olympic Games and other international sport competitions to prove their gender based on visual appearance or testing protocol to prevent males from competing against females because of their physiological advantages.

shaving points When athletes are paid by gamblers to manipulate the point spread to enable gamblers to win their bets.

show cause Requirement that an institution must justify to the NCAA Infractions Committee why a coach who has violated its rules should be permitted to coach during a designated period of time.

situational ethics ethical theory Advocates that love is the only absolute law, so as long as this is claimed, a person can do whatever is situationally desirable.

spirit of the rules Sporting behavior that displays conformity to the written and unwritten rules of the game, sportsmanship, and a commitment to not seeking unfair advantage over opponents.

sport ethics Study of how to teach character and moral values and model making morally reasoned decisions within competitive physical activities governed by rules.

sport specialization   Expectation, often imposed by coaches and sometimes by parents, that an athlete shows dedication to skill development and competition in only one sport.

sports agent   An independent contractor who acts on authority of and represents an athlete in negotiating playing and endorsement contracts and performing other agreed-upon services.

sports fix   Gamblers paying an athlete to influence the point spread that influences the outcome of a game to enable gamblers to make money on their bets.

sportsmanship   Conforming to the letter and spirit of the rules (sometimes called sporting behavior).

tanking   When tennis players or athletes in other sports put forth minimal effort in order to lose.

taunting   Ploys used in sports to attempt to distract and throw off an opponent's game.

tutoring   Assistance provided to athletes who are struggling to meet academic eligibility requirements for participation.

utilitarian ethical theory, or utilitarianism   Advocates that the ultimate standard of what is morally right is dependent on the greatest amount of good for the greatest number of people.

youth sport   Sport programs and competitions for children and adolescents sponsored by private or public, nonschool agencies and organizations.

Index

Note: italic page number indicates figure; t. indicates table.

About the Author

Angela Lumpkin is a professor in the Department of Health, Sport and Exercise Sciences at the University of Kansas in Lawrence, Kansas, where she previously served as Dean of the School of Education. She has served as Dean of the College of Education at State University of West Georgia, Department Chair at North Carolina State University, as well as Chair of NC State's faculty, and professor of physical education at the University of North Carolina at Chapel Hill. She holds a BSE from the University of Arkansas, MA and PhD from The Ohio State University, and a MBA from the University of North Carolina at Chapel Hill. She is the author of 20 books, including *Sport Ethics: Applications for Fair Play* in its third edition and *Introduction to Physical Education, Exercise Science, and Sport Studies* in its seventh edition. She has published over 40 scholarly refereed manuscripts and delivered over 170 professional presentations, including 18 invited lectures. She has served as President of the National Association for Sport and Physical Education, received the Honor Award from the American Alliance for Health, Physical Education, Recreation and Dance, and been selected as an American Council on Education Fellow.